The Whole Foods Kosher Kitchen
Glorious Meals Pure and Simple

Lévana Kirschenbaum
with Lisa R. Young, PhD, RD

Foreword by Dr. Tania Dempsey
Photographs by Meir Pliskin

Skyhorse Publishing

Skyhorse Publishing books may be purchased in bulk at special discounts for sales
promotion, corporate gifts, fund-raising, or educational purposes. Special editions can
also be created to specifications. For details, contact the Special Sales Department,
Skyhorse Publishing, 307 West 36th Street, 11th Floor, New York, NY 10018 or
info@skyhorsepublishing.com.

Skyhorse® and Skyhorse Publishing® are registered trademarks of
Skyhorse Publishing, Inc.®, a Delaware corporation.

www.skyhorsepublishing.com

10 9 8 7 6 5 4 3 2 1

Library of Congress Cataloging-in-Publication Data

Kirschenbaum, Lévana.
  The whole foods kosher kitchen : glorious meals pure and simple / Lévana
Kirschenbaum with Lisa R. Young.
     p. cm.
  ISBN 1-61608-292-5 (alk. paper)
  1. Nutrition. 2. Health. I. Young, Lisa R. II. Title.
  TX353.K556 2011
  613.2--dc22
                         2010052803

Printed in China

CONTENTS

> Throughout the recipes in this book, the following abbreviations are used:
> GF: Gluten-free
> GFA: Gluten-free adaptable
> P: Passover

ACKNOWLEDGMENTS

There are many people I would like to thank for always keeping me going.

- My mother, known as Maman to the whole family and even to all our friends, the ultimate artisan, and the original diva of glorious healthy meals: I wish to be in every way her disciple, and do her proud! I hope to continue to convey her genius at making quick, cheap, and healthy feasts to multitudes of grateful diners!
- My extended family of cooking demo students, not only for being my willing victims each time I subject them to a new creation, but who offer no end of insight, support, and friendship: They make working fun and delicious!
- Thanks to Lisa Young and her clear, practical, and no-nonsense language, I hope the reader will understand better all the obscure diet talk we are always trying to make sense of, and act on it.
- My husband Maurice, the poster child for soup-and-salad diet: how convenient is that for this cook? After all these years, he still looks with some amazement at the construction-site overtones of some parts of our home, and wonders what his wife might end up doing when she grows up: He is the ultimate patron of domestic arts!
- My children, not only the best captive audience, but great homemakers and hosts in their own right: My son Maimon and his wife Ruthie, my son Yakov and his wife Elisheva, my daughter Bella and her husband Meir; My grandchildren Musia, Sara, Chaya Rachel, Levi Yitzchok, and Tsofia, delightful whole-foods lovers all.
- My son-in-law and talented photographer Meir Pliskin.
- Tammy Polatsek, party planner extraordinaire, for letting us use her new stunning line of dishes, Carmona, for all the pictures in this book.
- Hannah Kaminsky, our talented food stylist and herself the author of two beautiful vegan desserts cookbooks.
- Abigail Gehring, the most devoted and talented editor ever. I am glad to have her not only as my most valuable assistant, but as a dear friend.

Lisa thanks her family, friends, and colleagues for their love, guidance, and support. Mom and dad, Bonnie and Luca, Teo, Celia, and Brando—you guys are so special to me. A special thanks to Joel Pelofsky, Adrienne Forman, MS, RD, and Renee Alster, MS, RD. And for research assistance, thank you Suzanne Natz, Jo Bartell, and Ilana Fishof.

And, finally, to Lévana who makes healthy eating taste delicious.

FOREWORD

by Tania Tyles Dempsey, MD

I met Rivka (who has allowed the use of her name in the hope of helping others) in September 1999 in a hospital while making rounds on my patient who shared her room. She asked me for my card while telling me that she was looking for a new primary care doctor. Rivka almost instantly became my patient, and over the past eleven years, I not only saw her weight balloon to 380 pounds but most importantly saw her successful journey to lose 200 pounds. Her story of transformation through integrating healthy food and lifestyle will undoubtedly be inspirational to all.

Rivka has what many of my patients suffer with: metabolic syndrome. Although metabolic syndrome can affect men and women, it is important to recognize certain features in women that can present as polycystic ovarian syndrome. Women with this syndrome often have insulin resistance and hormonal imbalances, including high male hormone levels, which can be controlled through diet, exercise, vitamin supplementation, and in some cases, medication. Some symptoms that these women suffer with include difficulty controlling weight, headaches, food cravings, irregular menstrual cycles, fatigue, and skin issues, such as acne, hair loss, or increased facial and body hair. These women are at risk for high cholesterol, high blood pressure, heart disease, and cancer. They often have numerous vitamin deficiencies that contribute to their poor health. With the right approach, many of their symptoms and risk factors can be dramatically improved. I have been committed to helping my patients, like Rivka, improve their overall health and reverse or prevent illness through a holistic approach to treatment. Food, I believe, is the first step in the right direction.

BEFORE

Rivka serves as a wonderful example of how a patient with metabolic syndrome/ polycystic ovarian syndrome can gain control over her life through a change in her lifestyle and diet. When I met Rivka, then twenty-seven, her life was spiraling out of control as was

AFTER

her weight. She had lost her mother many years earlier but was still trying to cope with the tragedy of it. She required multiple hospitalizations and many medications during that time that contributed greatly to her weight gain. The more distraught she became, the more she developed new ailments and problems requiring more medication. Instead of finding healing, Rivka was feeling worse. She gained a tremendous amount of weight as the dosages and the variety of her prescription medications increased. She developed an unhealthy relationship with food, using food to fill a void in her life and as a way to comfort herself during times of stress. Rivka developed elevated blood pressure, high cholesterol, and insulin resistance (pre-diabetes). When her weight reached 380 pounds, she decided it was time to take control. Up until then she had difficulty following through on the advice that I gave her, which included dietary changes and exercise. But she soon realized that it was really up to her to take the first step. Instead of crash or fad diets that she had tried before, Rivka began incorporating lifestyle changes and behavioral modification and was soon on the road to recovery. She started slowly doing yoga and swimming as it was difficult for her to do any other form of exercise at 380 pounds. She then began looking more closely at her diet. We spent hours in my office talking about the kinds of changes in her diet that would be easiest for her to make at first. Cutting out the processed carbohydrates made from white sugar and/or white flour was the most important first step. Learning about the many wonderful, tasty, and healthy foods that she could prepare on her own without feeling deprived was her next step. This quickly led to weight loss. She started making her own smoothies each morning, incorporating frozen blueberries and strawberries, soymilk, flaxseeds, and stevia sweetener. She ate salads with fish or chicken for lunch and used different types of seasonings to improve the taste so that she would enjoy her food more. She made stir-fried vegetables for dinner with olive oil or coconut oil. She snacked on nuts, such as almonds, walnuts, and cashews. She started seeing food as a way to heal her body instead of a way to deal with stress. She had used food both to comfort herself and to punish herself, but now she was using food as nourishment. As she shed more and more weight, I was able to take her off her medications, one at a time. And, most importantly, she started feeling healthier than ever. She began taking exercise classes and walking, which gave her more energy and helped her lose even more weight.

Rivka has lost 200 pounds to date and is now off all of her medications. Her blood pressure is normal, her cholesterol is much improved, and she has reversed her pre-diabetes. She still has some weight to lose, but she has learned to enjoy the food she eats and to cook her food in healthier ways. She continues to find alternative ways to heal her body, whether it is through eliminating certain types of foods (such as wheat) or incorporating more of other types of foods (those high in antioxidants), or through activities that help her achieve balance in her life (like exercise, yoga, meditation).

If we can all take a step back and think about what we are putting into our bodies and why, then we can all have the opportunity to improve our health.

INTRODUCTION

by Lisa R. Young, PhD, RD

Nutritious Tips for Becoming a Healthier You.

"Let nothing which can be treated by diet be treated by other means."
—*Maimonides*

As a nutritionist advising clients on healthy eating for over twenty years, below are some simple, healthy tips that I have recommended over the years. Even if you can only make one small change a day, you are still making progress. Do the best you can. Making small and realistic changes will help to ensure that you can stick to a healthy food plan for the long haul. Food should taste good, be enjoyed, and eating should bring you pleasure!

- Eat *whole* foods.
- *Cook* and eat at *home* more often.
- Try *new* foods.
- Eat a *balanced* diet by including a *variety* of foods from each food group.
- Choose an array of *colorful* fruits and vegetables.
- Eat *whole* grains instead of refined grains.
- Eat more *plant* based proteins.
- Include *heart-healthy* fats such as olive oil, fatty fish, nuts, and seeds.
- Use herbs and spices. They impart both flavor and nutrition to your foods.
- Practice *portion control*. Large portions contain more calories than small portions and, therefore, are a leading contributor to the obesity epidemic. *How much* you eat matters more than what you eat when it comes to weight control.
- Allow yourself to indulge in a *small* portion of your favorite treat.
- Eat small portions of high-fat meats and cheeses.
- Limit processed foods.
- Eat a small portion of "the real thing" instead of relying on diet food and using artificial sweeteners.
- Limit soda and large portions of other sweetened beverages.
- Limit packaged foods with ingredients you can't pronounce.
- Don't be fooled: While *"low-fat"* and *"organic"* are good terms to strive for when selecting certain foods (low-fat dairy and organic apples, for instance), they are

not foolproof and should not serve as a permission to overeat. Low-fat cookies, for example, still contain calories, and if you eat too many of them, you can—and *will*—gain weight. Organic junk food is still junk food, not health food. So don't be fooled. Proceed with caution when reading food labels.

Healthy tips when consuming fruits and vegetables:

Fruits and veggies are loaded with vitamins, minerals, fiber, and antioxidant photochemicals, which may help protect against chronic diseases. They are also relatively low in calories, making them a great choice for your waistline. Choosing a _colorful_ array of fruits and vegetables is best, as different antioxidants exist in the different color spectrum. The orange pigment found in cantaloupe, carrots, pumpkin, and sweet potatoes, for instance, contain the antioxidant beta carotene known to promote eye health. And, the deep red pigment found in tomatoes, watermelon, and pink grapefruit contain the antioxidant lycopene linked with prostate health.

- *It is best to EAT your fruits and vegetables from WHOLE foods.* Popping a pill—such as taking a beta carotene supplement—does not do the trick. Fruits and vegetables offer a combination of many health benefits that you will not find in a pill. So, remember to chew!
- *Go LOCAL and eat what's in season.* When you can, opt for local produce that's in season. Chances are it did not have to travel too far to get to you.
- *Go ORGANIC when you can.* The Environmental Working Group (www.ewg.org) offers a guide to shoppers on pesticide residues in produce and offers suggestions about when to buy organic produce. While organic ingredients contain the lowest pesticide residue, below is a list of the produce containing the highest and lowest pesticide residues if you are not able to always buy organic produce.

The *"Dirty Dozen"* contain the highest pesticide residues. Buy these organic:
Celery, peaches, strawberries, apples, blueberries, nectarines, bell peppers, spinach, cherries, kale/collard greens, potatoes, imported grapes.

The *"Clean 15"* are the lowest in pesticides. They include onions, avocado, sweet corn, pineapple, mangoes, sweet peas, asparagus, kiwi, cabbage, eggplant, cantaloupe, watermelon, grapefruit, sweet potato, and honeydew melon.

CHAPTER 1

EAT YOURSELF TO HEALTH!

When we were kids, there was nothing I felt our mother couldn't heal with food. Stomachache? She'd cook up a pot of oatmeal. A cold? Chicken soup. Nausea? A baked sweet potato. Sore throat? She'd boil milk with ginger and cloves. Hungry for a snack? She'd melt a dark chocolate square and spread it on toast. We so looked forward to the "cure" that we were always coming up with some urgent real or imagined booboo.

A few years ago, I came down with a grave case of IBS (irritable bowel syndrome) that necessitated a few days' hospitalization. After three months of trying a gamut of medications to no avail, I attempted to assist in my treatment. In my despair, I remembered my mother's familiar lines, which after sounding much too good to be true all these long years finally reasserted themselves: *"Just open your refrigerator!"* and *"The cure is in the pot!"* Why not work with the tools I knew best? After all, food was, and is, my life's work. I was excited to re-explore the whole spectrum of foods, this time focusing on cooking as a means to healing by using the darkest greens, the reddest fruits and vegetables, whole grains, lean proteins, and seaweed. Simple as that! In three short months, I felt wonderful and shed ten pesky extra pounds I had been lugging around, courtesy of having recently joined the club of middle-agers! Delighted with the results, I decided to apply the same intuitive logic with my arthritis, which I'd been treating with conventional medications that were only leaving me in great pain and greater confusion. I ate more and more dishes that included the powerfully antioxidant "yellow food" (turmeric: more about it later) the panacea I grew up with in my native Morocco.

In order to illustrate just what a long way whole foods have come, I would like to quote the late Bert Greene, who wrote in *The Grains Cookbook*, posthumously published in 1988, of his early experiences with starting an austerity diet program to shed many unwanted pounds:

> The meals were taken at an urban commune in New York City's East Village and were prepared by a group of very young men and women who viewed my age and ample size with ill-concealed mistrust. What I recollect best of that dim excursion into self-denial is not the meals (which, to be kind, were rudimentary), but the attitude of my fellow diners who so righteously consumed them. To a man and woman, every young person ate just what was placed before them—without

Fruits

(See page 88 for berries.)

Cantaloupe. This member of the melon family is rich in the antioxidant beta carotene, a plant-based Vitamin A precursor that helps with eye health among other conditions. It is also rich in the mineral potassium which may help lower blood pressure and the risk for stroke. And it is terrific if you are watching your waist; a one cup serving contains a mere 50 calories.

Watermelon offers a juicy sweet taste and a high water content, while packing in the antioxidants lycopene, beta carotene, and vitamin C, and the minerals potassium and magnesium.

Citrus fruits including **oranges** and **grapefruits** provide a significant source of vitamin C, folate, and potassium as well as fiber. Pink grapefruits are particularly

---

salt, pepper or any genuine relish. They all might have been denizens of some correctional facility, for there were tin plates and plastic forks and no conversation whatsoever. Since food is not (and never was) a penance for me, I left this cold commune fast.

The rest, for Bert Greene as well as for the future of grains and all whole foods, is history. Recently a *Wall Street Journal* food correspondent in Tokyo wrote a glowing article in the *Journal* about super healthy foods. I wrote to him, saying, essentially, hello, where have you been, I have been using these ingredients all along, long before they became hip. He replied, asking if I would consider giving demos in Japan. Wow, I thought, now we're talking!

On a basic level, unprocessed foods, in their original form, are foods packed with nutrients that promote and optimize good health. We city dwellers often wish we were fortunate enough to have better access to locally grown foods, but we can mitigate this disadvantage by getting our food minimally processed or unprocessed. It is most interesting to point out that all unprocessed foods nowadays marketed as "super foods" are in fact ancient foods, in vogue today by the grace of G-d. Finally, something good for us all is trendy to boot, and I hope and pray it never goes out of fashion. It's only the clutter of junk food on the market that has obscured, or even eclipsed, these foods from our line of vision for so long. Truly, whole and unprocessed foods are the ancient additions to the modern kitchen. One of my fondest memories is of drinking a glass of fresh-squeezed pomegranate juice, made from a rudimentary crank operated by a young Bedouin boy, at the entrance to the Old City in Jerusalem. Yes, I loved the boy and his curls and his grin and my ancient beloved City of Lights, but one certainly need not have all these props in order to enjoy a delicious glass of pomegranate juice, no sugar added please!

Countless students who attend my cooking demos tell me that, at my urging, at first they would timidly add a cup of flax meal to the cookie batter, a handful of barley flakes to the soup pot, or a cup of pomegranate juice to the smoothie, but that they soon dropped their apologetic attitude for good when they received rave reviews. Why apologize? For "depriving" your guests and family of white bread, gooey desserts, and heavy,

rich in the antioxidant lycopene. Eating these fruits whole yield more nutrients than drinking the juice.

Avocados are rich in heart-healthy monounsaturated fats, which may help raise levels of HDL (good cholesterol) while lowering LDL (bad cholesterol). They are also high in the antioxidant vitamin E.

Grapes. Consuming grapes may reduce the risk of blood clots, lower LDL cholesterol (the bad kind), and prevent damage to the heart's blood vessels, aiding in the maintenance of healthy blood pressure. Antioxidants called flavonoids may even increase HDL cholesterol (the good kind). The resveratrol found in the skins of red grapes may interfere with cancer development. Eating the whole fruit instead of consuming the juice contains the added benefit of fiber.

Kiwifruit with its brilliant green inside is packed with vitamin C and fiber.

Apples provide fiber along with the heart healthy antioxidant quercitin.

rich sauces with all their intractable, empty, useless calories? For serving healthful, nutritious, delicious, fun, and simple meals that everyone, *everyone*, will enjoy and benefit from immensely? My best walking advertisements are my family members: Although I cook (and serve) up a storm, they are all thin and fit! My reasoning is simple: Incorporate all the ingredients that are good for you into your daily food preparation—they are just as easy to procure as the bad ones—and you will find it very liberating to discover that in addition to tasting wonderful, your dinner didn't cost you a penny more, or take a minute longer to prepare than usual. The great difference will be in the results: You will feel truly wonderful. When was the last time you reported feeling great and losing weight *by eating?* Oh, you may ask, but what about the kids? The great war cry of the fretting mother—*They will never eat this!*—is receding to a remote and barely audible echo. You may know that I have just launched a line of spelt-based all-natural desserts, a sort of culmination of my life's work with natural foods (more on this later), and who do you think is clamoring for my cookies and muffins? Kids! They turn my mountain of all-natural spelt cookies to rubble in the blink of an eye, giving me—to say nothing of their moms!—endless pleasure, and lots of hugs.

All those ugly, grimy, bulbous, monolithic roots—rutabaga, celery root, turnips, and so on—don't let them daunt you. What need do they have of *looking* pretty? They contain endless reserves of inner beauty and flavor and produce dishes much superior to the prosaic and humble sum of their parts. All you need is a hammer (yes, a hammer) and a good knife to break them up in a snap. They cost pennies and are in many ways priceless, and so lean! As for the homely leaves you see piled on produce stalls—kale, collard greens, mustard greens, turnip greens, Swiss chard—they are veritable powerhouses and are very cheap and easy to cook. Do not let unfamiliar foods intimidate you—there is very little you can do to ruin them. Sauté them, throw them in soups, shred them raw, and add them to salads. When cooking a soup, consider adding a handful of barley, quinoa, or millet. Make your smoothies out of frozen raspberries and blueberries, powerful antioxidants. Add a teaspoon of turmeric to meat or vegetable stews. Use unfiltered apple cider vinegar (did you know it may work wonders on sore throats too?), easily available in health food stores, to create a great-tasting salad dressing. And when preparing a batch of cookies, add a handful of almonds, sunflower seeds, chia, hemp, or flaxseeds for extra crunch and flavor, and a whole lot more nutrition. Substitute barley, spelt, millet, or quinoa flakes for part of the flour in your cake or cookie batter. Agar or kuzu, natural gelling agents, are easily found in health food stores and make for soothing and delicious desserts in just minutes. I guarantee that you will become so attached to these ingredients you'll be using them all the time, as I do, in times of good health and in fun company!

Is it just coincidence that although you can find millions of recipes online, not everyone is a good cook? I suspect the reason is that recipes alone, without a real glimpse of the cook behind them (and his or her philosophy of cooking and eating), are quite limiting and aren't enough to make a good cook out of any of us. I simply can't start this book in earnest without first sharing my most basic policies about food shopping and conditioning, simple and nutritious cooking, and basic diet tools.

What happened to dinner as we once knew it? In a chapter of David Halberstam's wonderful book *The Fifties*, the young bride would doll herself up in the late afternoon and, at the first sound of the bell, race to open the door for her husband, hand him his favorite drink, usher him into the spotless dining room with fresh flowers adorning the table and the air fragrant with the promise of a delicious dinner. As we all know, this paradigm of conjugal bliss is gone, and who can honestly say they are sorry to see it go? Fast-forward to modern times: Many frazzled housewives run to the corner deli and buy a few pints of whatever drab institutional stuff they can get their hands on and then serve their purchases on paper plates, probably because they sense (correctly in my view) that the second-rate meal they are about to serve is not worthy of soiling the spanking new china and cutlery. (Remember the bridal registry? Gosh, it seems like eons ago!) And what about the many women who work long hours at the office and come home exhausted? You'd have to be a fool (or terribly inconsiderate) to expect a woman with a full-time job to spend her few free hours preparing and cleaning up after gourmet meals every night. It's no wonder there is a successful pizza delivery joint on every corner.

What a difference half a century can make in the politics of domestic life! The first model, in which the highlight of the housewife's otherwise uneventful day was the dinner hour when she brought all her charms and hard work to bear, was quickly discarded. The current model—and its attendant uninspired "treats"—is still hanging on. But let's hope and pray it is on its way out as well, never to return, and an alternative, sensible, stream-lined, and durable lifestyle will emerge in its place.

Prepared versus from scratch: Whenever there is an opportunity to save cooking or prepping time—and of course money—and still eat well with minimal or no loss of nutrition, I am the first to take it. Every so often, I play devil's advocate, and bring home the latest manufactured creations to let them face off against my own from-scratch ones, just to make sure I'm not missing any valuable shortcuts. A marinade, a salad dressing, a cake mix, a pancake mix, frozen fish sticks, frozen chicken schnitzels, and so on. And only the premium brands, mind you. But it invariably goes downhill as soon as I open the container; just one taste and I realize I've wasted my time and money. For example, store-bought dressings and marinades save only a minute or two and don't hold a candle to their homemade counterparts. Only a hopeless provincial would find polyester as sensuous as silk, copper as precious as gold, stainless steel as luxurious as silver. Why should it be any different with food?

I recently read an essay in which the author described his unhappy childhood revolving around a wheeling-dealing father who spent most of his days racking his brains on how to make lots of money *not* working and *not* spending and *not* providing and *not* getting caught "in the system," while he declaimed excitedly and relentlessly about his vision of a glamorous leisurely life to his wary and deprived family. The upshot was, predictably, that while all his neighborhood friends looked well fed, well adjusted, and well provided for, he and his siblings looked disheveled and were uprooted from house to house and from school to school.

Wouldn't it upset you, and then inspire you, I hope, to learn that cooks-from-scratch spend hardly any more time, money, or effort making *real* delicious, nutritious food than anyone spends who ends up with devitalized and devitalizing, boring food, using mixes, cans, and other dreadful ingredients? What could possibly beat the real thing?

Consider store-bought cake mixes and pancake mixes versus the from-scratch versions. Instructions for the store-bought varieties read roughly as follows: Preheat your oven, grease a tube pan (or heat your skillet), add an egg, add milk, mix, bake then clean up the bowl, pan, mold, or skillet; and you're done. This is *precisely* the same process used to make cakes, muffins, or pancakes from scratch! Using a mix is, oh, maybe a stitch or two less work, but besides being nutritionally worthless, it's more expensive and insipid. We always want a bargain, be it expressed in time or money saved, and we naively tell ourselves that if something comes in a package, it *must* mean it is saving us *something*. I understand using something bottled or packaged or powdered if we are, say, camping or traveling, stranded in the boondocks, or otherwise away from home and its amenities. Yes, in a pinch, we must do whatever it takes to subsist. But to live in a home equipped with the best appliances, to be surrounded with all the comforts a home can afford us, to be cornered by spectacular markets open at all hours and gorged with beautiful produce (my mother cried the first time she visited an American supermarket: she had no idea such plenty actually existed; she had thought of it as a Shangri-La fantasy), and to come home with such meager pickings as bottled dressings, precooked meals, cold cuts, and canned vegetables? In the Bible it says, *"Behold I have given you life and death. Choose life!"* And of course the reaction it begs is "Duh!" but what do you know, it is not so evident after all. Why condemn oneself voluntarily to a chronic on-one-foot position (excuse the imagery), a perennial "in a pinch" way of life? How disquieting this must feel! How it must downgrade and impoverish the quality of life!

A closer look at commercially prepared foods shows that all they are saving us is the "burden" of reaching for a pinch of salt, or a teaspoon of vanilla or baking powder. And as payment, we sacrifice good flavor, good nutrition, and pile on the preservatives, fat, sugar, alternative sweeteners, and goodness knows what else, some of which will almost certainly end up harming us. Take packaged fish sticks and chicken nuggets, for example: You bake them for seven to eight minutes and get a rubbery mess. Instead, you could heat a splash of olive oil in a skillet and sauté a few pieces of fish, chicken cutlets, or steaks two to three minutes on each side—it's ready in less time, and it's infinitely more delicious and more nutritious than the store-bought calamity you and I never need to settle for.

What are the benefits of eating a salad with homemade dressing? A piece of fish or chicken properly and briefly sautéed in a skillet or oven-roasted? A few crêpes whipped up in your own blender? A slice of cake or a muffin made from scratch in about five minutes? The answer is infuriatingly simple: It looks good and inviting, it tastes good, it feels good, it is healthier, it's ready in no time, and it yields ample servings. And the best part is, you have total control on the ingredients going into it. As importantly, it fosters a mood of wholesomeness, togetherness, and good cheer. You will want to eat this way more often and have everyone around you enjoy it as well.

Time your cooking differently: Joining friends for coffee? Instead of meeting at a café, invite them all to your house and prepare a fabulous cup of coffee for everyone in an eight-cup French press in the wink of an eye. A pitcher of iced coffee or tea is just as simple. While you're at it, whip up a great crêpe, omelet, corn bread, or muffin, which will be ready in a few short minutes, fragrant and inviting, with doggie bags for everyone, to boot. You don't have to start the baking hours before the guests arrive—do it once they're there, while you're chatting. Will your friends forgive you for multitasking ten minutes out of an hour or two? You bet, especially for a home-baked treat as the reward, and for skipping the dreary line behind the food carts at their corner! Likewise, you can turn on your stove and start some steel-cut oatmeal, which will serve eight and be ready to eat in only a few minutes. (For that matter, oatmeal is also great on a regular workday; begin cooking it just before you get into the shower and it will be ready and waiting for you when you get out.)

Feeding children: When my son Maimon was a little boy of seven or eight, he used to clamor for a playdate with his friend Nathan, and we always came away with the same disappointing answer from his mother: "Nathan can't come, he has great separation problems." One day after prodding the mother harder, they both showed up at my house. The mother put on her most solemn face, knelt by her son, and told him in a voice barely above a whisper: "Nathan, you understand I am leaving now, I won't be with you? You will be all alone with Maimon and Mrs. Kirschenbaum all day?"

"Yes, Mommy, that's all right, we are going to the park and then going for lunch. It will be fun."

Two steps from the door, the mother turned around again, this time looking positively mournful. "Nathan, in case there's any accident, emergency . . ." The rest of the sentence was drowned out by Nathan's bawling. Separation problem pinpointed! I am pleased to report that Nathan *stayed* and enjoyed himself immensely, that day and many subsequent others. Likewise, I encounter countless mothers who declare, "My children will never eat *this* in a million years. They are very fussy eaters. They only like white bread, sliced American cheese, spaghetti with ketchup, pizza, and fish sticks." I respectfully don't believe this.

I always wonder at how the very same mothers who will cry at the sight of a scratch on their child will think nothing of feeding him or her foods laden with chemicals: What presents the greater risk and inflicts the most damage? Just because the danger is insidiously incremental doesn't make it any less clear and present. Children will eat what their moms feed them, period. Kids are small adults, and we don't need to get them used (alas, even addicted sometimes) to packages with cartoon characters in order to ensure they will feed themselves. What would your children do after being served some homemade soup, a sandwich made with whole-grain bread, some roast chicken with brown rice or corn on the cob, and so on at home (or in school for that matter) several days in a row? Go on a hunger strike? Mount a mutiny with all the kids on the block? Make restaurant reservations? Of course not! On the second day, third at the most, they will sit down and eat, and yes, enjoy it! They eat junk only because that's what their friends eat, because that's what they were told was cool, because that's what their school feeds them, because that's what the vending machines heave relentlessly.

So, dear moms, unite, dare to be different, resist peer pressure, and do the right thing—your children will love you even more if that is at all possible. You will be rewarded with healthy and contented children at a minimal cost of money and time. My granddaughter recently created quite a stir at the supermarket when she asked her mother, at the top of her lungs, to please buy her some pumpkin and some peas; so you see, it is just what you get them used to. And no, she is not a geek, she is, in fact, quite a delightful and fun child, and so are her pumpkin-eating siblings and cousins.

Frozen versus fresh: Will it surprise you to hear that I actually *look* for frozen vegetables and fruits whenever I intend to use them in a dish where their looks won't matter (such as in soups, smoothies, and fruit sauces)? Frozen fruit and vegetables are picked at the height of their sweetness and freshness; and there are plenty of them. They are widely available, plus they are reasonably priced and require no cleaning. I throw frozen vegetables into soup (okra, peas, corn, broccoli, string beans, cauliflower, etc.) all the time and get great results. I make smoothies, fruit soups, and fruit sauces with frozen berries and other fruit, and even eat them with yogurt and granola. Using all frozen fruit eliminates the need for washing, for adding sweeteners (since the fruit is already so sweet), and for adding ice (for smoothies), leaving their intense flavors undiluted. Granted, they don't look as pristine as their fresh counterparts, but so what, as long as you are not using them for strawberry tart or chocolate-dipped fruit? Just make sure they have no sugar added (likewise, make sure your frozen vegetables have no sugar, salt, or other seasonings added).

Fruits and vegetables aren't the only frozen foods worth using. Recently, my fish market salesman repeatedly called me to promote a new item on his product list: frozen vacuum-packed tuna steaks that he assured me were sushi quality and as good as fresh-bought, at less than half the price. I was skeptical at first, but he kept raving about it and begged me to give it a shot. He was wrong about only one thing: It was *better* than fresh. He got me, and quite a few others, totally hooked on the tuna, which requires absolutely nothing but a sprinkling of salt and pepper, and searing one minute on each side. What a treat! I urge you, go for it. Likewise, my friend Georganne recently brought me a most improbable—and unforgettable—souvenir from a family vacation in Alaska: a slab of frozen vacuum-packed Alaskan salmon. I have never tasted salmon so fabulous before or since!

Reading labels—the whole picture: I think this little story of my childhood will preface my view perfectly. Growing up in Morocco, we had a town crier who served as a traveling lost and found. He haunted the streets with his strident daily cries, "Who lost a basket? Who lost a hat?" He made his modest living from the tips the grateful owners of whatever—sometimes even *whomever*—it was he found. One day he found a red rooster he got so attached to that he dreamed up ways to make it his for keeps while leaving his honorable name intact. So he beat the streets and screamed at the top of his lungs "WHO LOST" and ended in a whisper "a red rooster?" Since no one could hear what it was he'd found, no one claimed the rooster as his own. Feeling pangs of guilt, he decided to change gears. The next day, he started with a whisper "Who lost" and ended at the top of his lungs "A RED ROOSTER?" And that's how the rooster became his proud property.

Bags of sugar bearing the "vegan" seal, packaged meats with a "gluten-free" seal? Hmmm, it must be good, then, we tell ourselves in spite of the absurd labeling. Manufacturers perceive, correctly it turns out, that we won't take the time to read the whole *megillah* (affectionate Jewish for "nine yards") on the labels. If we did, we would probably never buy the products, laden as they are with all sorts of unpronounceable bad-bad-bad-for-you additives, preservatives, supplements, and whatnot. Low carbs, for example. I would hate to add myself to the glut of people who feed you a barrage of information on low-carb foods, which leaves me, for one, confused and not an ounce thinner. Most manufacturing powers that be, only too happy that hardly anyone reads labels thoroughly (if at all), pounce on the diet darling *du jour*, totally disregard the whole nutrition picture, take each ingredient out of its nutritional context, and replace carbs in their products with sugar and emollients, most often making them more caloric and infinitely less tasty. Is it any wonder that so often the public professes to be totally disillusioned with the so-called health foods and low-fat foods industry? Just try some low-fat peanut butter spread and you will immediately see why: It tastes revolting and has thirty *more, not less,* calories per serving than regular peanut butter. I ask you: Who needs it?

I recently saw a low-carb cookie that listed its nutrition information as "serving size: ½ cookie, 180 calories" (promise!) and found it a real chutzpah: Half a cookie? Who on earth eats half a cookie? What reckless manufacturer included 180 calories in half a cookie? Seriously, is the most important quality in a food that it be low in carbs, gluten-free, or even low in fat or high in fiber? On the face of it, labels that advertise such things make the product sound like a good deal—that is, until we read on and realize that lower carb or fat or higher fiber was achieved at the cost of whopping quantities of sugar, man-made unhealthy trans fats, enormous amounts of salt and, just as importantly, a great loss of flavor. (Same with fat-free cheese: shudder!)

Tomato juice is delicious all on its own, and it's loaded with vitamin C, lycopene, and other valuable nutrients. But the misguided manufacturers add shovelfuls of salt in a drink that is already naturally high in sodium to begin with. (The amount of sodium in a cup of commercial tomato juice is an absurd 654mg—nearly *half* of the total sodium daily recommendation for certain segments of the population!

Author M. F. K. Fisher wrote the following about commercial bread, circa 1942: "We continue everywhere to buy the packaged monstrosities that lie, all sliced and tasteless, on the bread counters of the nation, and spend money and more money on pills containing the vitamins that have been removed at great cost from the wheat."

Sixty-five years later, we only get more of the same, in more sophisticated packages. Take a look at the expensive "energy" drinks and vitamin waters invading the supermarket and health food store shelves—energy we could all be getting in endless supply and for free just by eating whole foods and nothing more.

I recently spotted yet another new hip drink: Acai Vodka. You'd have to drink yourself to a stupor before you get enough antioxidants out of this one! I agree it is too time consuming to go through the whole ingredient list on every food label (by the way, the longer the list, the farther you should stay away from the product; consequently you will be left with a short select list of minimally processed foods), but there are some items you should always watch out for. Ideally, we want our food to be low in saturated fat, sodium, cholesterol, calories, and sugar and high in fiber, vitamins, and minerals. And flavor—yes, flavor—bring it on down! Of course, no one single food group will accomplish that, but this is our homework: Any food item that has none of these assets (chips, fries, soda, hot dogs, store-bought cookies and cakes, and so on) is simply a waste of your time and calories and takes the place of something much more enjoyable and good for you (popcorn, dark chocolate, nuts, seeds, dried fruit, good fruit juices and teas, fruit, yogurt, whole-grain cereal, etc.).

Specialty food stores: Many food items take little or no room in your pantry or refrigerator and are worth having on hand to empower us with resourcefulness and creativity at a moment's notice: saffron and other exotic spices, unsliced cheese, dark chocolate, natural extracts and flavorings, whole grains and flours, teas (loose or in bags), coffees, whole-grain low-fat crackers, all-fruit jams and spreads, good olives, sun-dried tomatoes, dry wild mushrooms, natural oils, nuts, seeds, nut butters, dried fruit, vinegars, wine, rum, rice noodles. Whereas it would be daunting and expensive to try to get these items in a fancy neighborhood store, it would be much more fun and time- and cost-effective to go to a well-stocked health food, specialty, or ethnic foods store where you can get these items in larger amounts, straight out of bins or in generic containers, and without the hype of fancy labeling and packaging. Best of all, just do as I do: Go online and inquire about—and order—just about any specialty item you like!

Some unprocessed or minimally processed canned or bottled products are actually decent and very useful to have on hand: All-fruit jams, pineapple, cranberry sauce, beans, tomatoes, coffee, roasted peppers, beets, tuna, sardines, anchovies, and lemon juice are a few examples. Dry herbs are acceptable when fresh are not at hand—except for garlic and onion, which are acceptable *only* in their original whole fresh form (more on this later).

Imitation flavorings: I have the dubious distinction of living on top of a diner that is open 24-7. Yet in all the years I've lived here, I can't remember once being drawn to its unrelenting emissions. However, it does throw me back, albeit unwittingly, to an earlier period of my life when I lived near a bakery whose constant heavenly emanations made me weak at the knees. The little doggy in me (and, I'll bet, in all of us) is very attracted to aromas and sights first and to flavors second. What's there to get excited about in the diner's concoctions? Eggs and fries spewing noxious smells of rancid shortenings, melted fake cheese, neon-colored drinks, and mushy hot cereal. The bakery of my childhood, by contrast, positively vibrated with the aromas of real chocolate, real vanilla, real coffee, real butter, real lemon. Just thinking about it makes my tongue smile even after all these years. Nothing, *nothing*, replaces the real thing. Same goes for real versus imitation cheese food, wine versus cooking wine, dark chocolate versus commercial chocolate bars, to name just a few. Why, you might ask? Because they contain only trace amounts of cheese, wine, or chocolate, and the rest is a long tedious list of hideous things you should never put in your mouth.

The difference in price between the real thing and its lackluster commercial counterpart, if any, is negligible, but the rewards are infinite: Consider this line from an unknown but quite-often-noted author: *"The bitter taste of poor quality lingers long after the sweetness of low price is forgotten."* We are satisfied after a reasonable helping of something genuine and wholesome, and having hit the spot, we stop searching. I am always reminded of that song by the Rolling Stones, *"I can get no satisfaction / 'cause I try, and I try, and I try . . ."* A somewhat mischievous association. Or is it? Why eat globs of some mediocre institutional ice cream if you can have the proverbial perfect scoop and call it a day? Why eat a dozen institutional cookies in just a few minutes, when you can make four dozen perfect cookies, store them in a tin, and eat a couple at a time? Those muffins we buy with such abandon, thinking we are doing the healthy thing, often come from an insipid mix and have about 700 calories apiece. How about whipping up a baker's dozen from-scratch muffins in five minutes, eating one (about 300 calories) and freezing the rest for later use? Naturally less addictive because it contains much less sugar, fat, and salt, homemade is much superior in every way imaginable. Remember, a finished homemade product made from real ingredients is always much greater than the sum of its parts, however modest.

Mixed spreads: I recently spotted at the supermarket a big box of little boxes containing a mixture of peanut butter and jelly. The selling point, printed in bright bold letters, was that you need not bother to spread both peanut butter *and* jelly. Plus, it was portion-controlled, so you would not be tempted to eat more. In case, heaven forbid, we were too frazzled to spread some peanut butter on a piece of toast and then take another five seconds and spread jam over it. For this great service the manufacturer was providing, I did the math and found that the mixture cost, ounce for ounce, about eight times the price of peanut butter *and* jelly sold in separate containers. I can name many such examples, but I will keep the list short, and I have no doubt you will catch my drift: A carton of egg whites is about six times the price of its whole egg counterpart and saves you only the time it would take to separate the egg whites from the yolks (say, one minute). You can buy a container of yogurt topped with a tiny container of granola for about double what it would cost to stir a little granola from your cupboard into a container of yogurt. The latest innovation is an open-and-squeeze zipper bag of tuna, which costs more than double its canned counterpart, all because it affords me the luxury of not having to use a can opener: How nice! Then come the pre-soaped steel wool pads, the pre-sprayed polishing cloths, and many more: I throw up my hands! If you would allow me the slight digression, I often think, not very fondly, of the Clintonian reason for countless indiscretions, *"Because I could."* It just has to go, period.

Getting prepared meals delivered: Many diet programs make extravagant promises no one ever seems to cash in on, or at least not for very long, or else why do so many of us keep gaining all those unsightly pounds? Their appeal is roughly, "Lose weight on our diet, the delicious and inexpensive way, without ever cooking or doing the math or doing anything at all. In your sleep, as it were. Our talented chefs and expert nutritionists will do it all for you, and you will soon be joining the club of happy attractive trim men and women." It seems to me this is bound to set back our relationship with food even further. None of us has one solitary example of acquiring something without doing anything to earn it (even those fortunate few who hit the jackpot first had to buy a lottery ticket!).

The very few diet plans that call for our personal involvement in the preparation and consumption of our food are the most successful and get us the most lasting results. Plus, we have fun doing it and eating with our family and friends. No, we don't need to open our door and find a bag containing our daily food supply, unless we are old and incapacitated. Which reminds me—thank goodness for all those wonderful volunteer organizations that keep the elderly and home-bound well provided for and preserve their dignity at a nominal price. Incidentally, *these* are the very people who could use soap-soaked pads, nut-butter-jam spreads, and so on, but who, unfortunately, most often cannot afford these costly commodities! The single greatest diet and nutrition tool is behavior modification, and the single greatest behavior modification tool consists of acquiring a better knowledge of—and establishing a relationship with—what we are ingesting, for our sake as well as that of everyone entrusted in our care. Why not learn to relate to food, since we use it all day long, every day of our lives? Understanding our food is easy, fun, delicious, and liberating, and the health rewards are endless and permanent.

You will be pleased to find that many of my recipes are written in a way that empowers you, the cook, with many easy adaptations, according to your mood and preferences and the ingredients you might have on hand.

My Own Diet Tools

I wouldn't presume to wax nutritionist—there are many qualified people for that. Rather, since a whole lifetime of cooking and eating has somehow kept me and all mine healthy and trim, G-d bless, I decided I must be doing something right, and I would like to share some of my practices with you. After all, they are indeed the principles that inform the whole contents of this book.

Do the math: My first reaction each time I get a bank statement and am faced with the dismal numbers is to march straight to the bank and alert them that their mean giant calculator must simply be off its rocker. But no, it's not. It turns out that those withdrawals did take place and did add up—they always do—and the results are, alas, always accurate. When I peek at some fast-food restaurant customers' mountainous plates, I often find myself wondering, gosh, what would it take to work off this semi-industrial-size meal? Would swimming across the Hudson River be atonement enough? I remember when my sister Rackel had just moved to the States: she would look everywhere around her, bewildered, and say, "Gosh, everything is so *big* in this country—buildings, bodies, meals, drinks, *everything!*" My mother once exclaimed after a waiter placed an order of ice cream in front of her, "This is not ice cream, it's a monument!"

Too many "dieters" inhale a pint of frozen yogurt because the package claims to be fat-free, instead of enjoying half a cup of the real thing: *This* is the very reason so many people lament the fact they have not lost weight, or have even gained weight, on low-fat diets. Would you like two scoops of ice cream instead of two scoops of frozen yogurt? Go right ahead and enjoy them, just as long as you keep in mind that two scoops of ice cream are the caloric equivalent of almost a quart of frozen yogurt (incidentally, some very good brands of real ice cream are less caloric than others, so shop around. You might be able to enjoy the real thing more often after all!). After many graphic instances of low-calorie dishes facing off against their high-calorie counterparts, you can't help acquiring the good habit of counting. The good news is, after a while, you don't even need to count anymore; eating the right thing becomes second nature, and the occasional splurge is totally allowed and is not considered a terrible setback.

Snacks: The following remarks apply *only* to packaged commercial snacks. After so many years living in the States, I have become convinced that snacking is an American affliction masquerading as lighthearted and fun recreation. I blame it every bit as much as I do fast foods for causing all the havoc in so many people's figures and health: a sort of avatar of American opulence. I have calculated that you need about six lifetimes eating nothing whatsoever but commercial snacks and never eating the same snack twice in order to sample all of them available at an average supermarket. The problem is that the child in each of us has no idea where to start or when to stop. The very people who purport to have our nutrition foremost in mind keep coming up with all these snacks, fast and furious, promising heavenly tastes, a great energy boost, or worse, snacks that will replace meals. Seeing ads of beautiful girls ecstatically sipping their lunch from a can couldn't possibly help make it appeal to our senses any more than all the added strawberry or chocolate flavor in the world could help make it more palatable. Because snacking has such an unthreatening name, and we think of it somewhat affectionately, we do it mindlessly and hardly ever realize it will calorically (but of course not nutritionally) add up to a meal and then some. My mother tells me of a neighbor who had the annoying habit of "accidentally" dropping in on us at dinnertime. Each time we would ask him if he would like to join us, and he would vehemently protest, "Oh no! I couldn't put you to so much trouble. I just had dinner at home, all I want is a little snack," and proceed to eat himself silly. One day he was finally asked, gently but firmly, to please snack at home and then come and have dinner with us.

Why not forget about all the staggering variety of processed commercial snacks available on the market and stick to the natural snacks you love best and are best for you? Are you satisfied you had a meaningful breakfast, lunch, dinner? Wonderful, you still have a couple hundred calories to spend on something fantastic of your choice. That means about *one* treat. Yet another treat tempting you? Look forward to enjoying it tomorrow. We can't visit every place in the world or meet every wonderful person in the world. Neither can we sample every snack in the world. Life is much too short for that, so let's make our peace with it and narrow our choices to the very best.

Here is a list of healthy snacks I keep on hand to enjoy in small portions when I must have a treat between light meals, and which even indeed constitute a light and nutritious meal in their own right: yogurt, sunflower seeds, lightly oiled popcorn, natural granola, vacuum-packed roasted chestnuts, dried fruit, homemade cookies and muffins, dark chocolate, natural nut butters, all-fruit jams and hummus on whole-grain breads, coffees and teas, fresh and unprocessed frozen fruit, salad greens, and whole-grain low-fat crackers.

The kitchen is closed: I was never overweight, but for about five years I lugged around a pesky ten pounds I couldn't shake off. Ten unwanted pounds was too much to look my best but too little to do anything radical about, so I decided to do the equivalent of dropping the proverbial daily dime in the piggy bank, painlessly and effortlessly: every day I took out no more than fifty calories (half a glass of juice or milk, a third of a glass of wine, two crackers, half a slice of bread, etc.). Along the same lines, I moved most of my eating to the middle of the day, eating early dinners and making sure to eat late meals only when I absolutely couldn't help it (social events, business meetings, eating on the road, etc.); and if I suspected those late meals might be irresistible, I made room for them by eating extra light earlier that day. Not eating late as a rule, except for a cup of tea and a piece of fruit, aside of course for watching my portions during the day and taking long walks (my favorite form of exercise), was the single greatest change I made in my diet to this day (and yes, I kept those pesky ten pounds off: thanks for asking!).

Eat these in moderation: I used to think life wouldn't be worth living without pizza, pasta, bagels, and the like. But this love has always remained unrequited, and these foods wreak havoc on my system each time I succumb to them. I have the whole week of Passover to provide me with the ultimate litmus test: I feel great and light, even with the feasts I prepare, serve, and eat; and I don't miss the culprits for a moment. Of course, staying on this kind of diet year-round would be simply unrealistic, so I replace almost all white starches with whole-grain bread, brown rice, and other gluten-free grains, whole-grain cereal, and all the wonderful grains that are so easy to find in health food stores nowadays. Yes: spelt pizza, brown rice sushi, soba noodles. Yum! Likewise, I give my whole system a rest after a splurge that disagrees with me. Simple example: there is an infuriating ad on television about some antacid where the main character seems ready to keel over from heartburn, but about two seconds after popping an antacid tablet, he is back in "cannoli heaven," eating again and grinning. Why not have mercy on your tired stomach, forego the rest of the treat, have a nice cup of tea, and call it a day?

With, not _after,_ dinner: Do you love popcorn as much as I do? Don't eat it after dinner while you are watching a movie or reading a book. Have a light dinner of soup and salad . . . and popcorn! In other words, pace yourself. You can have all your favorites, only not all at once!

Eat at home whenever possible: What do nearly all people who look good and feel good have in common? They eat most of their meals at home. Their pantry is well stocked with healthy staples, fruit, and wholesome snacks, and when away at their office or on a trip, they work on replicating the feel of home food by finding the perfect salad bar and the perfect frozen yogurt place, and are not afraid to look like geeks just because they have some seeds, yogurt, or dried fruit stored away in a tiny space of the office refrigerator.

Learn to order in a restaurant: As a longtime (now former) restaurant owner, I can tell you with great authority that being a frequent restaurant-goer is no excuse for bad eating habits. Whatever dish I choose, I always order it with a whole grain and double the veggies, no gravy, mustard on the side, big pot of decaf tea, and bread to go. Are you simply dying to have that delicious bread? Great, only please don't have two rolls of it smeared with butter while you are waiting for your order to arrive (that's what doggie bags are for). Rather, have your treat for lunch or dinner the next day, with a good spread and a good salad.

Eat what takes time: My son Maimon, who used to look robust in his teenage years, to put it fondly, spent a year abroad in school, came back almost eighty pounds lighter, and never looked back. A dismal school dorm diet had jolted him into rethinking all his meals. Not only has he maintained his weight ever since, but he assures me he is never on a diet. So, what gives? Besides becoming more conscious of what he ingests, he shares a ridiculously simple trick with me, and with whoever asks him: *Eat things that take time to eat!* And what might that be? Well, to name a few valuable whole foods, watermelon, an apple, popcorn, sandwiches prepared with dense whole-grain bread, soup, salad, and so on. Then comes my (and my husband's) great favorite: sunflower seeds, in their shells of course. We simply couldn't live without them. They're the perfect eat-like-a-mensch-or-you-might-choke kind of food. Plus, they are delicious. They come in 2½-ounce vacuum-packed bags to preserve their freshness (and our self-control). We have done all the math: with all the painstaking shelling, it takes about an hour to finish a bag, a 230-calorie treat. And so good for you, with the perfect oils and vitamins. My husband and I hunker down to a bag (*each*, of course—there is a limit to sharing, even between husband and wife: *Don't touch my seeds, you hear?*) when reading a book, or making our calls, or even on short plane rides with meager offerings (yes, we dispose of our shells considerately!). You would think there was a famine, seeing how doggedly we comb areas where we think a stray seed may have gone into hiding, no doubt trying to escape the onslaught: under a bed, a table, a blanket. Sometimes I have trouble finding them in stores, and my first fear is that we Kirschenbaums might have depleted, or maybe even drained, the national supply. But no, they always reappear on the shelves, nice and crisp. Thank G-d for small blessings.

Never give up what you love: How in the world are we expected to enjoy a diet, let alone stick to it, if we are fed canned meal replacements or meals that arrive at our door in a sealed bag, as if we were maximum-security inmates? We want food that is vibrant, colorful, and fragrant, and I simply cannot imagine any of these ersatz "meals" being endowed in any measure with these attributes. Why not eat what you love and learn to love some other wonderful foods you may have been neglecting or ignoring? Whenever possible (which in my view is always), eat the lightest version of your favorites. Examples: thinly sliced medium-rare London broil for steak lovers; grilled chicken for barbecue lovers; bison (tomorrow's meat, I predict and hope) burgers for hamburger lovers; pasta with tomato or vegetable pasta sauce for pasta lovers; poached or grilled fish with lots of herbs and lemon for fish lovers; mountains of salads and veggies with homemade dressing; whole-grain bread with good spreads and nut butters, all-fruit jams and cheeses for sandwich lovers; frozen yogurt for frozen dessert lovers; perfect dark chocolate for chocolate lovers; and so on down the line. Likewise, eat smaller portions of calorie-dense foods (meat, fish, cheese, bread, etc.) and larger portions of lean foods (veggies, lightly dressed salads, vegetable-based soups, etc.).

What about the impossibly rich monstrosities we see so many people losing their figures on? That, in my view, is not a weakness but an absurdity: Give it up! PS: Dear gourmet coffee boutiques, how nice, how hip, how progressive of you to start off with a wonderful zero-calorie treat—coffee—and disfigure it (and us) by building it up to a 700-calorie drink, almost half of our daily caloric allowance in a tall glass. You're all the way up there with the déclassé fast-food joints, except with you, we haven't even started eating yet. Is this the best contribution your marketing wizards could come up with? No wonder the public is so confused and frustrated, and so often overweight! Yes, it is our responsibility to control our eating, but it is the manufacturer's responsibility—indeed mission; it should even be his pride and joy, his raison d'être—to offer safe delicious treats!

Use some restraint: A customer I catered a party for wrote me a thank-you note: "You are the only caterer I know with a heart!" Oh, I am sure there are a few caterers with a heart out there, but seriously: I often come across recipes (from fancy, well-informed cookbooks and food magazines, believe it or not) that read roughly as follows: "For 4 servings: 2 sticks butter, 1 cup heavy cream, 1 cup wine, etc." Stop right there, don't read on! It will be an orgy, not a dish! Come on, Chef, get real! We all know contractors who promise a beautiful kitchen, which I have no doubt they can deliver . . . for the modest sum of a quarter of a million dollars. But isn't it better to hire the less-expensive creative worker who makes the best use of the tools at his disposal and ends up with wonderful and affordable results? In the same way, why consume all those calories when you can have an equally delicious meal for half the caloric "cost" by using the right ingredients in the right amounts and the right combinations?

Get "stuck" with only the best: We all have at least *one* how-could-you-go-wrong-for-that-price? friend (a close relative of the indefatigable I-can-get-it-for-you-wholesale friend)—the friend who, with great glee, displays all his or her bargains of the day, while you try to keep your eyes kindly averted. Granted, the shirt or skirt or whatever was not exactly the color, or the size, or the style, or the fit they would have liked, but they just couldn't resist such an incredible steal. So they ask, how could they go wrong? And it screams for only one answer: You can go *very* wrong indeed, condemning yourself voluntarily to a wardrobe full of "shlock" items and their attendant frumpy look, all because of the prurient and short-lived thrill that comes from grabbing as many gimmicky cheap bargains as possible.

We all admire and seek to emulate the friend who has an uncluttered, well-chosen, and to-the-point wardrobe and who always looks wonderful while not spending a penny more than your bargain-obsessed friend (maybe even less: now wouldn't that be terribly vexing?). We feel the same about the speaker who carefully chooses his or her words to make a short-and-sweet presentation that hits the nail on the head each time. Likewise, your pantry, your table: just as the cheap plastic belt or the excess crude language obscures—indeed eclipses—all the good look and all the good message, so too, the garlic powder, the bouillon cube, the canned potato, the chicken nugget, the just-add-water soup. Even if you have no knowledge whatsoever of cooking, just by *not using anything wrong*, you will get great results. The deletions are every bit as crucial as the additions. Banish all those ingredients that might compromise or ruin your creation, and surround yourself with only what counts and will do you proud! *"Perfection is achieved, not when there is nothing more to add, but when there is nothing left to take away"* (Antoine de Saint Exupery).

On the jar labels:
lévana's grapefruit liqueur

lévana's preserved lemons

lévana's harissa

THE PANTRY: EDIBLE GIFTS TO YOURSELF AND BEYOND

A pantry stocked with your own artisanal condiments, liqueurs, sauces, or dressings will allow you to dress up simple foods at mealtime, minimizing preparation time when you need it most.

Let's talk about the other lucky beneficiaries—the neighbors and friends receiving your creations. "What shall we bring them?" That's what we invariably ask each time we get invited to someone's home, and of course, the question looms much larger when the invitation is for a weekend or even longer. To be sure, there's always the classic bottle of wine or liquor, the flowers, or chocolates, as dependable and welcome as the immortal little black dress. But suppose for a moment you are known (if you are not, you soon will be, with a little help from your friend!) for making the best marinade or liqueur or pickles or spice mixture. Imagine the excitement you will elicit when one of your signature healthy artisanal goodies is passed around and the sheer joy you will reap at watching everyone's delight! A triumph for you and a delicious reward for your healthy choices!

Of course you can consult with your hosts on whether you can help with the meal and what their needs might be, and end up whipping up a cake or a batch of cookies that will be served to the company. But if your hosts are all set with the menu, they will enjoy immensely a jar or a tin of something delicious that will remain a few days, maybe even a few weeks, after the party is over.

When the contents are fabulous, it's not necessary (it may even be excessive) to put it in a costly container or a frilly wrapping. Don't let the container eclipse the contents; rather, let the food do its magic!

The best thing about edible presents is that a batch will yield several of each item, making it possible to offer not one but several gifts to different friends on special occasions and to keep some for your own pantry! Yes, I know supermarket shelves are crammed beyond capacity with endless condiments, snacks, and whatnot; but they won't hold a candle to your own homemade, natural, and wholesome treats.

What might qualify as an edible gift? It could be any number of things, but they should have some important common traits:

- A food item that is capable of withstanding the rigors of transit for a few hours, without refrigeration, and is not so delicate that you are obsessing about it melting, crumbling, curdling, freezing, or oozing on the way. In other words, not a salmon mousse or chocolate truffles or lace cookies, but a relish, a marinade, a dessert sauce, etc.
- It should not be so large and cumbersome that it becomes more of an imposition than a welcome addition to a host's pantry; likewise, it shouldn't be something so perishable that it must be eaten that day. You are not looking to upstage the hostess.
- It should sound familiar, not outlandish, or worse, gimmicky: Did you mention you make the best chai spice mix, the best cranberry relish, or the best chocolate chip cookies? Bring it right on! Your originality will consist precisely in your making the most familiar goodie in the most unforgettable way.

Here, then, are some of my absolute favorite edible gift creations. These condiments and preserves are so fabulous the dish you use them on hardly needs any other adorning: Totally plain poached chicken breasts or baked fish or tofu, for example, will find their rightful place in the gastronomic world wearing a different but very becoming hat each time you decide to top them with another of the following foolproof preparations:

Gluten-free

People suffering from celiac disease can't have gluten in any amount, even minute. The following grains are totally off-limits to them: barley, malt, rye, triticale, wheat (all types: bulgur, einkorn, emmer, farina, spelt, and kamut). The grains allowed in a gluten-free diet are amaranth, arrowroot, buckwheat, cassava, corn, millet, quinoa, rice, sorghum, tapioca, teff, wild rice, oats labeled gluten-free (to make sure they were not processed in a wheat machinery). This part is clear enough. The more problematic part is the gluten (such as wheat, barley, rye, malt, and oats processed in wheat machinery) hidden in some condiments and prepared sauces, and some drinks (beer, bourbon, cider, vodka). When buying the following items, always make certain the label clearly states "Gluten-Free": BBQ sauce, curry, gravy, ketchup, malt vinegar, mustard, meat sauce, Non-dairy creamer, oyster sauce, peanut butter, powdered sugar, salad dressing, salsa, soy sauce, teriyaki sauce, tomato sauce, worcestershire sauce.

SALAD DRESSINGS

No bottled dressings, no matter how fancy and gourmet, come anywhere close in quality and flavor to homemade dressings, no matter how plain and boring. It's that simple. The food industry turns out hundreds of new dressings each year. You don't even need one of them. I always hear lame excuses like, "But we get more variety when we buy it!" "But it is easier when we buy it!" Let's do a little math here: Suppose you use just oil, lemon or vinegar, salt and pepper, and absolutely nothing more: If you have a dozen oils to choose from (canola, olive, sesame, toasted sesame, walnut, etc.) and a dozen vinegars (cider, balsamic, malt, wine, rice, raspberry, etc.) or lemon or lime juice, there is a whopping 144 varieties of dressing right there, all great!

Make a wonderful dressing in a flash. Better yet, make half a gallon of wonderful dressing in a flash, and store it in a glass jar. It is not perishable, and in any case, it will be used long before it gets a chance to get ruined. Remember, the dressing is good, the salad is good, so you will eat lots of the salad and use up the dressing faster!

All the following salad dressings are good enough to double as dips and sauces over unadorned fish, chicken, and tofu dishes.

OIL AND VINEGAR (OR LEMON) DRESSING GF, P

I am starting with the original bare-bones classic on purpose. This dressing is easier than even opening a jar! Don't use white vinegar because it has an acrid taste. All other vinegars are wonderful. Likewise, don't use the olive oil marked "light." You probably think it means light in calories (I was told this many times), but no—light only means it was stripped of its wonderful olive flavor, and left with all its caloric content, at about double the price of any other good olive oil. Who needs it?

Sea salt

I only use sea salt, throughout this book and everywhere; it is widely available and inexpensive, and all its nutrients are preserved intact. No need whatsoever to buy any fancy variety (such as gray, pink, etc.), except perhaps for an exceptional treat.

Ground pepper

Pepper: get yourself a peppermill, and play not only with the thickness of the grinds but with all the wonderful kinds of pepper: black, green, white, pink, mixed peppercorns! The lighter the color, the milder the flavor. No need to use a peppermill in every recipe that calls for ground pepper, but it will make a difference in a finished pasta or rice dish.

1½ cups oil, any except oil marked "light"
½ cup to ⅔ cup lemon juice or vinegar, any except white
Salt and pepper to taste

Mix all ingredients in a jar and pour over your favorite greens just before serving. Store refrigerated in a glass jar. Makes about 2 cups.

HERB MUSTARD DRESSING GF

Tofu has such an unctuous texture and results in such a good emulsion that it allows you to reduce the oil considerably, making it a leaner choice.

Tofu and other dairy-free products

Let's just say that it wasn't love at first sight between me and tofu, and who could blame me? The first time I spotted it at a supermarket, I thought, *What on earth is this pale, damp, jiggly, wobbly, rubbery slab doing in the produce section? Am I supposed to cook with it?* But that was many years ago, and I am writing now, many wonderful dairy-free dishes later. Soy and other dairy-free products (miso, dairy-free milks, etc.) have none of the attributes that naturally attract us to food—color, fragrance, texture. But while rarely visible, they work their unseen magic in the finished dish—whether a mousse, a soup, a pie, or ice cream. No calorie problems, no meat conflicts, just some great liberation. *Tofu,* for one, has such a creamy texture and bulk that it needs little or no help from the usual suspects (mainly, cream and eggs) to achieve the smoothness we crave in ice cream, sauces, dips, lasagna, and so on. Bland and unobtrusive, it obediently highlights the flavors with which it is paired, giving them an incomparable texture that opens the door to many sweet and savory possibilities. Likewise, many sweet and savory dishes, smoothies, and other drinks are prepared with dairy-free milks made from soy, rice, whole grain, almonds, hemp, or nuts, offering lots of nutrition without the lactose. You will note I make extensive use of the entire gamut, all of which are easy to find at health food stores.

1 soft or silken tofu cake, squeezed dry
4 large cloves garlic
¼ cup good olive oil
¼ cup Dijon-style mustard
½ cup orange juice or apple cider (settle for water or rice milk if you can't afford the extra fruit sugar)
⅓ cup wine vinegar, or any other vinegar except white
1 tablespoon oregano
Salt and pepper to taste

Blend tofu, garlic, and olive oil in a blender or food processor until smooth. Add all remaining ingredients and process until smooth. Makes about 2 cups. Store refrigerated in a glass jar.

FRUITY SHALLOT DRESSING GF, P

Believe me, bring this to a party and you will have everyone hounding you for your recipe. It happens to me all the time!

3 medium shallots
1 cup good olive oil
⅓ cup balsamic vinegar
⅓ cup apple cider, cranberry, or pomegranate juice
¼ cup pomegranate molasses or other all-fruit syrup (health food stores), maple syrup or agave
Salt and pepper to taste

In a food processor, finely grind the shallots. Gradually add all remaining ingredients and process just a few seconds. Makes about 2 cups. Store refrigerated in a glass jar.

CHINESE GREEN TEA DRESSING GF

The magic of Asian ingredients! With such intense and clean flavors, a little goes a long way. You will love this dressing not only with many salads, but also drizzled on grilled fish, tofu, or chicken. Makes about 2½ cups.

1 2-inch piece fresh ginger, peeled
½ cup toasted sesame oil
½ cup strong green tea (or red or white), decaf OK
2 tablespoons honey, agave, or maple syrup
⅓ cup soy sauce (GF, see page 21)
⅓ cup unfiltered apple cider vinegar, or brown rice vinegar
Dash of bottled hot sauce, or to taste

Grind the ginger finely in a food processor. Add all remaining ingredients and process until smooth. Makes about 2 cups. Store refrigerated in a glass jar.

CURRIED MANGO DRESSING GF

This dressing goes beautifully with salads that include fruit and nuts, even fruit salad. Mustard oil is available in specialty food stores; it is potent, so a little goes a long way.

1 ripe mango, peeled and cut in chunks
½ cup extra-virgin olive oil
2 tablespoons mustard oil (settle for Dijon-style mustard)
⅓ cup orange juice
⅓ cup lemon juice
1 tablespoon lemon zest
1 tablespoon curry, or to taste
Salt and pepper to taste

Place the mango chunks in the food processor. With the motor running, add the oils in a slow stream, then the juices and spices. Makes about 2 cups. Store refrigerated in a glass jar.

AVOCADO MINT DRESSING GF, P

This dressing will not keep as well as all the others avocado being so fragile and perishable; still it's delicious and I highly recommend it. Just use it on the day you make it, or no later than the next day or two. Throw the avocado pit in the jar: It will keep the dressing from discoloring.

1 medium ripe to ripe avocado, pit reserved
½ cup natural apple cider
¼ cup good olive oil
⅓ cup unfiltered apple cider vinegar
2 medium shallots
¼ cup mint leaves, packed
Salt and pepper to taste

Purée all ingredients in the food processor until smooth. Pour over salad greens just before serving and toss. Makes about 2 cups. Store refrigerated in a glass jar, with the pit.

CAESAR'S DRESSING GF

This dressing is much too good to be used only on salad, so go ahead and use it on grilled fish, or skip the anchovies in the dressing and use it on poached or grilled chicken.

Anchovies

Don't tell your guests that this dish, or any dish for that matter, contains anchovies until after they polish it off. The anchovies disperse and leave no trace of their controversial heritage except for a deep, smoky flavor. I'm reminded of a wonderful headline I once saw—"Anchovies: A blessing if disguised." Don't add salt to dishes including anchovies, as they are loaded with enough salt to season the whole dish.

Dashi powder

Also called Hondashi, it is a desiccated fish-seaweed powder: sort of like anchovies, only much more complex, and much easier to use. Dashi imparts an incredibly deep and luxurious flavor to dozens of dishes: Caesar salad, paella, fish soup, salmon mousse, fish terrine, pasta dishes, and fish sauces, to name just a few. Don't add salt to dishes including dashi, as it is loaded with enough salt to season the whole dish.

Capers

Capers are the buds of the caper bush, which grows in Mediterranean regions. They vary in size from very tiny (nonpareils) to as big as tiny olives with stems about an inch long (caper berries). Capers are pickled in brine or a mixture of water, salt, and vinegar, or packed in coarse salt (no added salt in the dish please!). They add tang and zip to salads and sauces at no caloric cost, and the berries look delightful as a garnish for martinis or other drinks.

6 anchovies, rinsed (or 2 tablespoons dashi powder)
3 tablespoons capers
½ bunch flat-leaf parsley, stems and leaves
3 tablespoons Dijon mustard
4 large cloves garlic
½ cup extra-virgin olive oil
¼ cup wine vinegar
½ cup water
1 tablespoon oregano
Ground pepper to taste

Place all the ingredients in a food processor and process until smooth, about half a minute. If the dressing gets too thick as it sits, thin it with a little more water. Makes about 2 cups. Store refrigerated in a glass jar.

YOGURT DILL DRESSING GF, P

Much leaner than ranch dressing, the insanely rich cousin that provided the inspiration for it.

1 cup yogurt or dairy-free yogurt, unflavored
1 small bunch dill, fronds and stems
4 large cloves garlic
½ cup olive oil
¼ cup prepared white horseradish, or 2 tablespoons wasabi powder diluted in ¼ cup cold water
¼ cup fresh lemon juice
2 tablespoons sugar
Salt and pepper to taste

Blend the yogurt, dill, and garlic in a food processor or blender until smooth. Add all remaining ingredients and blend until smooth. Makes about 2½ cups. Store refrigerated in a glass jar.

TAHINI DRESSING GF

You will love the ethnic twist in this dressing. Any excuse to use tahini (sesame paste)! It will perk up countless simple fish, poultry, and burger dishes.

¾ cup tahini (sesame paste)
4 large cloves garlic
1 cup water
½ cup fresh lemon juice
Salt and pepper to taste
Bottled hot sauce to taste
1 tablespoon ground cumin

Blend the tahini, garlic, and water in a blender or food processor until smooth. Add all remaining ingredients and blend until smooth. Makes about 2 cups. Store refrigerated in a glass jar.

ORANGE POPPY DRESSING GF, P

Orange and poppy seeds: Yum! Use this dressing in a salad that includes fruit, seeds, or nuts.

½ cup orange juice
1 cup olive oil
½ cup lemon juice
⅓ cup poppy seeds
Salt and pepper to taste
1 tablespoon each orange zest and lemon zest

Place all ingredients in a glass jar with a tight cover. Shake thoroughly before using. Makes about 2 cups. Store refrigerated in a glass jar.

BASIL HONEY DRESSING GF, P

I like to make this dressing in summer, when basil is plentiful, and use it in salad greens that include tomatoes, fennel, and/or olives.

Other herb uses

What's the matter, you have too much fresh basil, thyme, sage, rosemary, oregano, mint, or tarragon left over from cooking? Sounds like a wonderful problem to me. Do what my mother taught me: Put a generous handful (less for very intense herbs such as oregano or rosemary) in a cup, with a bag of your favorite unflavored tea if desired, and pour boiling water over it (one herb at a time please). Let the mixture infuse a few minutes and then enjoy it alone or with your favorite sweetener. It will taste and smell heavenly. If a cold drink is what you prefer, throw your herb in a pitcher of cold water. Just one more treat: throw your herbs in a food processor with olive oil and your favorite seasonings, and get a different pesto each time.

---

1 cup basil leaves, packed
¾ cup olive oil
2 medium shallots
½ cup natural apple cider
¼ cup honey
⅓ cup wine vinegar, or a little more to taste
Salt and pepper to taste

Place the basil, oil, and shallots in a food processor, and process until smooth. Add all remaining ingredients and process again until smooth. Makes about 2 cups. Store in a glass jar.

WALNUT DRESSING GF, P

For walnuts lovers. Sometimes we get lucky and find walnut oil at a decent price: Nothing like it!

⅓ cup toasted walnuts (12–15 minutes in a 300°F oven)
1 medium shallot, quartered
¼ cup walnut oil (if it's too hard to find, use ½ cup olive oil total)
¼ cup extra-virgin olive oil
¼ cup red wine vinegar
⅓ cup dry sherry (liquor stores) or mirin (rice wine: health food stores)
Salt and pepper to taste

Mix all ingredients in blender or food processor until smooth and perfectly emulsified. Makes about 2 cups. Store refrigerated in a glass jar.

REMOULADE DRESSING GF

This is an intensely flavored sauce with a robustness that is a good match for grated celery root, endives, watercress, as well as cold meats. It uses just a little fat and packs a great punch at a lower caloric cost.

⅓ cup low-fat mayonnaise (if mayo is a problem, substitute ⅓ cup silken tofu plus ¼ cup olive oil)
⅓ cup milk or dairy-free milk, low-fat OK, a little more if needed
Juice of 2 lemons
¼ cup prepared white horseradish (or 2 tablespoons wasabi diluted in a little cold water)
¼ cup Dijon-style mustard
Salt and pepper to taste
1 tablespoon sugar

Whisk all ingredients together in a bowl. Thin with a little more milk if necessary to make a creamy sauce. Makes about 2 cups. Store refrigerated in a glass jar.

RASPBERRY DRESSING GF, P

The most luxurious of all: You'll be delighted to have raspberry vinegar on hand!

1½ cups olive oil
¾ cup raspberry vinegar (recipe follows)
3 tablespoons honey, agave, or maple syrup
Salt and pepper to taste

Place all ingredients in a glass jar. Store refrigerated. Makes about 2½ cups.

RASPBERRY VINEGAR GF, P

You will make about 2 quarts in minutes. Beautifully colored and intensely flavored, a little goes a long way—mixed with a good olive oil in salad dressings, splashed into a fruit salad or a berry dessert sauce.

1 quart unfiltered apple cider vinegar
3 12-ounce packages fresh or frozen unsweetened raspberries (6 cups)

Heat the vinegar and the raspberries in a stainless steel pot until very hot, just below boiling hot. Turn off the flame, cover the pot, and set it aside for 2 days or more (if you think you will be needing this pot, just transfer the whole mixture to a glass bowl). Stir the mixture and strain it into glass jars, pressing gently on the raspberries to extract all the juice but not the pulp. If desired, add a few fresh or frozen raspberries. Makes about 2 quarts. Store in a glass jar at room temperature.

INFUSED OILS GF, P

This is so simple it requires no recipe whatsoever, and will cost you a fraction of their store-bought counterpart, and be infinitely superior.

Simply place your flavoring in a jar (one flavoring at a time please!) and complete with extra-virgin olive oil all the way to the top. Let the mixture infuse a few days at room temperature, then refrigerate. Use in salad dressings, stir-fries, and marinades. Still, I would like to give you an idea of proportions, just to get you started. Then feel free to adjust the amounts to suit your preferences.

All suggested amounts are for 1 quart oil.

Chili oil: 1 cup chili powder plus two tablespoons red pepper flakes (The powder will settle to the bottom; use only the clear liquid above.)

Lemon oil: grated zest of 4 lemons

Orange oil: grated zest of 3 oranges

Garlic oil: 2 dozen garlic cloves

Herb oils: a nice handful of your favorite herb: rosemary, thyme, sage, oregano, tarragon, chives, etc.

INFUSED VINEGARS

Exactly the same as for infused oils. Suggested flavorings above are for 1 quart apple cider vinegar.

LISA'S TIP

Oils (L.Y) Many healthy oils exist that add delicious aromas and texture to favorite dishes. Cooking oil is rich in flavor—and calories—so a little bit goes a long way. While many oils are rich in unsaturated fats and considered healthy, bear in mind that oil has lots of calories—approximately 120 calories per tablespoon—so if you are watching your weight, use it sparingly. But on the flip side, so many people have a "fear of frying" due to oil's high fat and calorie content. No need to ban oil completely for fear of getting fat. Many oils are actually linked to health and longevity. The key, as is with most foods, however, is to practice ***moderation.***

Here are some staples.

Olive oil contains monounsaturated fat, considered a "healthy" fat as it may actually lower your risk of heart disease. It also contains antioxidants including vitamin E and flavonoids. It is a great substitute for saturated fats such as butter or trans fats such as margarine. It is great drizzled on salads, sauces, and sautéing at low temperatures. Pure, virgin, or extra virgin olive oil can all work. However, extra-virgin is the least processed and preserves the most nutrients.

Canola oil is a neutral tasting oil made from rapeseeds and is rich in heart-healthy monounsaturated fats and omega-3 fatty acids. Known for its high smoke point, it is good for frying.

Sesame oil is high in polyunsaturated fats and vitamin E and is a terrific oil for adding a zest of flavor to many dishes.

Walnut oil has been shown to lower triglycerides that may reduce the risk of heart disease. It is delicious sprinkled on salads and can be substituted for some of the butter in baked goods.

Peanut oil is rich in resveratrol, the substances found in red grapes and wine, which has been associated with a reduced risk of heart disease. It is often used in cooking, because it has a mild flavor and a relatively high smoke point. Its high mono-unsaturated content makes it heart-healthy and resistant to rancidity.

Sunflower oil is a rich source of vitamin E and is low in saturated fat.

Coconut oil is high in saturated fat and should, therefore, be used sparingly. Yet it has become quite the rage; the fatty acids are medium chain triglycerides (MCTs) that are thought to be more easily metabolized by the body. However, while coconut oil certainly merits more research, based on the current research, I'd suggest using this oil, like other saturated fats, in moderation.

Butter is high in saturated fat and cholesterol. However, because it contains no trans fat, it is a better alternative to stick **margarines** that are hydrogenated (trans fat).

CONDIMENTS, SAUCES, AND MARINADES

DRY SPICE RUB GF, P

I can see you recoil at the sheer size of this recipe, and of course, you can divide it, but I don't think you will: After you taste a dry-spice-rub roast chicken or roast turkey or roast anything, you'll be glad you have plenty on hand! I use this magical rub in countless dishes. It never fails me. I even roast turkey and capon with it.

Since all ingredients are dry, I never have to worry about having to use it up quickly. I make a large batch, about a year's supply (just a few months if you use it as gifts to your delighted friends!) and store it just as I do spices, at room temperature, away from heat. Mine has no salt whatsoever, so that you might feel free to use it liberally with kosher meat and poultry, or if you are limiting your sodium intake.

Of course you can adjust the proportions any way you wish until you arrive at your favorite balance. For Passover: Skip whatever spices might not be available and double up on the ones you can find.

2½ cups dry cilantro flakes
2½ cups dry parsley flakes
1¼ cups paprika
1¼ cups oregano
2 tablespoons red pepper flakes
⅔ cup ground cumin
⅔ cup ground coriander
⅔ cup ground pepper
¼ cup ground bay leaf
⅔ cup tamarind powder
⅔ cup turmeric

Mix all ingredients thoroughly. Store in perfectly dry and perfectly clean glass jars. You will need 3 to 4 tablespoons of the mixture for roasting a chicken (page 141), 8 servings salmon or tuna, a 3-pound London broil, or 3 pounds thickly sliced tofu. Store it with your spices. Makes about 10 cups.

Tamarind powder

Literally, *tamar Hindi*, which means "Indian date". Made from the pulp found in the large bean pods of the tamarind tree, tamarind powder is very sour and adds a wonderful tang to many Indian dishes and Indonesian dishes. I love to use it here and in many other dishes where I don't want the moisture of lemon juice.

Garlic powder—more exactly, no garlic powder

My culinary nemesis: as jarring as the missing tooth or the slipped stocking stitch. Please don't! You will never ever miss it. Someone once asked me at a cooking demo, "If I ever run out of garlic powder, can I settle for fresh?" Which prompted, besides lots of laughter, the subsequent gift of a gorgeous silver life-size garlic-head necklace from my dear friend Joe. I wear it at my demos: it helps me exhort the crowds and has become my trademark.

Ground bay leaf

I always use my bay leaves ground: It saves you the part where you have to fish them out and spares you the suspense of getting one stuck in your throat (I saw it happen a couple times, and it was not pleasant). You can buy them ground, or you can grind them in a spice grinder or in a food processor. They will disperse safely and beautifully in your dish.

PRESERVED LEMONS GF, P

*There is no Moroccan cooking without preserved lemons, and the store-bought variety
doesn't even begin to compare with homemade. They take minutes to prepare and two weeks to
"incubate," totally unassisted, and the result is a few months' supply of the single element that
will convert many of your dishes from plain to glorious. The fragrance is intoxicating: a pure
lemon quintessence for lemon lovers only.*

*When lemons are plentiful, buy a dozen or two, a box of coarse salt, and a couple of wide-
mouth glass jars. That is all you need, along with some elbow grease to cram the lemons into
the jar and force the juices out. That is the secret of their swelling and pickling, as well as their
heady aroma. Do not let the amount of salt daunt you. Much of it gets washed away, and you
can reduce, or even eliminate, salt from the dish you are preparing with the preserved lemons.*

8 to 10 large thick-skinned lemons
Coarse sea salt

Wash and dry the lemons thoroughly. Remove any green points attached to the ends
of the lemons. Cut them in quarters lengthwise. Place 2 to 3 pieces in a clean wide-mouth
quart-sized glass jar, top with a thick layer of salt. Repeat. Lemon, salt, lemon, salt, and so
on, all the way to the top, pressing down hard as you go to draw out the juice. Don't worry
if the juices don't appear immediately; they soon will with all that salt. The lemons should
be totally submerged by their own juice and reach all the way to the top of the jar. Top with
an extra layer of salt to ensure that no lemon skin is exposed (or it will mold). If the lemons
are very large, you might need 2 jars.

Place the jar (or jars) in a dark cool place (I keep mine under the sink). They will be
ready in two weeks, at which point they should be refrigerated. To use, take out a quarter
of a lemon at a time. Discard the pulp, rinse the skin thoroughly, and mince. Add to fish
and chicken dishes, bean soups, salads, and salsas. Makes about 2 quarts. After the two
weeks of pickling at room temperature, store refrigerated.

HARISSA GF, P

We Moroccans (and honorary Moroccan friends and neighbors) couldn't live without it. Some like it hot: Hello, this is for you! Although connoisseurs (including this one) will insist that authentic harissa is made with water-reconstituted dried red hot peppers, I find that they are not readily available, so I devised this fabulous recipe with dried hot pepper flakes, with near-identical results.

This condiment is the classical accompaniment to couscous and is also delicious served with fried fish and grilled chicken. Diluted with a little water and lemon juice, it is also a superb marinade for beef, fish, or chicken, even vegetables. (In marinade form, it is called chermoula.)

¾ cup crushed red pepper flakes, mixed with two cups boiling water (use up to 1 cup if you want it extra hot), and reserved
1 large bunch cilantro, stems cut off
1 head garlic, cloves separated and peeled
1 cup olive oil
1¼ cups paprika
3 tablespoons cumin
Salt and pepper to taste

Grind the cilantro and garlic in a food processor. With the motor running, add the oil gradually. Add the paprika, cumin, salt, pepper, and the reserved red pepper flake mixture and process for a few more seconds. Store in refrigerated glass jars. Makes about 4 cups.

Variation: Halbah

A great Yemenite favorite, which gets its name from its trademark ingredient—fenugreek, called halbah in Arabic. No paprika. Double the cilantro and add ¼ cup ground fenugreek.

COCKTAIL SAUCE GF, P

What excuse could there possibly be for buying this? Ready in a minute! Low in calories and very high in flavor, it goes beautifully with natural (no nitrites) smoked turkey, poached chicken breasts, or roast fish, or as a spread for sandwiches.

1 cup good natural-brand ketchup
½ cup Dijon-style mustard
½ cup prepared white horseradish (or ¼ cup wasabi powder plus ½ cup cold water)

Whisk all ingredients until smooth. Makes 2 cups. Store refrigerated in a glass jar.

Natural smoked turkey

Natural (no nitrites) smoked turkey is a great lean choice for jazzing up many dishes, or in sandwiches. Make an extra effort to secure the natural, no-nitrites kind and enjoy it as often as you would like!

CHOWCHOW GF

This is what I call my funky-chunky mustard spread. It always reminds me of my dear late father, Z'L, who loved it. Similar to Piccalilli, both of British origin. The recipes vary greatly, but the main idea is constant: small chunks of vegetables in a spicy mustard base. This is my own version, and I am confident even the Queen of England might be pleased with it. Here, finally, is one lean condiment you can slather with much greater abandon than mayo wherever you want more zing and texture! Do all your cutting and slicing in the food processor, it won't take a minute. Frozen cocktail onions are delicious and very cute, and save you the pesky task of blanching and peeling.

1 pound fresh or frozen cauliflower florets
2 Granny Smith (green) apples, unpeeled, cored, and quartered
6 ribs celery, peeled
1 small white cabbage, quartered, center cores cut off
2 cups fresh or frozen corn kernels
1 pound tiny frozen cocktail onions
3 tablespoons salt
¾ cup flour, any flour
½ cup dry mustard powder
2 tablespoons turmeric
2½ cups unfiltered apple cider vinegar
3 cups natural apple cider
2 cups sugar or Sucanat

In a food processor, finely chop the cauliflower and apples, but don't let it get too fine: Use the pulse button to control it better. Transfer the chopped mixture to a nonreactive bowl. Switch to the fine slicing blade and slice the celery and cabbage. Transfer to the bowl; add the corn, onions, and salt. Toss the mixture thoroughly and set it aside while you do the rest of the recipe.

Place the flour, mustard, turmeric, and vinegar in a wide-bottom stainless steel pot, and whisk until perfectly smooth. Turn on the flame, add the cider and sugar, and bring to a boil, whisking. Reduce the flame to low, and cook 5 more minutes. Pour this mixture over the vegetables, and combine thoroughly. Pack into glass jars. Let the mixture cool a little before refrigerating. Makes about 3 quarts.

CRANBERRY RELISH GF, P

Here is a treat you can make year-round, since frozen cranberries are always available and delicious. This match is unbeatable: cranberries, mint, and orange. Delicious with poultry dishes. No cooking!

1 pound bag fresh or frozen cranberries
1 bunch mint, leaves only
1 navel orange, skin and all, quartered
½ cup fresh lime or lemon juice
¾ sugar
½ teaspoon cayenne, or to taste
Salt to taste

In a food processor, coarsely grind the cranberries, mint, and orange using the pulse button so the mixture remains chunky. Add all remaining ingredients and pulse until just combined. Makes about 2 cups. Store refrigerated in a glass jar.

OLIVE SUN-DRIED TOMATO DIP GF

My own take on tapenade. From this fabulous mixture, you can go in several directions:
- *Spread it as is on toast or bruschetta.*
- *Mix with a little low-fat mayonnaise, silken tofu, or yogurt (dairy-free OK), and get a dip.*
- *Boil some noodles and mix 1 cup of the cooking liquid into the mixture, and get a pasta sauce.*
- *Mix with a little white wine and get a sauce for chicken or fish.*

Olives

Ignore those inferior brands of tinned olives (overripe and watery), and look for good-quality olives, firm and meaty and full of flavor: oil-cured or in salt or vinegar brine. For olives you'll be using in sauces, try your best to find pitted: It will save you some labor and blackened fingernails!

½ cup pitted Moroccan or Niçoise olives
1 cup basil leaves, packed
6 large cloves garlic
½ cup sun-dried tomatoes, rinsed, packed
½ cup capers
1 cup olive oil
2 tablespoons wine vinegar
Ground pepper to taste

Cream all ingredients in a food processor. Makes 2 cups. Store refrigerated in a glass jar.

TERIYAKI SAUCE GF

I live in the vicinity of several Chinese restaurants (who doesn't?). Every morning I watch the mountain of trash at their back door, and it always includes enormous jerry cans of teriyaki sauce: No wonder all those dishes look like a container of motor oil has accidentally landed there. This unwelcome sight has totally cured me of any urges to order teriyaki dishes at restaurants. Why, oh why don't they make it themselves? Nothing could be easier! Use it on fish, chicken, London broil, tofu, Portobello, to name just a few possibilities.

Sake

Sake is a wine made from a fermenting process using rice. The advantage of using sake in cooking, besides its wonderful flavor, is its high alcohol content: Whereas table wines have an alcoholic content that vary from 11 to 13½ degrees and must be drunk promptly after opening, sake has a higher alcohol content (around 16 degrees) and therefore is shelf stable, making it a great choice if you are not a wine drinker and use wine beverages in great moderation or only for cooking. If you don't have sake, dry sherry or dry vermouth will be equally suitable as they are also shelf stable at 16–17 degrees.

⅓ cup toasted sesame oil
¼ cup olive oil
¼ cup grated fresh ginger
½ cup fresh lime or lemon juice
½ cup soy sauce (GF, see page 21)
½ cup dry sherry, mirin or sake
⅓ cup honey 2 teaspoons ground black pepper
2 tablespoons bottled hot sauce or to taste
Good pinch ground cloves

Place all ingredients in a glass jar. Makes about 3 cups. Store refrigerated in a glass jar.

THAI SAUCE GF

Peanut butter is intensely flavored, a little goes a long way and combines beautifully with the other stars: lemongrass, coconut milk, cilantro. Wonderful as a dipping sauce or as the sauce for cold sesame noodles.

1 cup strong Lapsang Souchong tea (1 tea bag steeped in ½ cup boiling water)
½ cup coconut milk
½ cup peanut butter
¼ cup toasted sesame oil
¼ cup soy sauce (GF, see page 21)
¼ cup brown rice vinegar
2-inch piece ginger
1 stalk lemongrass, 2–3 outer leaves removed, or 2 tablespoons powder
2–3 tablespoons bottled hot sauce
4 scallions, sliced
6 sprigs cilantro, stems discarded

Cream the first set of ingredients in a food processor. Pulse in the scallions and cilantro. Transfer to a glass jar and store in the refrigerator.

Japanese pickle press

This nifty, inexpensive round or square box is the secret of professional-tasting pickles and kim chi easily made in your own kitchen. Mine is 3½ quarts and is easy to order online. It is equipped with a vise that comes down on the seasoned vegetables you are pickling. Place your seasoned vegetables in the press, press down hard to lock the press, and turn the vise down as low as it will come. You will be amazed how the vise will compress the veggies, separating the liquids from the solids.

After a couple hours, the pickles are ready: You are left with a fabulous handful of pickles. Transfer the pickles to a glass jar with only enough of the pickling liquid to cover them completely, discarding the rest of the liquids. Or simply leave them in the pickle press, liquid and all.

JAPANESE PICKLES GF, P

You'll love 'em! They have a small fraction of the salt and the vinegar of their commercial counterparts, and ten times the flavor. Crunchy and pungent with just a hint of sweetness, and really good for you too, like all fermented foods. I whip them out anytime I need a quick fix but can't afford anything too caloric, like after dinner when the kitchen is closed.

The simple secret here is to force the mixture into a wide-mouth glass jar or a pickle press (see box) so it disgorges its juices and you are left with a reduced and powerfully condensed bowl of pickles.

½ small head green cabbage, diced about 1 inch
2 large carrots, diced about 1 inch
1 medium purple onion, diced small
4 Kirby cucumbers, or one long seedless cucumber, unpeeled, diced about 1 inch
1 large turnip, diced about 1 inch
6 ribs celery, peeled and diced small
½ cup brown rice vinegar, or unfiltered apple cider vinegar
3 tablespoons salt
3 tablespoons wasabi powder (For Passover: grated fresh horseradish)
3 tablespoons sugar

Place all the vegetables in a glass or stainless steel bowl. Whisk the vinegar, salt, wasabi, and sugar in a cup. Pour over the vegetables and toss thoroughly. Force the mixture into clean glass jars or in a pickle press (see page 38 about how to use). Allow a few hours to pickle. Store refrigerated up to two weeks. Yields about 3 quarts.

Variation: Kim Chi GF, P

This great crowd pleaser is exactly our condiment above, with some added sliced garlic cloves and red pepper flakes and some sliced fresh ginger if desired. Proceed just as above.

The Japanese Pickle Press

MANGO-PINEAPPLE SALSA GF, P

Refreshing and colorful, and so versatile: use it on sliced tuna, roast salmon, poached chicken breasts, grilled tofu, and even by itself!

3 medium-ripe mango, diced small
1 ripe pineapple, diced small
2 jalapeño peppers, minced
¼ cup minced cilantro
1 small red onion, minced
2-inch piece fresh ginger, grated
⅓ cup olive oil
Salt and pepper to taste

Mix all ingredients in a bowl. Transfer gently to a glass jar, without pressing so as not to bruise and crush the fruit. Store refrigerated in a glass jar. Yields about 5 cups.

COCONUT CILANTRO CHUTNEY GF, P

I love chutney: sweet, sour, hot—yum! I have included some delicious chutneys in my book Levana's Table. *Here's one more, and this one doesn't even need cooking. Pure coconut magic!*

Coconut milk

Coconut milk is the strained mixture of coconut water and grated coconut meat, with water added to give it its creamy consistency. Ideally suited to enrich and flavor many dishes without the addition of heavy cream. Not to be confused with cream of coconut, which contains many unwanted emollients and sweeteners.

1 small onion, quartered
1 cup unsweetened grated coconut
¼ cup fresh lemon juice
1 jalapeño pepper, more if you like it really hot
1 tablespoon cumin
1 bunch cilantro, stems removed
Salt and pepper to taste
½ cup coconut milk, a little more if needed

Blend all ingredients in a food processor until fine, adding a little coconut milk if necessary to make it all stick together. Store in a glass jar in the refrigerator. Makes about 2½ cups.

SOFRITO GF, P

A valuable building block in many Latin and Sephardi dishes, you will always be happy to have it on hand. Multiply the recipe and freeze it in 1-cup containers and take them out as needed, using the whole 1-cup container for any recipe calling for it.

- *Toss it into 3 cups cooked rice or any other grain.*
- *Use it as a base for bean, fish, or vegetable soups.*
- *Dilute it with a little water and wine and use it as topping on grilled fish, poached chicken breasts, even pasta.*
- *Use it as a topping for focaccia or mix it with a good tomato sauce and use it as a topping for pizza.*

⅓ cup olive oil
12 large cloves garlic
2 large onions, quartered
6 ribs celery, peeled and cut in thirds
2 large bunches flat-leaf parsley
1 bunch cilantro, tough stems discarded
2 red bell peppers, seeded and cut in chunks

Heat the oil in a large skillet. In a food processor, finely grind the garlic. Add the remaining ingredients, in batches, and grind coarsely, using the pulse button so the mixture doesn't get watery. Add the mixture to the skillet as it gets ground and sauté until all liquids evaporate. It will take about 10 minutes. Store the mixture in three 1-cup containers: glass containers for the mixture you are refrigerating and using in the next few days, plastic containers for the mixture you are putting away in the freezer for future use. Makes about 3 cups.

RED PEPPER COULIS GF, P

Pronounced Coo-lee, a fancy French word that just means a thick uncooked sauce (sounds more intriguing in French, now, doesn't it?). Raw and bold and exuberant, perfect with plain-cooked fish and chicken, fish cakes and terrines, even as a spread for sandwiches.

2 red peppers, seeded and cut in chunks
½ cup basil leaves, packed
2 large cloves garlic
½ cup olive oil
2 tablespoons paprika
Salt and pepper to taste
Bottled hot sauce to taste

Purée all ingredients in a food processor a full minute until perfectly smooth. Makes 2 cups. Store refrigerated in a glass jar.

Variation: Tomato coulis

Substitute 4 plum tomatoes for the peppers, and proceed just as above.

WATERCRESS WASABI SAUCE GF, P

Watercress and wasabi: that's one bold pairing! Try it with seared or broiled fish or chicken, or vegetable terrines.

1 bunch watercress, stems and all
3 tablespoons wasabi powder (or ¼ cup prepared horseradish)
½ pound silken tofu (or ¾ cup low-fat mayonnaise, and skip the olive oil listed below)
¼ cup olive oil
1 tablespoon sugar
1 tablespoon green peppercorns in brine, drained (settle for 1 teaspoon ground pepper)
Salt to taste

Bring water to boil in a saucepan and plunge the watercress for just a few seconds. Immediately rinse in cold water. Squeeze thoroughly dry. Transfer to a food processor with all remaining ingredients and process until smooth. Makes 2 cups. Store refrigerated in a glass jar.

MOCK HOLLANDAISE SAUCE GF

Never mind what the heavy-cream-and-egg-yolks hollandaise sauce aficionados will say: I played with it and ended with something super easy, lean, and wonderful, and quite close to the classic hollandaise. This works, and that's what counts! A friend of mine, who has just undergone heart surgery, told me how delighted he was to be reunited with this great favorite food of his. Talk about going to one's heart through one's stomach!

Use the sauce on asparagus or poached chicken breasts, or as a dip with a little added curry powder. No one will ever know they are eating something that is so good for them!

1¼ cups plain yogurt or dairy-free yogurt, low-fat OK
⅓ cup Dijon-style mustard
⅓ cup low-fat mayonnaise
1 teaspoon turmeric
Pinch nutmeg
Pinch cayenne
Salt and pepper to taste
If you would like a curried sauce: 1 tablespoon curry powder

Whisk all the ingredients in a bowl until smooth. Makes about 2 cups. Store refrigerated in a glass jar.

PESTO AND ALL VARIATIONS GF, P

The perennial favorite is based on basil, olive oil, and toasted walnuts; but we have seen it recast with a different herb or nut, and tasting just as delicious and interesting. Use not only as a pasta sauce but as topping for cooked chicken or fish, or a dip. I find that toasting the nuts intensifies the pesto's flavor, so don't skip that step!

2 cups basil leaves, packed
½ cup good olive oil
⅓ cup toasted walnuts (about 15 minutes in a preheated 300 °F oven)
4 garlic cloves
Salt and pepper to taste

Process all ingredients in a food processor until smooth but still a little chunky, not a complete paste. Makes about 2 cups. Store refrigerated in a glass jar.

Variations

In the same proportions:
- Substitute parsley, cilantro, mint, spinach, arugala, and watercress for the basil.
- Substitute pecans, pine nuts, hazelnuts, and pistachios for the walnuts
- Add some freshly grated Parmesan. In this case, omit the salt.

SESAME DIPPING SAUCE GF

You will be using it all the time!

½ cup toasted sesame oil
½ cup soy sauce (GF, see page 21)
½ cup brown rice vinegar
½ cup dry sherry, mirin, or sake

Place all ingredients in a jar. Store in the refrigerator. Makes 2 cups.

PRESERVES, LIQUEURS AND DESSERT SAUCES

ALL-FRUIT JAMS AND PRESERVES

I am a jam lover, so I am pleased to see there are a couple new and wonderful all-fruit jams in the market. *All-fruit* means no added sugar of any kind, so ignore the preserves made with artificial sweeteners. Rather, it means that all sources of sweetness are fruit. Not only does it mean a much lower calorie content per serving but also a much more intense fruit flavor.

Just one word of advice: homemade natural jam might be somewhat more perishable than store-bought jam prepared with sugar, so freeze some of it, and use the open container within 4 to 6 weeks.

Apple pectin is to fruit what cornstarch or arrowroot is to vegetables—a natural thickener, easy to find in health food stores.

Get racy and throw in your favorite flavoring (one at a time please!) in a batch of jam for some extra zing, depth, and mystery: rosemary, ginger, thyme, sage, lavender, juniper, orange flower, and so on.

Most of the herbs come in powerful extracts, easy to find at health food stores or online; a few drops will go a long way. Likewise, you might want to add a spice, again one at a time: ground black or white pepper, cinnamon, cardamom, cloves, nutmeg, ginger, anise, and so on.

I do love to use frozen berries—for jams, sauces, and smoothies—as they are at the height of their ripeness and flavor. Always ready for you whenever you are.

ALL-FRUIT ORANGE MARMALADE GF

That's right—skin and all. I recently gave a taste to my mom, the original master artisan, who wouldn't dream of straying from the time-honored equal-parts-fruit-and-sugar classic. Her grudging praise was, it doesn't look quite as pristine as the one made with sugar, but it is just as delicious: Good looks in a marmalade? *Please! If I am keeping all of the flavor intact, who cares?*

Stainless steel pots

I won't say a word about what brand pots to pick, simply because I never want you to think that in order for you to be a good cook you need to invest in some extravagantly priced cookware. What I do want to recommend for your pots, though, are these:

- Heavy gauge, called in the business 18/10.
- The layer directly in contact with the food must not be aluminum, as it is reactive and will leach into your food, resulting not only in a metallic off-taste but in real health hazards. (Which is the reason, by the way, you shouldn't be cooking or baking in disposable aluminum pans. Only warming up is acceptable in disposables.) It's OK, it's good even, if the bottom or intermediate layer of

---

your pot is aluminum, as it is a great heat conductor—meaning your food will cook evenly—just as long as the inside of the pot is not. We want our food to be in direct contact with stainless steel, copper, enamel. Recently my daughter Bella replied to my question "Did you make sure you used a real cake pan?" with "Come on, Mommy. I'm your daughter. How could I use disposable?"

- A wide bottom. It makes all stove-top preparations a pleasure, as there is minimal piling and therefore allows for much better control. There's nothing you can't do with a broad and shallow pot: Instead of the impractical 9-inch round, 12-inch-high stock pot, get a 12- or even 14-inch, 6-inch-high pot. Same goes for skillet: Nice and broad please! This cute Aesop fable will make my point in full: The fox invited the stork to his house and served her food in a wide shallow bowl; and of course she couldn't get to it, so the foxy fox polished off her meal as well, just as he had planned all along. When she invited him, she served him in a long narrow bowl, and feasted on her food . . . and his. You have guessed it: We are the foxes!

3 12-ounce containers frozen orange juice concentrate
3 12-ounce containers frozen apple juice concentrate
3 large navel oranges, unpeeled
4 large thick-skin lemons, unpeeled
¼ cup apple pectin powder, mixed with a little water until smooth
Optional: a flavoring of your choice (see recipe intro)
¼ cup fresh lemon juice

Place all the fruit concentrates in a wide-bottom stainless steel pot and bring to a boil. Immediately reduce the heat to medium- low and cook uncovered about 1 hour, stirring occasionally. The juice will reduce by about half.

Rinse the fruit very well and cut in quarters. Remove any pits. Grate coarsely in a food processor. Stir the fruit into the pot with the pectin mixture and cook one more hour, stirring occasionally, never allowing the mixture to stick or darken. Turn off the flame and stir in the lemon juice. Store in pint-size glass jars in the refrigerator. Makes about 8 cups.

ALL-FRUIT BERRY JAM GF

Same recipe as the marmalade. Substitute 12 cups frozen berries of your choice for the citrus, and 3 12-ounce containers frozen cranberry juice for the orange juice concentrate. Optional: Throw in 1 teaspoon cayenne pepper if you like berry jam with a kick. All other ingredients listed are the same, and the preparation is identical. Store in pint-size glass jars in the refrigerator. Makes about 8 cups.

ALL-FRUIT APRICOT JAM GF

Same recipe as the marmalade. Substitute 10 cups packed chopped dried apricots for the citrus. All other ingredients listed are the same, and the preparation is identical. Store in pint-size glass jars in the refrigerator. Makes about 8 cups.

RED WINE JELLY GF

Here is a good place to throw in some ground pepper and the extract of your choice! A snap to make.

2 bottles dry red wine
3 12-ounce containers frozen cranberry juice
1 teaspoon ground black pepper
¼ cup apple pectin powder, mixed with a little water until smooth

Optional: the extract of your choice (see recipe intro)

Bring the wine and juice to a boil in a wide stainless steel pot. Reduce the flame to medium and cook uncovered, stirring occasionally about 1 hour, or a little longer, until you are left with about 8 cups liquid. Stir in the pectin mixture and cook 20 more minutes. Store in pint-size glass jars in the refrigerator. Makes about 8 cups.

WHITE WINE JELLY GF

Same ingredients and recipe, using dry white wine, frozen apple juice, and ground white pepper.

LEMON CURD GF, P

This is pure lemon seduction, eaten as a jam or used as a filling on a baked pie crust and topped with berries (lemon blueberry tart: page 287).

3 tablespoons lemon zest
¾ cup fresh lemon juice, strained
1½ cups sugar
4 eggs, beaten
¾ cup margarine spread

Bring water to boil in a saucepan, then turn the heat down to low, keeping the water at a simmer. Set a bowl securely on top of the water and add the zest, lemon juice, and sugar, whisking. When the mixture is hot, add the eggs, whisking constantly until thick. This step will take 3 to 4 minutes. Add the margarine spread and whisk just one more minute until it is incorporated and the mixture looks smooth. Cool completely.

Store refrigerated in a glass jar. Makes about 3 cups.

GRAPEFRUIT LIQUEUR GF, P

For many years, I have made liqueur from etrog, a very rare citrus fruit—"the fruit of a goodly tree," as it is reverently referred to—used in the celebration of the Jewish holiday of Sukkot. Every year at the end of the holiday, I call all my friends in the nick of time to bum their etrog before it gets discarded and proceed to make gallons of a fascinating liqueur, diligently and resignedly removing the myriad pits contained in the fruit before slicing it and combining it with other ingredients. This year I decided that since the fruit is so rare and the liqueur made from it so labor-intensive, I would experiment with the fruit that comes closest to it in flavor—the more reliable and widely available grapefruit. I even pushed my luck and made it with agave syrup and made a gallon of fabulous liqueur in no time. After about a week, I sampled the delicious dram: It was a triumph!

LISA'S TIP

Agave nectar is a sweetener that is making a splash in the culinary world. Agave is a syrup from the Mexican agave cactus, the same plant that gives us tequila. It is higher in fructose, and therefore, sweeter, than table sugar. While not calorie-free, it is an all-natural sweetener that boasts a low glycemic index, which means that the body absorbs it more slowly. However, agave is still a sugar, with the same 16 calories per teaspoon as other sugars, so we need to watch it as carefully as we would other sugars.

---

2 large grapefruit
4 cups white agave syrup
8 cups vodka (generic brand OK)

Scrub the fruit thoroughly with warm water and a vegetable brush, cut it in eighths, then in thin slices, by hand or using the slicing blade of a food processor, removing any occasional pits. Place in a nonreactive mixing bowl such as stainless steel or glass (no plastic or aluminum), add the syrup and vodka, and mix thoroughly. Transfer to clean wide-mouth jars. Let the mixture sit for a week at room temperature. Before using, strain the amount you intend to use and leave the rest in the jar, fruit and all.

Don't just discard the fruit when most of the liquid has been used: Throw in a little more vodka and agave in the jar and let the mixture steep again a few days. The longer it sits the more intense the flavor. Serve chilled. Makes about 1 gallon mixture, 2 quarts clear liqueur. Store at room temperature.

GINGER LIQUEUR GF, P

Strictly for ginger lovers. My club is quite large, and always expanding! I know you can find ginger liqueur on the market, but sorry, guys, it doesn't come close! No need to use expensive vodka—even a generic brand will do. Here again agave works like a charm. If you are left with lots of ginger slices after you use most of the liquid, throw in a little more vodka and syrup.

8 cups water
3 cups peeled ginger, sliced thin a food processor
2 cups fresh lemon juice
2 cups white agave syrup
3 cups vodka (generic brand OK)

Bring all but last ingredient to a boil in a stainless steel pot. Reduce to medium and cook uncovered about 1 hour. The mixture will thicken and get syrupy. You will be left with about 3 cups liquid. Let the mixture come to room temperature. Stir in the vodka and transfer the mixture to glass jars. Store at room temperature. The liqueur is ready to use in about a week. The longer it sits, the more intense the flavor. To serve: You will notice that some white-ish sediment will settle in the bottom of the jar. Do not shake the jar, so as not to get the liquid cloudy. Ladle the clear liquid into a pitcher, making sure you don't reach to the bottom (or strain through a very fine strainer). Serve chilled. Makes about 3 quarts clear liqueur.

CHOCOLATE SAUCE GF, P

No commercial chocolate sauce comes anywhere close to this one. So simple to make, and so versatile: Serve it on cake or ice cream, dip strawberries and orange slices in it as soon as it cools off, and before it hardens, pour it on cake or spread it on a finished cake as a glaze. Yum!

I urge you to experiment with the gamut of dairy-free milks available at health food stores and better supermarkets.

Natural margarine spread

Ever since I can find several new brands of acceptable non-hydrogenated margarines, (called trans-fat-free-margarine spreads, to be exact: we will call them margarine spreads throughout the book), I no longer have the qualms I used to have about occasionally using margarine spread when oil won't do the job. Only, please read the labels and be sure you are picking the non-hydrogenated trans-fat-free type. They rarely come in sticks, mostly in tubs, and even though they look less firm than their hydrogenated counterparts, they absolutely do the job. Don't use the "light" ones that use water in the mix—they don't work for baking.

---

1 cup dairy-free milk, low-fat OK
½ cup agave syrup, light or dark
1½ cups semisweet best quality chocolate chips
⅓ cup pure cocoa powder
¼ teaspoon salt
¼ cup natural non-hydrogenated margarine spread, at room temperature

In a medium saucepan, whisk all but last ingredient until smooth. Turn on the heat to medium, and cook until hot, but not boiling, whisking constantly. Turn off the heat and add the margarine spread, whisking until smooth and glossy, about one minute. The sauce will thicken as it cools. Microwave very briefly it if has thickened too much, or stand the jar in a larger container of warm water. Makes about 3 cups. Store refrigerated in a glass jar.

CARAMEL SAUCE GF

Another glowing example of a treat known as dairy that doesn't at the least suffer from a dairy-free adaptation, au contraire! (Go ahead and multiply the recipe if you would like—it keeps very well.)

Reinventing cream

For a richer texture, I use a simple trick, which you will often encounter throughout the book, to augment the "milk" fats in many dishes: I add soy or rice milk powder (easy to find in health food stores or online) to my dairy-free milk and obtain the rich and dense texture of cream, or quite close. It is also much less caloric than the dishes containing dairy cream.

---

1 cup Sucanat
½ cup agave syrup
⅓ cup water
¾ cup dairy-free milk, low-fat OK
⅓ cup soy or rice milk powder
3 tablespoons brandy or rum
1 tablespoon vanilla extract
1 teaspoon salt

Bring the Sucanat, agave, and water to boil in a small saucepan, stirring. When it comes to a boil, stop stirring and cook until thick and a deep amber color, 2 to 3 minutes. Whisk the remaining ingredients in a small bowl until perfectly smooth, then carefully add to the saucepan (to avoid splattering). Cook another 3 minutes on a medium flame, whisking. Store refrigerated in a glass jar. (Shake before using.) Makes about 2½ cups.

CRANBERRY COULIS GF, P

You will find at your health food stores very good brands of natural cranberry sauce with a short list of very decent ingredients, and none of the offending corn syrup—just about what you would make in your own home. Throw it in a berry compote for added zing or blend it with some juice, as in this ridiculously simple preparation, and you get a wonderful ruby-colored cranberry coulis that will go beautifully with chocolate and many other desserts.

1 15-ounce can cranberry sauce, smooth or whole
2 cups cranberry or pomegranate juice

Blend in a food processor or blender until smooth. Store refrigerated in glass jars. Makes about 4 cups.

STRAWBERRY SAUCE GF, P

Frozen berries are so sweet that I find I need no added sugar in the sauce, but feel free to sweeten it a little if you think the finished sauce needs a little sugar. I use it with plain cakes and frozen desserts, and even as a dipping sauce for mixed berries.

Immersion blender

A wonderfully nifty tool, inexpensive and portable (it will fit in a drawer), that allows you to blend your soup directly and in one shot right in your pot. No transferring, no mess. Just make sure there are no bones in the soup, or you will break your blade.

---

1 12-ounce bag frozen unsweetened strawberries
1 cup cranberry or pomegranate juice
¼ cup crème de cassis (liquor stores; for Passover: any nice Passover berry liqueur)
¼ cup fresh lemon juice
2 tablespoons tapioca flour or arrowroot (Passover: potato starch), mixed with a little water until smooth

Optional: Add a little sugar to the finished sauce if you think it needs it.

Bring all but last ingredient to a boil. Reduce the flame to low, add the starch mixture, and cook, stirring—until just thickened and the mixture is no longer cloudy—about 1 minute. Purée in a blender or with an immersion blender until smooth. Adjust the sweetness to your own taste. Cool completely before serving. Store refrigerated in a glass jar. Makes about 3½ cups.

Variation: Raspberry sauce

Proceed exactly as above, but strain the final sauce to get rid of the seeds, pressing down on the solids.

HONEY ALMOND SPREAD (AMLOU) GF, P

The treat of my childhood: peanut butter and jelly Moroccan-style called Amlou. Talk about healthy—a nutritional powerhouse, besides being fabulous.

2 cups toasted almonds (about 15 minutes in a preheated 325°F oven)

⅔ cup extra-virgin olive oil

⅔ cup dark honey

½ teaspoon salt

Process all ingredients until smooth. Spread on bread or toast.

Store what's left in a glass jar at room temperature. Makes about 2 cups.

HOT CHOCOLATE MIX GF, P

A friend recently brought me a box of insanely expensive hot chocolate mix. I couldn't wait to try it, and . . . I was frankly underwhelmed. What's the big deal, I thought. It certainly didn't beat boiling some milk or dairy-free milk with some good cocoa powder, a little sugar, and maybe a little vanilla extract or other flavoring. Yes, that's the whole story! No problem making your own natural mix the instant way, using milk powder—dairy or not—and mixing it with boiling water, making a delicious cup of hot cocoa in a jiffy. I still make it for my children, who now enjoy it with their children. Love of hot chocolate is forever. Thank G-d for small blessings!

2 cups cocoa powder, Dutch-processed

3 cups sugar

For mocha: Add 1 cup instant coffee powder, decaf OK

Optional flavorings: Add only in your individual cup; choose one: pinch cayenne, cinnamon, nutmeg, vanilla, etc.

Mix thoroughly and store in a glass jar. For 1 cup hot cocoa: whisk 2 tablespoons of the mix into 1 cup very hot milk. Makes about 6 cups mix. Store in a glass jar at room temperature.

Note: If you find boiling the milk too much of an imposition, add 3 cups milk powder, dairy or dairy-free, to the mix.

For 1 cup hot cocoa: Whisk 3 tablespoons mix into 1 cup boiling water. Makes 9 cups mix.

CHAI MIX GF, P

Delicious in hot or cold tea. Even in hot cider! Even in hot chocolate: Hello! It will take you minutes to put together, and it will last you months. Passover: Skip any spice you can't find and double up on what you have, just as long as you have the cardamom (a must!).

2 tablespoons ground anise

2 teaspoons finely ground pepper

1 tablespoon nutmeg

2 tablespoons cinnamon

⅓ cup cardamom

2 tablespoons ground ginger

1 tablespoon ground cloves

Mix all ingredients thoroughly in bowl, then transfer to a perfectly clean and dry glass jar. Store with your spices. Makes 1 cup mix.

For 1 cup chai: Start with about ¼ teaspoon of the mixture per cup of hot tea (or hot chocolate, or hot cider) and increase it to your own taste. Add milk and sugar to taste.

SOUPS

I develop all my recipes with the home cook foremost in mind; and from every comment I hear, I have come to the conclusion that most cooks find making homemade soup stock before proceeding with a recipe a real imposition—maybe even a deterrent. Almost all cookbooks use stock as the essential ingredient for a good soup, which at the outset excludes the earnest but busy cook, or forces him or her to settle for an inferior commercial base.

The good news is that you can make a delicious soup from scratch using water as "stock." Until recently, I used to trick my untrickable mother (who fed us wonderful soups made with chicken or meat every other night: that was practically our dinner) and tell her a soup she liked was made with stock, and she would invariably say, "Ha! See what a difference it makes?" Trust me. If I could make a convert out of her, you should be no problem at all. You will never miss homemade stock in these recipes.

Making soup is the ultimate showcase for you as a cook. You have much freedom and flexibility and room for creativity, provided that you keep a few basic principles in mind.

Choose full-flavored vegetables and grains: Your choice of ingredients matters. For example, a vegetarian cream of broccoli soup will be wonderful, whereas an unadorned cream of zucchini is apt to be ordinary. The reason is quite simple: Broccoli has flavor that stands on its own while zucchini tends to be bland. The best vegetarian soups use intensely flavored vegetables such as celery root, cabbage, turnips, parsnips, carrots, watercress, spinach, mushrooms, and tomatoes. Combine milder vegetables such as zucchini, string beans, and red peppers with more assertive ingredients such as tomatoes, garlic, and basil.

Combine ingredients effectively: Resist the temptation to make soup (or any dish for that matter) with a very long list of ingredients. First of all, you do not want all your soups to taste and look the same. Second, you should always give a particular ingredient and/or seasoning the chance to be the "star." A short, well-chosen selection of ingredients will yield infinitely better results than an enormous indistinguishable medley.

Exercise caution with cooking times: Al dente does not work for soup (miso soup is in a class by itself and is awarded a full chapter in this book). Vegetables must be tender yet not mushy. Beans must be soft enough to release their starch yet retain their character. In a pinch, use good quality canned beans rather than end up with tough incompletely cooked and indigestible beans. All root vegetables require longer cooking times to fully release their flavors and fragrance. Add delicate vegetables, such as zucchini and bell peppers, halfway through the cooking process so they don't get mushy or discolored, or worse, tasteless. Add very delicate leafy vegetables—such as spinach, watercress, lettuce, and scallions—at the very end of the cooking process. A minute or two is all they need to wilt yet retain their bright color.

Modulate the texture of the soup: In order to avoid thin, watered-down soup, start with less water and err on the side of thickness. All the recipes in this chapter will result in soup you might have to thin, so before serving, adjust the texture by adding a little liquid if you need to.

Sauté in olive oil: Leeks, onions, celery, and garlic, properly sautéed in very good olive oil, guarantee a delicious soup. I allow about ⅓ cup olive oil for three to four quarts of soup, which gives the soup the richness and smoothness it needs without making it too caloric. Do not try to reduce this amount further out of a desire to make it leaner, as it will result in an undistinguished "boiled" baby-food-like soup with no texture to speak of. You will note all my soups yield a large batch, so the oil will add no more than 30 calories per serving, in exchange for lots of good flavor and texture.

Season the soup: Think about all the wonderful herbs and spices at your disposal when making soup: thyme, sage, oregano, tarragon, basil, bay leaves, and lemongrass, to name but a few. Add herbs toward the end of cooking so their flavor does not diminish. To enrich a soup, a cup of wine or coconut milk; a dollop of miso paste; a strip of kombu; or a few drops of soy sauce, mirin, or toasted sesame oil will do wonders.

Experiment, and get different results each time. Also, because it is hard to gauge how your soup will respond to seasoning, be sure to taste before serving, and adjust the seasonings. Lastly, you will notice that in all my soup recipes I instruct the reader to add ground pepper at the very end of the cooking process, unless the total cooking time of the soup is very brief. That's because I find that ground pepper added to a large amount of liquid for an extended cooking time tends to give the soup an acrid taste, whereas a little added pepper stirred in at the end tastes clean and strong.

Thicken the soup appropriately: If you want a clear soup, make a concentrated chicken, beef, or vegetable broth that you will serve as is, or to which you will add garnishes, such as dumplings, croutons, noodles, or shredded greens. If you are making a smooth creamed soup, include one or two of the following starchy vegetables: potatoes, sweet potatoes, corn, parsnips, or peas. When blended with other ingredients, they will create a thick, rich soup. If you are making a chunky soup, just a handful of barley, rice,

Storing, freezing, and reheating the soup

Never divide a soup (or any) recipe. Why should you once you've got that pot going? Making a large batch and freezing it means great savings of time and labor. Just as importantly, don't serve it all week until it comes out of your (and your family's) ears: *Freeze it*! Set aside the amount you think will be eaten, plus a little more for the cook to eat the next day. Pour the rest in one-quart plastic containers equipped with tight lids, filling them half an inch from the top to make prevision for their expansion in the freezer, then label and date each container. Don't forget this last step, or you will be stomped by some UFOs: unidentified frozen objects. You will be delighted to find a quart of several kinds of soup in your freezer, each enough for two ample servings, before embarking on a trip, or when you come home late some evening. To reheat: Run your frozen container under warm faucet water for just a few seconds and slide it in one block into a pot with just a little water added. Reheat on a low flame, stirring occasionally. It will only take a few minutes total, well worth avoiding microwave reheating (which might scorch the outside before it gets to the center: I never recommend it for anything but small quantities).

split peas, or lentils will add the necessary starch and impart a wonderful taste. Grains such as bulgur, oats, millet, cornmeal, or farina will disperse in the liquid and produce a delicious soup with a somewhat less starchy texture. Each grain produces unique results, so experiment with different combinations.

Another mixture used to thicken soups lightly without making it starchy is sofrito, which is widely used in Latin cooking (see page 41).

Use only the best: Notice I didn't say the most expensive or the fanciest, just the best. It is perfectly all right to use leftover vegetables or beans in soup, but it is not acceptable to use wilted greens or blemished vegetables. Your soup will reflect the high standards you apply in selecting your ingredients, so use seasonal vegetables—or frozen unprocessed vegetables—at the peak of their perfection whenever possible.

THE MOST BASIC GRAIN SOUPS

If the following three soups don't convince you of the magic of soups with no stock or broth, nothing will. Nothing but the grain and seasonings!

SEMOLINA (OR CORNMEAL) SOUP GFA

In my native Morocco, this is often breakfast. It takes minutes from beginning to end, and it is so satisfying. I have whipped it up countless times when I needed to round out a meal in a jiffy. You can save even more time by grinding the garlic and cilantro in a food processor. If you are making this for breakfast, the quick way, throw in the garlic and the cilantro whole. The garlic will be easy to fish out, or enjoy whole in your bowl, and you can discard the cilantro at the end of cooking. Gluten-free: Look for brown rice farina, or simply use fine or medium cornmeal. For an occasional splurge, add some freshly grated Parmesan.

3 quarts (12 cups) water
A dozen cloves garlic
1 bunch cilantro, tough stems cut off
⅓ cup extra-virgin olive oil
Salt and pepper to taste
1½ cups semolina (or farina; gluten-free: fine cornmeal)

Put all but last ingredient in a heavy pot and bring to a boil. Reduce the flame to medium. Stir in the grain, pouring gradually. Cover and cook ten more minutes. Adjust the texture and seasonings. Serve hot. Makes a dozen ample servings.

STEEL-CUT OAT SOUP GF

This is a most unusual combination of flavors, and it works beautifully. When we were children, we were often given this soup to fortify our diet. I have listed only dry herbs, because I was hoping you would make it, as we did in my native Morocco, for breakfast, when we need to use our time most judiciously; but of course, if you happen to have the fresh herbs on hand and a little more time, by all means use them. Fenugreek is the essential secret ingredient here, so don't skip it

3 quarts (12 cups) water
1½ cups steel-cut oats, or millet
⅓ cup olive oil
2 tablespoons ground fenugreek
8 cloves garlic, halved lengthwise
¼ cup dry cilantro
¼ cup dry parsley
¼ cup dry mint (Attention, Middle Eastern friends: Look for *flayo*, also called *zuta levana*, dry or fresh, a wild variety of mint, at your food markets or shuks: heavenly!)
2 teaspoons turmeric

Bring all ingredients to a boil. Reduce the flame to medium and cook covered, 30 minutes. Adjust the texture and seasonings. Makes a dozen ample servings.

Note: If you are using fresh herbs—one bunch cilantro (stems cut off), 1 bunch parsley, 1 bunch mint (leaves only), all minced by hand or in a food processor. You can also just throw them in whole and discard them at the end of cooking. Proceed just as above.

Steel-cut oat soup

Oats

Many containers of oats of all shapes and sizes are marked "gluten-free." You might conclude that it means the gluten has been removed from a grain that originally contains gluten. In fact the exact opposite is true: In and of themselves, oats have no gluten whatsoever. They might contain traces of gluten only because they are often counter-intuitively processed in machinery that also processes gluten grains. Fortunately, grain processors are increasingly processing oats in gluten-free machinery, letting our gluten-free friends enjoy them to the fullest and allowing the confusion to dissipate.

Fenugreek

If you believe that unappealing mudpacks give your skin its renewed glow, then you should have no trouble believing that fenugreek does wonders for some dishes: Bitter, pungent, and acrid by itself, it has none of the inviting qualities of its fellow spices (fragrance, color, flavor); yet it is delicious combined with other ingredients in soups and many condiments. Very healthy too! We used to sneak it into drinks and soups for upset stomachs and complexions.

FAVA BEAN SOUP GF

There is no substitute for these funky and incredibly flavorful beans. You will find them in Indian, Italian, and Middle Eastern grocery stores, or simply go online—well worth looking for. You will love them, so get a nice supply and store them in glass jars.

Don't get it into your head to peel them, which would be pure slavery. Buy them peeled!

4 cups peeled dry fava beans
3 quarts (12 cups) water
½ cup olive oil
Salt to taste
8 large cloves garlic
2 tablespoons paprika
1 teaspoon cayenne, or to taste
2 tablespoons cumin
¼ cup fresh lemon juice

Bring the beans, water, oil, and salt to boil in a wide-bottom pot. Reduce the flame to medium and cook covered for 2 hours. Whisk the paprika, cayenne, cumin, lemon juice, and a little water in a bowl to make sure you have no spice lumps, and throw the mixture in the pot. Cook 15 more minutes. You will find that the beans have almost completely dissolved all by themselves; but just in case you want a more elegant presentation, cream the soup with an immersion blender. Adjust the texture and seasonings. Makes a dozen ample servings.

Variation: Cold fava bean soup GF

Stir in a 15-ounce can coconut milk in the chilled soup, and serve cold.

MISO SOUP WITH ALL THE FIXINGS GF

Miso soup is a marvel: Quick is not even the word. By the time it comes to a boil, it's done, a whole pot full. It's also an incredibly nutritious and versatile low-calorie treat. I am giving you here a basic recipe, but I am including as many variations as I can think of, and let you play with it and get another exciting soup each time. It will all be ready as soon as it comes to a boil. The miso, ginger, toasted sesame oil, bottled hot sauce, and scallions are a constant with all variations.

You may never go back to the Chinese-restaurant variety, unless you do as I do from time to time—order it to your specifications: First, make sure it has no MSG. Then, no canned veggies please! Banish the canned baby corn, bamboo shoots, and water chestnuts. Who needs them? Instead spread the fresh good stuff thick: fresh mushrooms, broccoli, zucchini, snow peas, and so on.

2 quarts (8 cups) water
1 pound shiitake mushrooms, caps only, sliced thin
1 pound firm or extra-firm tofu, cuts in small cubes
1 bunch Swiss chard, leaves only, cut into ribbons
1 cup miso paste, dark for a stronger taste, white for a milder taste
2-inch piece ginger, grated
¼ cup toasted sesame oil
1 tablespoon bottled hot sauce, or more to taste
4 scallions, sliced very thin

Bring all but last ingredient to a boil, then turn off the flame. Stir in the scallions. Serve hot. Makes a dozen ample servings.

Variations:

- Choose from sliced celery, sliced zucchini, sliced carrots, frozen corn kernels, sliced nappa cabbage, sliced bok choy, etc. Nothing canned whatsoever please! Proceed as above.
- Throw in a nice handful or two of rice noodles or soba noodles, left whole (get ready for slurping) or cut into smaller pieces (no slurping). Proceed as above.
- Throw in a handful of seaweed: crumbled nori, wakame, arame, hijiki. Proceed as above.
- Include 3–4 cups either cubed chicken breasts or fish: They will cook in the same time the soup does. Proceed as above.
- Add bright green vegetables such as snow peas, spinach leaves, watercress leaves, asparagus sections, broccoli spears, or string beans all the way at the end of cooking, after the soup comes to a boil, so that they retain their bright color.
- Throw in a 15-ounce can of coconut milk for a richer soup. Proceed as above.
- Throw in a cup of sake for added punch. Proceed as above.

MSG

I almost didn't include this information, thinking by now it is clear to everyone they should stay away from MSG (no, not Madison Square Garden—I wish: monosodium glutamate) with a vengeance, until my son-in-law Meir recently reported mysterious and repeated blinding headaches. Concerned, we recommended complete tests and asked him what changes might have taken place in his diet. Oh, not much, he said . . . except maybe some big bowls of soups served at catered affairs (in catering halls where he works as photographer) that he had started eating daily and was happy to find since his late work hours so often mean eating on the fly and settling for institutional fare. Well, that did it. We urged him to stop eating them altogether, and needless to say, the headaches disappeared after a couple weeks, and thank G-d, never came back. Interesting information: In case you started getting headaches, rule out the MSG first: It may well be the culprit. I simply cannot get anywhere near it.

Miso Soup

VEGETABLE-BASED SOUPS

CURRIED APPLE KALE SOUP GF

Oh, you'll be eating your leaves now that you are cooking them in such exciting ways! The demure kale is paired with green apples and vibrant seasonings: How can you miss?

¼ cup olive oil
1 large onion, quartered
4 ribs celery, peeled
1–2 tablespoons curry powder
1 tablespoon grated fresh ginger
1 tablespoon cardamom
1 tablespoon cinnamon
2–3 tablespoons sugar
2 Granny Smith (green) apples, unpeeled, grated
1 large bunch kale, stems, and leaves, chopped medium fine
2 cups green split peas or mung beans, picked over and rinsed
3 quarts (12 cups) water
Salt to taste
1 15-ounce can coconut milk
6 sprigs cilantro, tough stems cut off, minced

Heat the oil in a wide heavy pot. In a food processor, coarsely chop the onion and celery. Add to the pot and sauté until translucent. Add the curry, ginger, cardamom, cinnamon, and sugar, and cook just a few more seconds. Add all but 2 last ingredients and bring to a boil. Reduce the flame to medium and cook covered about 1 hour, or a little longer, until all beans and vegetables are perfectly tender. Add the coconut milk and cilantro and cook 5 more minutes. Adjust the texture and seasonings. Makes a dozen ample servings.

LISA'S TIP

Legumes

Legumes—a class of vegetables including beans, peas, and lentils—are a terrific food to include in the diet. Legumes are rich in fiber and chock-full of vitamins and minerals, including folate, manganese, iron, potassium, magnesium, and copper. They are also economical and easy to store, and can be used in to many dishes. A terrific substitute for meat, legumes offer a nutrient-dense plant protein that is much lower in saturated fat and a good source of fiber and phytochemicals. No wonder they have been linked to lower rates of heart disease, diabetes, certain cancers, and lower body weights. (Note: beans are not fattening when consumed in place of high-fat meat!)

Here are a few pointers on several legumes.

Kidney beans are chock-full of fiber, protein, vitamins, and minerals, including potassium and the B vitamins folate and thiamin.

Green peas offer a significant source of fiber and protein. They also contain lutein and zeaxanthin, compounds that are essential for good eye health and have been shown to lower rates of cataracts. Peas also pack vitamin K, which helps with bone health and blood clotting.

Chickpeas are a great option for plant protein and fiber; they also contain magnesium, manganese, iron, and folate.

Lentils. In addition to the benefits from the soluble fiber, protein, and complex carbohydrates that all legumes offer, lentils also offer the added benefit of being a significant source of iron. Lentils are also high in the B vitamin, biotin, which aids in the body's metabolism and growth.

Black beans, like other legumes, are high in fiber and protein and offer a great alternative to the saturated fat found in meat. What sets black beans apart, however, are their at least eight different flavonoids, called anthocyanins, which serve as cancer-combating antioxidants in the body.

Peanuts are rich in heart-healthy unsaturated fat, and contain protein, fiber, vitamins, and minerals, as well as antioxidants. It is no surprise that regular consumption of peanuts has been associated with lower risk for coronary heart disease in people who eat them in place of other high-fat foods.

If I had a hammer . . .

Hammer

If I had a hammer . . . I would eat my veggies more often. You may find the use of a hammer in the kitchen somewhat odd and unbecoming, but you will quickly change your mind when you see how many thankless tasks it performs in a jiffy. A hammer makes short work of cutting all those monolithic items that usually cause us so much grief in the kitchen: butternut squash, pumpkin, chocolate blocks, big turnips, and more. No force and no pressure whatsoever. Simply place a cleaver with the blade poised on the spots where you want to cut. Hit the cleaver with a hammer, with one clean strike to the brute, and voilà!

Artichoke hearts and bottoms

For serving artichokes plain with a vinaigrette (trimming the tips with scissors would look neater and prettier), simply boil them until the leaves come off easily, about 25 to 30 minutes, then enjoy warm or cold by dipping the flat tips of the leaves and then the heart in your favorite sauce or dressing. But quite often we want to include artichokes as one of the ingredients in a larger dish, and getting at the hearts or bottoms before we can even get on with the recipe can seem rather daunting.

Someone in the food industry, bless him, has done all the pesky job of snapping the leaves off the artichokes, and the even peskier job of scraping the fuzz off the artichoke bottoms, leaving us only with exactly what we want (perfect artichoke bottoms or baby artichoke hearts) in order to sail through the preparation of quite a few artichoke-based treats. Lean, nutrient-packed, different, and delicious. Did you know there was an artichoke liqueur called Cynar? Not for the fainthearted: Try it, it might grow on you!

Saffron

I'm just mad about saffron. Not just an old hippie song, saffron is an essential spice in Mediterranean cooking. It is the stamen of the crocus flower, that adorable flower that spells out the arrival of long-awaited spring and which can be harvested only by hand, hence its infamous reputation for being as expensive as gold. But in my book, the delicate color and flavor it imparts to a dish makes it every bit as valuable as gold. Besides, a little goes a very long way. Ignore the impossibly expensive vials sold at produce stores and get an ounce-sized box at Indian or Italian grocery stores, which will last you months and months and will cost you a small fraction of the price.

ROASTED GARLIC, ARTICHOKE, AND CELERY ROOT SOUP GF, P

The elegant and silky soup you will end up with will belie its scant preparation time—all thanks to the perfect pairing of ingredients and the availability of frozen hearts and bottoms.

4 heads garlic
2 tablespoons olive oil
3 quarts (12 cups) water
3 10-ounce boxes frozen artichoke hearts, or 2 1-pound bags artichoke bottoms
1 large head celery root, grated
⅓ cup olive oil
3 sprigs fresh rosemary, leaves only
3 sprigs thyme, leaves only
Good pinch saffron
1 teaspoon turmeric
Salt to taste
Ground pepper to taste
¼ cup chopped chives

Preheat the oven to 400°F. Cut off the points of the garlic heads. Rub with the olive oil. Wrap in foil, cut sides down, and roast until browned and soft, about 45 minutes.

Meanwhile, make the rest of the soup. Bring the water to boil in a wide heavy pot. Add the artichokes, celery root, olive oil, rosemary, thyme, saffron, turmeric, and salt to taste. Bring back to boil, then reduce to medium. Cook covered for 30 minutes. Squeeze the flesh out of the garlic heads into the pot whenever it's ready and cool enough to handle. Purée the soup with an immersion blender. Add ground pepper to taste and chives. Adjust texture and seasonings. Serve hot. Delicious chilled too. Makes 12 ample servings.

Food processor

My mother loves to joke that I would never have gotten married if the food processor had not been popularized in the nick of time (roughly in 1976, which is when I got engaged). She is only half kidding: I honestly don't think I would have become a professional cook without its priceless performance. Thank you, dearest class, for your recent birthday gift to your cooking teacher—a giant twenty-cup food processor! No gift was ever more appreciated, or amortized. My beast of burden, I give it all my grinding, blending, grating, and slicing to do in seconds. Do we need more reason than that to own one? It obediently and quickly does all my bidding: chopping, slicing, shredding. Good brands come with a small opening (for slicing small cucumbers, thin carrots, etc.) and a large opening (for slicing a whole onion, shredding large wedges of cabbage, shredding whole cored apples, etc.). Be sure you buy the brand with the largest large opening so you can throw apples, onions, and other large fruit or vegetables whole without having to cut them first. Get a large one—the larger the better: Its base always remains small no matter what the capacity, which means it won't take more room on your counter. Ignore all the inferior brands, which behave like toys and will ultimately cost you more if you count the number of times you will have to replace them, and finally go for a premium large container brand. The best investment you ever made in your kitchen and with your time: you will amortize the costs in the preparation of half a dozen meals at the most!

Peeling celery

Always peel the rounded side of a rib of celery with a vegetable peeler, just as you would a carrot. You will be surprised at how much more pleasant the celery will be to cook with, especially in recipes where you have to cream a soup, as peeling it rids it of all its fibrous, bitter, tough threads. This step will also make your salads much more palatable and scooping dips and spreads with celery sticks a real treat.

QUICK BORSCHT GF, P

A triumph of sweet-and-sour match. I call it quick, because I have no intention (and neither do you, I'll bet!) of spending half the day making the classic high-maintenance beef-based original. Experience the magic of cranberry sauce in this soup! The food processor will make short work of grating, grinding, and slicing all your ingredients—30 minutes of cooking is all I need, as the flavors are so intense and all ingredients are shredded fine.

⅓ cup olive oil
8 large cloves garlic
1 large bunch dill
1 large onion, quartered
4 ribs celery, peeled
1 large carrot, grated
1 small white cabbage, sliced very thin
2 large beets, grated fine
1 large can (3 cups) crushed tomatoes
2 tablespoons paprika
12 cups (3 quarts) water
1 15-ounce can natural smooth cranberry sauce (health food stores)
¼ cup sugar
Salt and pepper to taste
⅓ cup unfiltered apple cider vinegar

Heat the oil in a wide-bottom pot. In a food processor, finely grind the garlic and dill. Add the onion and celery and mince using the pulse button. Add the mixture to the hot oil and sauté until translucent. Add all remaining ingredients and bring to a boil. Reduce the flame to medium and cook covered about 30 minutes. Adjust texture and seasonings. Makes a dozen ample servings.

CABBAGE CARAWAY SOUP GF, P

Cabbage and caraway have a natural affinity and team up with the potatoes to produce this delightfully funky soup.

⅓ cup olive oil
2 medium onions, quartered
2 large leeks, white part and the soft green parts, sliced thin
6 large cloves garlic
3 ribs celery, peeled and cut in chunks
2 large potatoes, peeled and cut into large chunks
1 bunch dill, fronds and stems
1 large head cabbage, cut into large chunks
4 cups canned crushed tomatoes
3 tablespoons paprika
Salt to taste
12 cups (3 quarts) water
3 tablespoons caraway seeds
Pepper to taste

Heat the oil in wide soup pot. In a food processor, coarsely chop onions, leeks, garlic, and celery and add to the hot oil. Sauté until translucent. Add all remaining ingredients except caraway seeds and the pepper, and bring to a boil. Reduce the flame to medium and cook covered for 1 hour. Add the caraway seeds and the pepper and cook another 10 minutes. Cream with an immersion blender until smooth. Adjust the texture and seasonings. Serve hot. Makes a dozen ample servings.

Slicing leeks

Leeks are very grimy, so be sure to slice them before washing. In recipes where you would like to serve the leeks unsliced, like leeks vinaigrette, which are just boiled leeks with a plain oil-and-vinegar dressing, I would still recommend cutting the leeks across their whole length—it's the only way to get at their inside layers and wash them properly. When serving, display them with cut side down so they look nice and "whole."

LISA'S TIP

Leeks are part of the allium vegetable family—which also include **onions, garlic,** and **scallions**—and have been associated with a lower risk of heart disease. They are rich in vitamins A and C, and phytochemicals that may also be prevent certain kinds of cancers.

CARROT GINGER SOUP GF

Starring the humble carrot, with all the flavorings that compliment it. Don't be afraid of serving it to guests—it doesn't taste nearly as modest as the ingredient list reads.

⅓ cup olive oil
2 large red onions, quartered
2-inch piece ginger, grated
1 tablespoon curry, a little more if you like it hotter
3 large carrots, grated (about 4 cups packed)
¼ cup maple syrup
3 quarts (12 cups) water
½ cup millet (or other quick-cooking grain: steel-cut oats, teff, amaranth, etc.)
1 teaspoon allspice
2 teaspoons cinnamon
1 tablespoon orange zest
Salt to taste
Freshly ground pepper to taste

Heat the oil in heavy pot. In a food processor, coarsely grind the onions and add to the hot oil. Reduce the flame to medium and fry, stirring occasionally until very dark brown. This step will take about 20 minutes. Add the ginger and curry and cook, stirring 2 more minutes. Add all but last ingredient. Bring to a boil. Reduce the flame to medium and cook covered for 30 minutes. Adjust the texture and seasonings. Makes a dozen ample servings.

LISA'S TIP

Carrots are a good source of fiber, which helps to maintain bowel health, lower blood cholesterol, and aid in weight maintenance. The orange pigment found in carrots are due to the antioxidant, beta-carotene, also found in other deep orange foods such as **sweet potatoes, pumpkin, butternut squash, papaya,** and **cantaloupe.** Beta-carotene is converted to vitamin A in the body, helps to maintain healthy eyes, support your immune system, keep your skin healthy, and protect against certain cancers.

CHESTNUT MUSHROOM SOUP GF

Chestnuts and mushrooms: What could be more seductive?

> ## Chestnuts
> I just can't be bothered with boiling and peeling chestnuts before I could get on with this or any dish, so I buy them vacuum-packed roasted and peeled, and they are easy to use and delicious: my granddaughter Chaya Rochel munches on them all the time. They come in 3- or 5-ounce sealed bags. I prefer using the 3-ounce bags as they make a better size serving snack, especially for children.

> ## Cooking wine and sherry
> Ounce for ounce, cooking wines and sherries are priced exactly as a moderately priced good bottle of table wine. So I beg you, please don't settle for these hideous imitations; go into a liquor store and get yourself a good bottle of wine that will do your dish proud! No need to get anything expensive, just *real*! Mirin, a wonderful rice wine, is easily found at health food stores and will do a great job as well.

⅓ cup olive oil
4 large leeks, white and light green parts, sliced
1½ pounds cremini or portobello mushrooms, sliced
1 cup dry sherry or sake (liquor stores)
8 cups water
1 pound total vacuum-packed roasted chestnuts
6 sprigs thyme, leaves only
2 good pinches saffron
4 bay leaves, or ½ teaspoon ground
1 cup white miso paste
4 cups milk or dairy-free milk, low-fat OK (soy, rice, almond, oat)
Good pinch nutmeg
Ground pepper to taste

Heat the oil in a wide heavy pot and add the leeks. Sauté until translucent. Add the mushrooms and sauté until all liquids evaporate. Add the sherry, water, chestnuts, thyme, saffron, and bay leaves and bring to a boil. Reduce to medium and cook covered for 30 minutes. Add the miso, milk, nutmeg, and pepper and heat through another 3–4 minutes. Cream with an immersion blender. Adjust the texture and seasonings. Makes a dozen ample servings.

Variation: Potato mushroom soup

Substitute 3–4 large Yukon gold or other good potatoes, cut in large chunks, for the chestnuts and proceed as above.

CHICKEN VEGETABLE SOUP GF, P

I have a wonderful recipe of chicken matzo ball soup in my first cookbook, Levana's Table. *I am giving you here a variation my mother lives on almost daily—chicken soup as a meal: Nothing gets discarded. It's the best! If you would rather use chicken breasts, then add ⅓ cup olive oil to the pot.*

1 large onion, quartered
1 large bunch dill, fronds and stems
1 bunch flat-leaf parsley
8 ribs celery, peeled
1 large carrot
1 large sweet potato
1 large parsnip
1 large turnip
1 large zucchini
12 chicken thighs, skins off
1 teaspoon turmeric
2 good pinches saffron
5–6 bay leaves, or 1 teaspoon ground
Salt to taste

Put three quarts (12 cups) water to boil in a large pot. While the water is heating, coarsely grind the onion, dill, parsley, and celery in a food processor. Throw the ground mixture in the pot. Grate all the vegetables in a food processor and add to the soup with all remaining ingredients (if you have more time to spend on the preparation, dice all the vegetables small). Bring to a boil. Reduce the flame to medium and cook covered for 1 hour. Adjust the texture and seasonings. Makes a dozen ample servings.

Note: For more presentation, take out the thighs, discard the bones, dice the meat, and return to the pot. Or simply use boneless thighs: Your butcher will do it for you.

CORN CHOWDER (ALL VARIATIONS) GF

A chowder almost always signals the presence of potatoes, and a hearty creamy-chunky texture. This one has an added appeal: a lovely pale yellow color. Make this soup only with fresh corn please, when it is tender and sweet. Did you know the cobs impart great flavor to soup? I am including a fish as well as a chicken variation.

⅓ cup olive oil
4 leeks, white parts only, sliced
4 ribs celery, peeled
6 large cloves garlic
1 bunch dill, fronds and stems
2 yellow peppers, cut in large chunks
4 cups fresh corn kernels, from about 6 ears corn (Reserve the stripped cobs.)
3 quarts (12 cups) water
2 large potatoes, cut in small cubes
2 cups dry white wine
Good pinch saffron
6 bay leaves, or 1 teaspoon ground
1 cup white miso paste, a little more if the finished soup needs to taste saltier
4 cups milk or dairy-free milk, low-fat OK
Good pinch nutmeg
Pinch cayenne
Ground pepper to taste

Heat the oil in a wide heavy pot. In a food processor, coarsely grind the leeks, celery, garlic, dill, and peppers. Add the ground mixture to the hot oil and sauté until translucent. Add the corn, water, reserved cobs, potatoes, wine, saffron, bay leaves, and salt and bring to a boil. Reduce the flame to medium and cook covered for 30 minutes. Whisk in the miso, milk, nutmeg, cayenne, and pepper and cook 2–3 more minutes until just hot—do not boil or it might curdle. Discard the cobs. With an immersion blender, directly in the pot, purée about a third of the soup, leaving the rest chunky. Adjust the texture and seasonings. Serve hot. Makes a dozen ample servings.

Tomato corn chowder GF

Reduce the water to 8 cups and add 4 cups canned crushed tomatoes; cook as above.

Corn fish chowder GF

Use either the basic corn chowder or the tomato corn chowder recipe; throw in about 2 cups small salmon cubes after puréeing the soup and cook 10 more minutes.

Corn chicken chowder GF

Use the basic corn chowder recipe and throw in 2 cups diced chicken breasts after puréeing the soup and cook 10 more minutes.

KABOCHA SWEET POTATO SOUP GF, P

My daughter Bella's favorite. I brought her a vat of it when she had her baby. Still she doesn't seem to tire of it and now enjoys it with her baby. I always notice with pleasure that all kids love it! A snap to make: All aboard, then cream it at the end of cooking.

Kabocha squash

My favorite squash of all. Lean, dense, deeply flavored, nutritious—there's nothing you can't do with it: soups, stews, even salads, grated raw, skin and all!

---

1 kabocha squash, about 2 pounds, unpeeled, seeded, and cut into large chunks (use a hammer)

2 large sweet potatoes, cut into large chunks

1 large red onion, cut into large chunks

2 cups red lentils or yellow split peas (Passover: 2 large potatoes, cut in large chunks)

6 ribs celery, peeled

1 large bunch dill, fronds and stems

⅓ cup olive oil

6 bay leaves, or 1 teaspoon ground

1 tablespoon turmeric

Sea salt to taste

3 quarts (12 cups) water

Ground pepper to taste

Bring all ingredients to boil in a wide heavy pot. Reduce to medium, cover, and cook 1½ hours. Cream with an immersion blender. Adjust the texture and seasonings. Makes a dozen ample servings.

QUICK MINESTRONE GF

I trust you should have no trouble whatsoever finding dozens of delicious minestrone recipes. My original idea for this quick and incredibly satisfying version of the classic was: How can I play with the same ingredients and get a great soup in a fraction of the time? The answer: the incredible selection of frozen vegetables available in supermarkets and dry herbs. This soup requires no prep work at all. Please note the optional grains I have suggested cook quickly and need no soaking, to keep up with the brief cooking time of the soup.

3 quarts (12 cups) water

3 pounds of any frozen unprocessed cut vegetables—short and sweet selection: cauliflower, broccoli, string beans, zucchini, turnips, onions, corn, peas, carrots, okra, spinach, kale, lima beans, edamame, pidgeon peas, etc.

½ cup of steel-cut oats, red lentils, barley, or spelt (or 2 cups canned white beans or chickpeas, drained and rinsed)

⅓ cup olive oil

Salt to taste

Good pinch red pepper flakes

3 cups canned crushed tomatoes

1 teaspoon turmeric

2 tablespoons paprika

6 bay leaves, or 1 teaspoon ground

2 tablespoons dry basil

Bring all ingredients to a boil in a wide heavy pot. Reduce and cook covered for about 30 minutes. Adjust the texture and seasonings. Makes a dozen ample servings.

LISA'S TIP

Broccoli is a cruciferous vegetable, and part of the Brassica family that also includes **kale, collards, cabbage, bok choy, brussel sprouts, turnips,** and **cauliflower.** Members of the brassica family are rich in phytochemicals, believed to have antioxidant properties. Broccoli is a true nutrition powerhouse; it is chock-full of vitamin C, the mineral calcium, fiber, and vitamin A. Broccoli is also rich in sulforaphane, a health-promoting compound that can fight cancer.

ROASTED TOMATO SOUP GF, P

If you love tomatoes as much as I do, this soup is for you. Who knew the modest tomato could produce such a luxurious dish? Don't change anything: Every single ingredient does its magic in this heavenly soup. I often serve it at Seder dinners, or other long and elaborate dinners, not only to knock their socks off but also to mitigate the length and richness of the feast. Try the soup cold too sometime!

Do not attempt to make the soup with other varieties of tomatoes, which won't stand up to roasting.

5 pounds best-quality tomatoes (about 7–8 large beefsteak, or 18 plum tomatoes), split across, quartered if using the beefsteak ones
3 heads garlic, points sliced off, leaving the cloves exposed
4 medium purple onions, peeled and split across
3 red peppers, halved and seeded
Coarse sea salt to taste
Vegetable spray
10 cups water (2½ quarts)
½ cup olive oil
1 cup dry white wine
2 cups tomato juice
¼ cup tomato paste
1 tablespoon paprika
4 sprigs rosemary, 2 if they are very large, leaves only (left whole OK)
6 sprigs thyme, leaves only (left whole OK)
2 good pinches saffron threads
Freshly ground pepper to taste

Preheat the oven to 425°F. Spread the first set of ingredients on a cookie sheet lined with foil or parchment and spray generously with vegetable spray. Roast for about 45 minutes until the vegetables look charred (the garlic heads might take a little longer). As soon as they are cool enough to handle, squeeze the garlic heads until all the flesh is forced out of its skin into a wide heavy pot. Add the other roasted vegetables and all remaining ingredients except pepper, and bring to a boil. Reduce the flame to medium and cook covered for 30 minutes. Add the ground pepper. If you used whole rosemary and thyme sprigs, discard them at this point. Cream with an immersion blender until perfectly smooth. Adjust the texture and seasonings. Serve hot as is or with croutons (page 102). Makes a dozen ample servings.

THAI SWEET POTATO PEANUT BUTTER SOUP GF

Rich and silken—Asian flavors at their best. Half a cup of peanut butter will be ample enough to impart a rich nutty flavor to the whole batch.

¼ cup olive oil
2 stalks lemongrass, tough ends removed, or 1 tablespoon lemongrass powder
2-inch piece ginger, peeled
2 large onions, cut in large chunks
3 tablespoons sugar or Sucanat
2 tablespoons curry powder
1 tablespoon cinnamon
2 teaspoons turmeric
3 large sweet potatoes (or a 3-pound butternut or kabocha squash, or 4 large carrots), cut in chunks
12 cups (3 quarts) water
1 15-ounce can coconut milk
Salt to taste
½ cup peanut butter
Ground pepper to taste

Heat the oil in a wide heavy pot. In a food processor, finely grind the lemongrass and ginger. Add the onion and pulse until coarsely ground. Add the mixture to the pot, reduce the flame to medium, and fry, stirring occasionally until dark brown. This step will take about 20 minutes. Add the sugar and sauté 1 to 2 more minutes until caramelized. Add the curry, cinnamon, and turmeric and sauté just a few more seconds. Add all remaining ingredients and bring to a boil. Reduce to medium and cook covered for 30 minutes. Cream the mixture with an immersion blender. Adjust the texture and seasonings. Serve hot (but try it chilled too sometime). Makes a dozen ample servings.

CREAM OF VEGETABLE SOUP GF, P

No need to cut, dice, or sauté anything here either. All those large veggies will start breaking during cooking, so, all aboard, just peel and throw in the pot and cream at the end of cooking. About ten minutes of prep work for a huge potful of delicious soup! Another great children favorite.

3 quarts (12 cups) water
2 large potatoes
1 large sweet potato
1 large carrot
1 large turnip
2 large zucchini
1 large onion
1 large bunch parsley, leaves and stems
1 large bunch dill, fronds and stems
6 ribs celery, peeled
⅓ cup olive oil
Salt to taste
1 teaspoon turmeric
4 bay leaves, or 1 teaspoon ground

Bring all ingredients to a boil, reduce the flame to medium, and cook covered for 1 hour. Cream with an immersion blender. Adjust the texture and seasonings. Makes a dozen ample servings.

FISH SOUP GF, P

Although this soup is included in my first cookbook, Levana's Table, *I just didn't have the heart to leave it out. You can easily make a whole meal out of it. Oh, I know you will be told there's no good fish soup unless you include all that shellfish, but wait till you taste this one! It simply has too much going for it to be missing anything. I have no quarrel with mock crab, which is made of all-natural pollock and adds great texture and flavor, which suits kosher diners as well as diners reluctant to use shellfish just fine.*

I eliminate the broth-making step by wrapping the heads and tails of fish loosely in cheese-cloth, cooking them with the soup and then discarding them without any mess. Cooking the soup with the heads intensifies its flavor and imparts a light gelatinous texture. This is every bit as interesting as the traditional French version containing shellfish: Besides, the Moroccan version never had any. If you have dashi powder, no need to use the head or tail—it will do the job beautifully.

⅓ cup extra-virgin olive oil

4 large leeks, sliced

4 ribs celery, peeled and cut in thirds

4 large cloves garlic, peeled

1 bunch flat-leaf parsley

1 small bunch cilantro

1 red bell pepper, seeded and cut in chunks

Head and tail of a large salmon, tile fish, or any other big fish, quartered, loosely but securely wrapped in cheesecloth (if you have dashi powder, skip this step and use ¼ cup dashi powder, and no added salt in the recipe)

4 cups canned crushed tomatoes

2 large potatoes (or 1 medium celery root instead), cut in ½-inch cubes

1 cup dry white wine

½ to 1 teaspoon cayenne

Good pinch ground cloves

3 bay leaves

1 tablespoon paprika

2 good pinches saffron

Salt to taste

2½ quarts (10 cups) water

2 tablespoons anisette or arrack

3 pounds boneless, skinless fish such as salmon, tile, or snapper, cut in 1-inch cubes

1 pound of frozen mock crab, thawed and flaked (if you don't have it, just add a little more of the fish you are using)

Freshly ground pepper to taste

Heat the oil in a wide heavy pot. Coarsely grind the leeks, celery, garlic, parsley, cilantro, and red bell pepper in a food processor. Add to the oil. Sauté the ground mixture until all liquids evaporate. Add the cheesecloth (if using a fish head; otherwise add the dashi), canned tomatoes, potatoes, wine, cayenne, cloves, bay leaves, paprika, saffron, salt, and water. Bring to a boil again. Reduce the heat to medium and cook, covered for 45 minutes. Add the anisette or arrack, the fish, and pepper and cook another few minutes, just until the fish is cooked through. Press on the cheesecloth to release as much liquid as you can before discarding. Adjust the texture and seasonings. Makes a dozen ample servings.

LISA'S TIP

Fatty fish

Fatty fish, including salmon, sardines, and tuna, are a great protein choice and contain the healthy fats, omega-3 fatty acids, which contribute to heart health and reduce inflammation.

BEAN AND GRAIN SOUPS

QUICK BLACK BEAN CHOCOLATE SOUP GF

Beans and chocolate? I recently teased my friend Sara into identifying the odd ingredient in this soup, which she loved. I enjoyed watching her racking her brains, and didn't feel any guilt about it: After all, she was working for food and was kept guessing through a second bowl. PS, she never did identify it; she said all she could tell is that this was like no other bean soup she ever had. That's the magic of chocolate!

Canned beans will work here just fine as the soup has lots of fabulous flavors going for it.

Sofrito:

⅓ cup olive oil
1 large onion, quartered
4 large cloves garlic
4 ribs celery, peeled and cut in thirds
1 large red pepper, seeded and quartered
1 bunch flat-leaf parsley, stems and all
½ small bunch cilantro, stems cut off

6 cups good-quality canned black beans (2 large cans), drained and rinsed
½ cup tomato paste
2 cups dry red wine
3 tablespoons bottled hot sauce
6 bay leaves, or 1 teaspoon ground
3 quarts (12 cups) water
⅔ cup grated semisweet chocolate or chocolate chips
1–2 tablespoons ground cumin
1–2 tablespoons oregano

Heat the oil in a heavy pot. Make the sofrito: In a food processor, coarsely grind the onion, garlic, celery, pepper, parsley, and cilantro. Add the ground mixture to the hot oil and sauté until translucent (if you have sofrito in your freezer, page 41, skip this step; use 1 cup thawed sofrito and proceed with the recipe from this point). Add the beans, tomato paste, wine, hot sauce, bay leaves, and water and bring to a boil. Reduce the heat to medium and cook 30 minutes. Add the chocolate, cumin, and oregano and cook for 15 minutes more. Adjust the texture and seasonings. Serve hot. Makes a dozen servings.

MOROCCAN LENTIL SOUP GF

All my favorite flavors are in. Costs pennies and takes minutes, and tastes like a million bucks: You just can't miss with these assertive flavors! It is also very versatile: Using the exact same base, you might want to substitute other grains for the lentils, just as long as they don't take longer to cook (barley, azuki, brown rice, mung, etc.).

2 large onions, quartered
1 large bunch flat-leaf parsley
1 bunch cilantro, tough end stems cut off
6 ribs celery, peeled
4 cups canned crushed tomatoes
⅓ cup olive oil
Salt to taste
3 quarts (12 cups) water
2 teaspoon turmeric
2 cups green or brown lentils
Pepper to taste

In a food processor, coarsely grind the onion, parsley, cilantro, and celery. Transfer the mixture to a heavy wide-bottom pot. Add all but last ingredient and bring to a boil. Reduce the flame to medium and cook covered for 1 hour, or a little longer until the lentils are perfectly tender and the soup looks thick and creamy. Stir in the ground pepper and adjust the texture and seasonings. Makes a dozen ample servings.

Variation: Buckwheat, bulgur, teff, or millet soup

These grains take only a few minutes to cook. Proceed with the recipe just as above, substituting 2 cups of the suggested grain for the lentils, but with one change: Add them in the last 20 minutes of cooking.

Moroccan
Lentil Soup

CHICKPEA SOUP GF

The French term for chickpeas *is "pois chiches," meaning something like pea's poor relatives. Wow, if poor and modest could always taste like this (I for one think it always does), just give it to me! So many hummus joints have recently sprouted all over the city: chickpea spreads with all the fixings. But has anyone thought, as I did, about a liquid version? Rah-rah! By the way, it is not entirely my invention, as we grew up with chickpea soup at home made with meat and served as a whole dinner. But this meatless and no-less-delicious version is (entirely) my idea, and I am so proud of it I made it on a recent CBS morning show segment I was invited to. My plan was to knock their socks off with something very plebeian that tastes marvelous, and it worked: gastronomy sans argent! Is it any wonder Moroccan food is my first and most lasting culinary love?*

1 pound dry chickpeas, soaked overnight and drained
12 large cloves garlic
½ cup tahini (sesame paste)
1 large bunch cilantro, stems cut off
1 large bunch flat-leaf parsley, leaves and stems
6 ribs celery, peeled
Salt to taste
2 teaspoons turmeric
1 teaspoon ground coriander
12 cups (3 quarts) water
Ground pepper to taste
¼ cup fresh lemon juice

Bring all but last 2 ingredients to a boil in a wide-bottom pot. Reduce the flame to medium and cook covered for 2 hours. Add the lemon juice and the pepper. Cream until smooth with an immersion blender. Adjust the texture and seasonings. Makes a dozen ample servings.

MUSHROOM BARLEY SOUP GF

The hearty and wonderful classic. Gluten-free—this is for you too! Brown or wild rice or steel-cut oats will be a great substitute for the barley.

⅓ cup olive oil
6 large cloves garlic
1 large onion, cut in large chunks
5 ribs celery, peeled
1 large bunch dill, fronds and stems
1½ pounds domestic, portobello, or cremini mushrooms, diced
3 quarts (12 cups) water
1¼ cups barley (gluten-free: short grain brown rice or wild rice)
2 large carrots, diced ½ inch
1 large parsnip, diced ½ inch
1 large turnip, diced ½ inch
6 bay leaves, or 1 teaspoon ground
Salt to taste
1 teaspoon dry thyme
Pepper to taste

Heat the oil in a wide heavy pot. In a food processor, finely grind the garlic. Add the onion, celery and dill, and grind coarse, using the pulse button. Add the ground mixture to the pot and sauté until translucent. Add the mushrooms and sauté until most liquids evaporate. Add all but last ingredient and bring to a boil. Reduce the flame to medium low and cook covered for 1½ hours. Stir in the ground pepper. Adjust texture and seasonings. Makes a dozen ample servings.

OAT QUINOA CHILI GF

For all of us whose love of beans remains, alas, unrequited, let me say you can make a perfect chili substituting oat, quinoa, and lentils in any proportion for the feisty beans, so you can have your chili and eat it too! You can easily make this dish vegetarian: It has lots of great flavor going for it even without the meat. If beans are no trouble, by all means use them—3 cups in all—but soak them overnight and cook the dish a little longer until the beans are tender.

Sofrito:

3 tablespoons olive oil
2 medium onion, quartered
2 ribs celery, peeled and cut in thirds
4 large cloves garlic
1 bunch flat-leaf parsley
1 small bunch cilantro, stems discarded
1 red bell pepper, seeded and cut in chunks

1½ pounds ground turkey, beef, lamb, or bison (skip for an all-vegetarian dish or substitute 1 pound seitan, diced)
4 cups canned crushed tomatoes
⅓ cup tomato paste
2 cups dry red wine
6 bay leaves, or 1 teaspoon ground
⅓ cup chili powder
1 cup steel-cut oats
1 cup quinoa, thoroughly rinsed and strained
1 cup short grain brown rice or barley
2 tablespoon ground cumin
2 tablespoons oregano
Salt and ground pepper to taste

Heat the oil in a wide heavy pot. Make the sofrito: Coarsely grind in a food processor the onion, celery, garlic, parsley, cilantro, and red pepper and add the ground mixture. Sauté until translucent. (If you have sofrito in your refrigerator or freezer, page 41, use 1 cup, thawed, and skip this whole first sautéing step; proceed with the recipe from this point on.) Add the meat and sauté, breaking up any large chunks, until no longer pink. Add the crushed tomatoes, tomato paste, wine, bay leaves, chili powder, sugar, oats, quinoa and lentils, and 12 cups (3 quarts) water. Bring to a boil. Reduce heat to medium and cook covered for 1 hour. Add all remaining ingredients and cook 10 more minutes. Adjust texture and seasonings. Serve alone or with the usual garnishes: white or brown rice, guacamole (recipe follows), or corn chips. Makes a dozen ample servings.

MOROCCAN PEA SOUP GF

Practically my granddaughter Tsofia's first food after the baba. And guess who fed her: Who better than yours truly, her Tuesday babysitter and occasional personal chef? All the delighted toothless smiles were ample reward to me, dribble and all. All children, big and small, love this soup. I have noticed that children are, inexplicably, more attracted to "yellow food" than to "green food," and this is why I make this soup with yellow split peas: The flavor remains very much the same, sweet and mild.

Listen to what my friend Chaya Minna (Helen) Schwimmer wrote me about the soup: "Moroccan pea soup is the new Jewish penicillin! I have been cooking chicken soup for my family for almost forty years, but it has been displaced by your Moroccan pea soup. We all love it, from our three-year-old granddaughter to her grandfather and everyone in between. When I brought a serving over to a neighbor who was ill and she found that it was the only food she could tolerate, I gladly made her a batch each week. It is definitely the new chicken soup in our house!"

2 large onions, quartered
8 ribs celery, peeled and cut in large chunks
3 large carrots, cut in large chunks
1 pound bag green or yellow split peas, picked over and rinsed
1 large bunch flat parsley, stems and leaves
1 bunch cilantro, stems cut off
⅓ cup olive oil
1 teaspoon turmeric
3 quarts (12 cups) water
Salt to taste
Pepper to taste

Put all but last ingredient to boil in a wide heavy pot. Reduce the heat to medium and cook covered for about 1 hour, or a little longer until the peas are very tender. Add pepper to taste. Cream with an immersion blender. Adjust the texture and seasonings. Makes a dozen ample servings.

INDIAN RED LENTIL SOUP GF

I think you can tell: I adore lentils (dahl), and why not? Ready in minutes, easy to use, inexpensive, and a nutritional treasure. Try your very best to get to an Indian grocery store and check out their dizzying array of lentils (or just go online!).

⅓ cup olive oil
2 tablespoons curry, or more to taste
1 tablespoon cumin
1 tablespoon ground cardamom
1 teaspoon turmeric
1 tablespoon grated fresh ginger
1 stalk lemongrass, minced, or 1 tablespoon lemongrass powder
4 large cloves garlic
8 sprigs cilantro, stems cut off
1 small bunch flat parsley
1 tablespoon tamarind powder
4 cups tiny red lentils
3 quarts (12 cups) water

Heat the oil in a heavy wide-bottom pot. Reduce heat to medium and add the curry, cumin, cardamom, and turmeric. Sauté until just fragrant, about 1 minute. Coarsely grind the ginger, lemongrass, garlic, cilantro, and parsley in a food processor. Add the ground mixture to the pot and sauté 2 to 3 minutes, stirring occasionally. Add all remaining ingredients and bring to a boil. Reduce the heat to medium and cook covered for 30 to 40 minutes. Adjust the texture and seasonings. Makes a dozen ample servings.

HERB WHITE BEAN SOUP GF

I am mighty proud of this rustic creation—a low-cost and low-maintenance feast, and a meal in itself. I might surprise you by asking you: No substitutions whatsoever in this soup, please. I tried playing with it (using dried herbs, skipping the smoked turkey), and it was pretty good, yes, but nowhere near as fabulous as when I made it the way I am instructing you here. It's okay to put in the fresh herb sprigs whole and discard them at the end of cooking.

1 pound large dry lima beans, soaked overnight and drained
3 quarts (12 cups) water
⅓ cup olive oil
8 large cloves garlic
1 large carrot, cut in large hunks
4 ribs celery, peeled
4 large leeks, sliced
1 large wedge Savoy or white cabbage, hard core removed
2 cups natural (no nitrites) smoked turkey, about 1 pound, white or dark, diced small
1 cup dry white wine, sake, or dry vermouth (liquor stores)
6 bay leaves, or 1 teaspoon ground
2 good pinches saffron
6 sprigs thyme, leaves only
2 sprigs rosemary, leaves only
3 sprigs sage, leaves only, chopped
Salt to taste
Ground pepper to taste

Bring the beans and water to boil in a wide heavy a pot. Reduce to medium and cook covered for 1 hour while you prepare the rest of the soup.

Heat the oil in a large skillet. In a food processor, finely grind the garlic. Add the carrot, celery, leeks, and cabbage and grind coarsely. Add the ground mixture to the oil and sauté until translucent. Transfer the sautéed mixture to the bean pot and add all but last ingredient. Bring to a boil, reduce, and cook 1 more hour, or a little longer until the beans are very soft and the soup looks creamy and thick. Stir in the pepper, and adjust the texture and seasonings. Makes a dozen ample servings.

MOROCCAN LIMA BEAN SOUP GF

Here's the simple secret of this wonderful and super simple soup: preserved lemon. You'll be glad you have your little stash of the great stuff in a jar! If you don't have it, simply choose from all the other soups I have included, but don't settle!

⅓ cup olive oil
2 large onions, quartered
6 ribs celery, peeled
8 large cloves garlic
3 quarts (12 cups) water
1 pound large lima beans, soaked overnight and rinsed
4 cups canned crushed tomatoes
3 tablespoons paprika
½ teaspoon cayenne, or to taste
Salt to taste (use sparingly: the preserved lemon is salty)
½ preserved lemon, peel only, rinsed (page 33)
1 bunch flat-leaf parsley, leaves and stems
1 small bunch cilantro, tough ends discarded
2 tablespoons ground cumin

Heat the oil in a wide heavy pot. In a food processor, coarsely grind the onions, celery, and garlic. Add to the pot and sauté until translucent. Add the water, beans, tomatoes, paprika, cayenne, and salt and bring to a boil. Reduce to medium low and cook covered for about 2 hours or until the beans are very soft and start breaking up and dispersing in the liquid. In a food processor, finely grind the preserved lemon, parsley, cilantro, and cumin and add the mixture to the pot. Cook another few minutes. Adjust the texture and seasonings. Makes a dozen ample servings.

COLD SOUPS

COLD FRUIT SOUP GF, P

This wonderful ruby-colored soup is equally at home in a soup bowl as a first course or in a martini glass as a dessert.

Even in the heart of summer, I make this soup with frozen berries and rhubarb, just because nothing could beat their sweetness and ease of preparation. Frozen berries would not be just an acceptable substitute: they would be quite wonderful, as frozen fruit are picked at their sweetest and ripest. Try them in this recipe. The fact that they are a little bruised by freezing will not matter in the least since we are cooking them.

Of course, if you have lots of beautiful fresh berries and/or rhubarb on hand, go ahead and use them. In season, add plums, cherries, etc.

2 Granny Smith (green) apples, peeled and cut in chunks

10 cups total fresh or frozen (I prefer frozen) strawberries, raspberries, blueberries, peaches, pitted cherries, plums (in any combination you like)

A mixture of the following spices, tied in a cheesecloth: 1 large piece lemon peel, 1 large piece orange peel, 6 cloves, 10 black peppercorns

2 cups dry red wine (liquor stores)

4 cups unsweetened cranberry or pomegranate juice

Juice of 2 limes or lemons

½ to ⅔ cup maple syrup (start with less and wait until you taste the finished soup to add more)

½ cup tapioca flour, whisked with a little cold water until smooth (for Passover: potato starch)

Bring all but last ingredient to boil in a heavy pot. Reduce the heat to medium low, add the tapioca mixture, and cook 10 more minutes, no more. Remove the cheesecloth. Cream the soup with an immersion blender, but not completely. Leave about a quarter of it chunky. Adjust the texture and seasonings. Chill completely before serving. Serve as a first course, alone or with a scoop of plain yogurt (dairy-free perfect too), or as a dessert, alone or with a scoop of coconut sorbet. Makes a dozen ample servings.

Variation: Strawberry rhubarb soup GF, P

Use 10 cups combined strawberries and rhubarb, and no other berries. Proceed exactly as above. You might need to add more maple syrup, rhubarb being quite tart.

Cold Fruit Soup

Berries

Eating a diet high in fruits and vegetables has been correlated with a reduced risk of various chronic diseases. And for good reason: they are low in calories and rich in nutrients. Berries, in particular, are a nutrition powerhouse. Many reasons exist to put berries on your shopping list and to cook with them.

Naturally low in calories, berries contain vitamins and minerals, including vitamin C, folate, potassium, and calcium. The pigments that give berries their beautiful colors turn out to also contain phytonutrients and antioxidants that are good for health. Fruits rich in phytonutrients are linked to lower rates of cardiovascular disease, strokes, and cancer in the people who eat them.

Berries are also high in fiber that can aid digestion. One cup of raspberries, for instance, contains only 65 calories plus a healthy 8 grams of fiber. So feel free to fill up on them, guilt free. Pectin, one of the soluble fibers in berries, also has cholesterol-lowering properties and contributes to heart health.

Berries are a terrific fruit group to include in the diet because of its high ORAC (oxygen radical absorbance capacity) value, a measure of antioxidant capacity. Diets high in antioxidants are beneficial and help fight chronic diseases because they protect the body from free radicals associated with aging and inflammation, among other conditions. Blackberries, strawberries, cranberries, and blueberries are among the foods that top the chart for containing the most antioxidants per serving. So feel free to enjoy these colorful jewels.

Berries—in particular, blueberries, cranberries, and mulberries—contain the polyphenol, resveratrol, associated with heart health, anticancer activity, and reduced inflammation. Berries known for their deep concentrated pigment contain the flavonoid, anthocyanins, which contain many health benefits that may help ward off diseases such as diabetes and cancer. Raspberries, strawberries, and cranberries also contain the polyphenol antioxidant, ellagic acid, which seems to have some anti-cancer properties.

Good news for berry lovers. You can get them year-round without worrying about price. While fresh berries eaten immediately after harvest are the best choice in obtaining essential nutrients, unfortunately today's lifestyle does not always allow us to find them easily or to grow our own fresh berries. Frozen berries are the next best thing and allow us to indulge year-round, and at a modest price. Berries frozen right after harvest preserve many of their nutrients and phytochemicals, making them a terrific and nutritious choice.

Here are some **berry bites**:

Blueberries are rich in antioxidants and vitamin C and may benefit heart health and brain function associated with aging. Research suggests that consuming blueberries may keep your blood pressure in check.

Cranberries contain flavonoids that may protect against inflammation and may help prevent urinary tract infections. Furthermore, the procyandins found in this berry contains antioxidant and antibacterial properties.

Raspberries contain the antioxidant quercetin that has anti-inflammatory benefits and the phenolic compound, ellagic acid, and can help fight cancer. And even more good news: 1 cup contains only 65 calories and 8 grams fiber.

Blackberries top the chart for containing the most antioxidants per serving, so put them on your shopping list.

Strawberries are a terrific source of vitamin C; 1 cup of sliced strawberries contains more than a day's worth of this antioxidant nutrient. A cup of strawberries also contains 3 grams dietary fiber and is low in calories (less than 50 calories per cup).

Berry tip: Beware of HYPE

While the juice from the **acai berry**, for example, may be high in antioxidants, little evidence actually exists that it has special weight loss or other powers, often touted on Internet ads. Save your money and stick with the good ole regulars.

COLD MINTED HONEYDEW AND KIWI SOUP GF, P

Please don't throw in any fruit that will alter in any way the lovely pale green color of the soup (in other words, no berries, mangoes, etc.). No cooking: So little work, so much taste and presentation!

1 large honeydew melon, peeled and cubed
6 ripe kiwis, peeled and halved
3 cups green grapes
½ cup fresh lemon or lime juice
2 tablespoons lemon zest
1 cup mint leaves, packed
¼ cup maple syrup, or a little more to taste
4 cups pure white grape juice

Blend all ingredients in batches in a blender until perfectly smooth. Thin the soup if necessary with a little more grape juice. Serve chilled. Garnish each bowl with a nice mint sprig and a slice of lime. Makes a dozen ample servings.

GAZPACHO GF, P

Dare I include this tired horse of the cold soup repertoire? Yes! Because I have a couple of wonderful secret ingredients that do wonders with this perennial favorite: watercress and capers. The upgrade will certainly not be lost on you—liquid salad never tasted so good. Do not be tempted to substitute stem tomatoes or grape or cherry tomatoes, no matter how luscious they look. We want much meatier tomatoes here, like plum or beefsteak.

8 plum tomatoes, halved (or 4 beefsteak tomatoes, quartered)
2 red peppers, cut in large chunks
1 medium red onion
4 large cloves garlic
Half a bunch watercress, stems and leaves
¼ cup capers (Passover: might be hard to find, in that case just skip them)
4 cups tomato juice
½ cup olive oil
½ cup fresh lemon or lime juice
3 tablespoons bottled hot sauce, or a little more to taste
1–2 tablespoons cumin
3 tablespoons paprika
Salt and pepper to taste

In a blender or food processor, in batches, blend all ingredients until smooth. If you like it chunkier, stop blending before it gets completely smooth. Add enough cold water to give the soup the right texture. Serve chilled, topped with lemon or lime slices. Makes a dozen ample servings.

Variation: Gazpacho with mock crab and guacamole.

If you would like to make a main course out of this soup, top the soup with a handful crumbled mock crab and a generous dollop of guacamole (page 83).

LISA'S TIP

Yogurt is full of vitamins and minerals—calcium, protein, riboflavin, phosphorus, vitamin B12—and friendly bacteria called probiotics that may improve immunity and aid in digestive health. Best to choose low-fat or nonfat varieties, and add your own fruit instead of purchasing the flavored yogurts full of added sugars. Try experimenting with Greek yogurts as they are creamier and contain more protein.

COLD AVOCADO CUCUMBER SOUP GF, P

Is chilled and spicy what you are after? Nothing to it, and no cooking! Just one recommendation: Try your best to make it on the day you intend to serve it, or make it in advance without the avocadoes, and mash the avocadoes and stir them in just before serving.

4 cups unflavored yogurt or dairy-free yogurt
4 avocadoes, peeled and halved
4 ribs celery, peeled
1-2 jalapeños
1 large seedless cucumber, peeled
1 large bunch dill, fronds and stems
1 medium purple onion, quartered
Salt and pepper to taste
6–8 cups water (start with less, adding gradually to thin the soup to a good texture)

In a blender or food processor, mix all ingredients, in batches. Chill the soup. Makes 8 ample servings.

COLD MINTED ESCAROLE PEA SOUP GF

Peas and escarole are natural partners: The sweetness of the peas offset the bitterness of the escarole in this rustic French soup. I love to serve it cold, but try it hot too sometime (in this case, bring to just below boiling so as not to allow the milk to curdle).

Escarole is a member of the lettuce family, rather neglected in America. It has a delightfully bitter edge that makes it a big salad star and lends itself perfectly to quick cooking, paired as it is here with milder ingredients.

⅓ cup olive oil
4 large leeks, sliced
4 ribs celery, peeled
1 small bunch flat-leaf parsley
1 large onion, quartered
1 large zucchini, cut in large chunks
3 quarts (12 cups) water
Salt and pepper to taste
4 cups frozen peas
1 large head escarole, chopped
1 small bunch mint, leaves only
4 cups milk or dairy-free milk, low-fat OK

Heat the oil in a wide heavy pot. In a food processor, coarsely grind the leeks, celery, parsley, onion, and zucchini and add the mixture to the hot oil. Sauté until translucent. Add the water and salt and pepper and bring to a boil. Reduce the temperature to medium and cook covered for about 20 minutes. Add the peas, escarole, and mint and cook 10 more minutes. Add the milk, and cream the soup with an immersion blender until perfectly smooth. Adjust the texture and seasonings and chill. Serve cold. Makes a dozen ample servings.

COLD RED AND YELLOW PEPPER SOUP GF

Pretty, light, and nutritious. The whole idea here is to end up with a yellow mixture and a red mixture, and pour them simultaneously and steadily from 2 pitchers to get this gorgeous red-and-yellow palette.

4 large red bell peppers, cores and seeds taken out
4 large yellow bell peppers, cores and seeds taken out
Vegetable spray
⅓ cup olive oil
6 large cloves garlic, minced (use the food processor)
4 leeks, dark leaves discarded, sliced
2 large potatoes, diced
2 quarts water
1 cup dry white wine (liquor stores)
Salt to taste
A little ground pepper
1 tablespoon paprika
2 tablespoon tomato paste
½ cup basil leaves, packed

Peppers: Broiling by roasting

Peppers can get quite pricey, but the good news is they are easily roasted, and after roasting, they freeze very well. Here is a much easier and much less messy way of "broiling" them: no charred skins and no turning over. When they are plentiful and well priced, buy lots of them (remember, roasted peppers will greatly reduce in bulk so they will take much less room in the freezer), rinse them thoroughly, cut out the cores, and tap them cut side down onto a counter to rid them of their seeds. Spray them with vegetable spray and place them cut-side down on a baking sheet lined with foil or parchment. Roast them at 450 degrees about 30 minutes. When they are cool enough to handle, peel only the dark-looking skins and ignore the lighter-colored ones. Divide them in manageable quantities in small zipper bags and freeze them. You will be delighted to find them when you need them!

Preheat the oven to 425°F. Spray the peppers with the vegetable spray and place cut-side down on a cookie sheet lined with foil or parchment. Roast about 45 minutes until the skins look blistered. The peels will be very soft—peel off only the darkest ones.

Meanwhile, make the soup. Heat the oil in a wide heavy pot. Add the garlic and leeks and sauté until wilted. Add the remaining ingredients and bring to a boil. Reduce the heat to medium and cook covered for 30 minutes. Divide the mixture in two. In one pot, add the yellow peppers. In the second pot, add the red peppers, paprika, tomato paste, and basil. Cook each mixture 10 more minutes. Process each mixture separately with an immersion blender until smooth (start with the yellow mixture so you won't have to rinse the immersion blender when you switch to red). Adjust the texture and seasonings in each pot. Chill completely.

To serve: Pour simultaneously, slowly and steadily from 2 containers equipped with a spout. Makes a dozen ample servings.

Cold Red and Yellow Pepper Soup

SALADS

Whenever I ask my husband on weekdays what he would like to have for dinner, he answers without fail: a salad, or soup and a salad. If I say I have some delicious fish or chicken or rice, he says, OK, throw it into the salad. Yes, salad is a very big deal in my house. I make it in vats, and the vat gets all cleaned up each time; my husband's portion is as large as all our guests' combined. You might think his diet is boring and his wife's skills are wasted on him, and the answer to all of the above is exactly the opposite! It is exciting and full of surprises, and it keeps him thin and fit, G-d bless!

Salad possibilities are endless (including salad sandwiches, yum!), but I will give you just a few guidelines:

- **A short selection:** Pick only a few ingredients and a few colors, leaving plenty of room for variety on other salad days. You can even select one ingredient and do perfectly well: all romaine or all watercress and so on. If you are choosing salad as a main course, you can make the selection a little, not much, longer. How short can the selection get? Here are just a few suggestions that seem so ridiculously simple you might not think of them by yourself, each starring just *one* salad ingredient: a whole bunch of celery, all ribs peeled and very thinly sliced, oil and lemon, salt and pepper to taste; a whole head of fennel, ditto (no peeling); lots of red radishes, very thinly sliced, with brown rice vinegar and salt.

- **Just a little dressing:** Use just enough dressing to coat the greens lightly, and just before serving, or you will make it soggy.

- **Only the best:** Select the freshest, crispest, most colorful leaves. Washing the leaves and herbs ahead of time keeps them crisp and fresh longer: drain them thoroughly and roll them in paper towels before storing them in a zipper bag. Likewise, grate carrots, cabbage, and beets; store them in a zipper bag lined with paper towels; and use them as needed.

- **Salad as main course:** What a treat! Take a good look at your leftovers and do some good flavor and texture matchmaking.

- **Leaves:** No iceberg: There is simply no excuse for such a mediocre choice, unless all you want your salad to be is crunchy (I doubt it!). Choose from romaine, watercress, arugala, mesclun, endives, spinach, kale, mustard greens, escarole, Boston lettuce, etc.

- **Raw veggies:** Let me set apart the delicious, nutritious, and much-maligned avocado. So many of us have all but crossed it off our lists because it is fattening. Half an avocado has 130 calories, or as many as in a pat of butter, and is a real nutritional powerhouse. So what's wrong with that? Put it back on ASAP! Slivered red peppers, sliced cabbage, slivered fennel, grated carrots, grated red or golden beets, sliced radishes, sliced daikon, sliced mushrooms, sliced zucchini, raw corn kernels in season, scallions, sprouts, cucumbers, tomatoes, celery, etc.

- **Cooked ingredients:** This is where your leftovers will come in very handy and will turn a salad into a main course—different, personalized, and exciting each time: Just knowing this will prevent you from eating beyond the point when you are full because you are afraid "it might go to waste" (it won't!). Sliced fresh or bottled roasted red peppers, diced cooked eggs, diced potatoes, rice, kasha, quinoa, couscous, oats, noodles, diced chicken, flaked fresh cooked or canned fish, diced cooked or natural (no nitrites) smoked turkey, smoked salmon, sliced steak, canned beans and chickpeas, fresh roasted or canned beets, string beans, frozen corn, etc.

- **Garnishes:** Grated cheese, capers, gherkins, good olives, granola, etc.
- **Fruit and nuts:** Diced apples, pears, mango, fresh figs, papaya, grapefruit, orange, raisins, cranberries, toasted nuts, sunflower, pumpkin, flax, chia, hemp seeds, etc.
- **Herbs:** Coarsely chopped basil, parsley, dill, cilantro, mint, chives, etc.

Just a last remark on my personal preference on the choice of "container" for serving salad: I find that placing salads, especially leafy ones, in deep salad bowls, presents two disadvantages: the lower leaves tend to get bruised by the weight of the upper ones, and the dressing runs all the way to the bottom, creating dry upper leaves and soggy bottom leaves. This is why I prefer to serve salads in platters or very shallow bowls instead of in deep bowls—the uncluttered and lightly dressed leaves remain crisp, and you have no compulsion to add more dressing!

Please dress only the amount of salad you think will get eaten, adjusting the amounts of dressing used accordingly. Save the rest, undressed, sealed, and refrigerated—it will be most welcome for next meal.

Short and Sweet Salad Greens Selection

APPLE WALDORF SALAD GF, P

Waldorf in a dish signals the presence of apples, celery, and nuts. Besides these constant trademarks, there's so much you can do with a Waldorf salad, so let's start with my favorite, then take it places! Passover: Adjust the dressing ingredients using what you have on hand.

2 gala or other fragrant apples, unpeeled, diced small

4 ribs celery, peeled and sliced very thin

½ small red onion, minced

Optional: ½ cup golden raisins

½ cup walnuts, cashews, or pecans, toasted and chopped coarse

1 cup remoulade dressing (page 29)

Place all salad ingredients in a bowl, adding the nuts just before serving so they don't lose their crunch. Pour the dressing over the salad and toss. Makes 8 servings.

Variations: Play with the possibilities and enjoy an exciting dish each time.

- Add shredded romaine, thinly sliced endive or fennel or grated celery root (in this case, make a little more dressing as the salad will get bulkier).
- Throw in some freshly grated Parmesan
- Substitute other kinds of nuts: pistachios, peanuts, almonds, pine, etc.
- Turn the salad into a main course by adding some diced cooked salmon or sliced poached chicken breast or diced natural (no nitrites) smoked turkey or both.
- Throw in some diced avocado.
- Throw in some frozen corn, thawed.
- Throw in some cooked brown rice, or any cooked grain you might have on hand.

Endive Waldorf Salad

HUMMUS, ALL VARIATIONS
Basic hummus GF

I bet you thought hummus comes in pint containers and no other way. That's how ubiquitous commercial hummus has become—a marked improvement over many mediocre commercial offerings, but commercial nonetheless. But wait till you see (a) how simple it is to whip up and (b) how many hats it wears and how many exciting hummus variations you can make throwing in small leftover portions of some interesting ingredients. It is super healthy, so enjoy—as a dip or spread or in a sandwich. Let me also say, at the risk of appearing somewhat disingenuous, since hummus *literally means "chickpeas" in Hebrew and Arabic, that you can substitute cooked tiny lentils (ready in just a few minutes) or canned white beans and proceed exactly as instructed. My secret ingredient for delicious basic hummus: ground coriander. So here comes!*

> 1 15-ounce can good-quality all-natural chickpeas, liquid and all
> ⅔ cup tahini (sesame paste)
> ¼ cup fresh lemon juice
> 4 large cloves garlic
> 1 tablespoon ground cumin
> 1 tablespoon ground coriander
> Ground pepper to taste (no salt please: the chickpeas are salty!)

Process all ingredients in a food processor until perfectly smooth. Pour into a flat platter. Just before serving, drizzle with a little olive oil and sprinkle with paprika and minced parsley. Serve with good olives and pita bread.

Variations GF

Consider these additions or substitutions at blending time, if you have any of the following on hand. As always, one at a time please!

- **Roasted garlic hummus:** Substitute 1 head roasted garlic (page 173) for the fresh garlic.
- **Roasted pepper hummus:** Throw in 2–3 roasted red peppers, bottled OK.
- **Nutty hummus:** Substitute peanut or other nut butter for the tahini.
- **Spicy hummus:** Make it as hot as you like, with jalapeño or chili powder to taste, and maybe some chopped cilantro and/or parsley.
- **Avocado hummus:** Substitute an avocado for the tahini.
- **Spinach hummus:** Throw in a handful frozen spinach, thawed and squeezed dry.
- **Tofu Hummus:** Throw in a cup tofu, and a little more tahini.
- **Sun-dried tomato olive hummus:** Omit the tahini, cumin, and coriander and throw in some good pitted black olives, basil, and sun-dried tomato, rinsed and squeezed dry.
- **Artichoke hummus:** Omit the cumin and coriander and throw in a 10-ounce box frozen and thawed artichoke hearts and some fresh or dry rosemary.

- **Roasted vegetable hummus:** Throw in a handful of roasted veggies. No need to make them just for the purpose of this recipe. Just take them from a batch you might have on hand.

My granddaughter Tsofia enjoying hummus

ARTICHOKE WHITE BEAN DIP GF

I often notice that as soon as we don't talk about trimming artichokes and getting our hands grimy, we find more people amenable to trying them. So frozen hearts or bottoms, in salads, soups, or dips: way to go! This dip is simply fabulous. The ingredients work beautifully together, so as much as I like to play with my food and urge you to play with yours, I say, leave this one exactly as is!

1 head roasted garlic (page 173)
⅔ cup extra-virgin olive oil
1 10-ounce box frozen artichoke hearts or bottoms, thawed
1 cup canned white beans, rinsed and drained
Juice and zest of 2 lemons
Ground pepper to taste
2 tablespoons fresh rosemary leaves, or 1 tablespoon dry
Good pinch red pepper flakes

Process all ingredients in a food processor until smooth. Store refrigerated in a glass jar. Makes about 4 cups.

SPICY CHICKPEA LETTUCE SALAD GF

One of my favorites! All of you out there always asking how we turn a same old, same old salad into an exciting main course salad: You can glorify it even further by throwing in some leftover diced fish or chicken, or make it dairy, and throw in some crumbled feta.

8 cloves garlic
3 ribs celery, peeled
1 jalapeño, stem cut off
1 bunch flat-leaf parsley
½ preserved lemon, skin only, rinsed (page 33) (settle for zest of 2 lemons if you don't have any on hand)
½ cup olive oil
⅓ cup fresh lemon juice
2 tablespoons cumin
1 tablespoon oregano
Bottled hot sauce to taste
3 cups canned chickpeas (1 large can), strained and rinsed
6 plum tomatoes, seeded and diced small
1 cup pitted Moroccan (oil-cured) olives
¼ cup capers
3 romaine hearts, sliced very thin

In a food processor, finely grind the garlic, celery, jalapeño, parsley, and preserved lemon. Add the oil, lemon, cumin, oregano, and hot sauce and pulse just 1 to 2 times until combined but still chunky.

Place all the salad ingredients in a platter. Toss with the ground mixture. Serve at room temperature. Makes 8 servings.

BEAN CORN SALAD GF

Those of you trying to reduce your animal protein intake will do excellently with this dish, as beans have a high protein content—plus they are high fiber, an asset fish or meat are not endowed with. Use any other beans you might have on hand: white beans, cranberry beans, navy beans, etc. Get good-quality canned beans with minimal processing. (How can you tell? When the ingredient list is extra short: beans, salt, water!)

Serve this salad with guacamole on the side and make a main course of it!

2 cups canned black beans, rinsed and drained
2 cups canned red kidney beans, rinsed and drained
2 cups fresh corn kernels (or frozen and thawed)
2 large tomatoes, halved, seeds squeezed out, diced small
¼ cup chopped flat parsley
¼ cup chopped cilantro
½ small red onion
4 large cloves garlic
1 tablespoon cumin
2 tablespoons capers
⅓ cup olive oil
¼ cup fresh lemon juice
2 tablespoons bottled hot sauce
Salt and pepper to taste (taste first: you might not need any added salt)

Place the beans, corn, and tomatoes in a bowl. Finely grind the parsley, cilantro, onion, and garlic in a food processor. Add the cumin, capers, oil, lemon juice, hot sauce, salt, and pepper and pulse just 1 to 2 times to combine. Pour the mixture over the salad and toss. Serve at room temperature. Makes 8 servings, or 4 main course servings.

CAESAR'S SALAD GF

If there was ever a time Caesar salad went out of fashion and was eclipsed by a new salad on the block however briefly, I can't remember it. The queen, albeit with a king's name. What is the secret of its enduring popularity? In my opinion, a short but unbeatable classic ingredient lineup. Only the best: crisp romaine, croutons made from good-quality bread, freshly grated Parmesan—all totally attainable! Make a double batch of the dressing and enjoy it with many other goodies.

6–8 slices good-quality bread, gluten-free OK, cut in ½ inch cubes
3 romaine hearts, torn into bite-size pieces
½ small purple onion, sliced very thin (food processor)
½ cup *freshly* grated Parmesan, a little more to taste
1 cup Caesar's dressing (page 26)

Preheat the oven to 375°F oven. Make the croutons: Place the bread cubes in one layer in a baking sheet and toast until light brown, about 12 to 15 minutes. Reserve.

Place the romaine, onion, and cheese on a platter. Just before serving, add the croutons. Pour the dressing over the salad and toss.

Makes 8 servings.

Caesar's Salad

CABBAGE CUCUMBER APPLE SLAW GF, P

Look what happened to coleslaw! And why not? A slaw being nothing more than shredded cabbage as the first building block—have fun adding all the good stuff, with minimal effort on your part, thanks to the food processor. I can't tell you enough how good and good-for-you green apples are in salads and side dishes! You want this salad to be pale green and white, so nothing brightly colored such as carrots or red peppers or radishes!

1 small head cabbage or nappa, shredded thin (slicing disk)
4 ribs celery, peeled and grated (slicing disk)
1 seedless cucumber, grated coarse (shredding disk)
2 Granny Smith (green) apples, unpeeled, cored, and grated coarse (shredding disk)
1 bunch scallions, sliced very thin
1 bunch dill, minced (chopping blade)
Dressing:
½ cup olive oil
¼ cup unfiltered apple cider vinegar (health food stores)
2 tablespoons prepared white horseradish, or 2 tablespoons wasabi diluted in a little cold water
Salt and white pepper to taste
2 tablespoons sugar

Place all the vegetables in a mixing bowl. Mix the dressing ingredients thoroughly and pour over the mixture. Toss gently so as not to extract moisture. Store refrigerated in glass jars. Makes about 2 quarts. Serve at room temperature.

Variations
- Throw in some grated daikon, or some sliced endive or fennel.
- Thrown in some diced orange or grapefruit slices.

CABBAGE SALAD WITH GARLIC AND LEMON GF, P

So simple it doesn't even look like a recipe. I throw it in my sandwiches or serve it with my main course.

1 small head white cabbage, quartered, tough cores discarded, sliced very thin in a food processor
4 large cloves garlic, minced
⅓ cup fresh lemon juice
½ cup olive oil
Salt and white pepper to taste

Mix all ingredients in a bowl. Store refrigerated in glass jars. Makes about 2 quarts. Serve at room temperature.

KALE, BEET, AND SEAWEED SALAD GF

With this dish, I am doing nothing more than group the veggies many of us wouldn't imagine eating raw. The result is a real triumph, so get ready to adopt them wholeheartedly into the family! You would enjoy beets and turnips much more often, even raw, if only you would grate them very fine in a food processor. The salad will keep well a good couple days.

> **LISA'S TIP**
>
> **Kale** is a nutritious green packed with calcium, beta carotene, vitamin C, and fiber.

1 bunch kale, tough stems removed, leaves cut into very thin ribbons
1 large beet, red or golden, grated very fine (food processor fine shredding blade)
6 scallions, sliced very thin
¼ cup hijiki (or other seaweed: wakame, arame, etc.) or other seaweed (health food stores), soaked in hot water to cover
½ cup sesame or other seeds (chia, flax, hemp, etc.), toasted
1 cup Chinese green tea dressing (page 24)

Place all salad ingredients in a mixing bowl. Pour the dressing over the salad and toss. Store refrigerated in glass jars. Makes 8 servings.

Variations

- Substitute other greens for the kale—mustard, collard, turnip, spinach, even nappa cabbage.
- Substitute rutabaga (yellow wax turnip), daikon, carrots, or zucchini for the beet.
- Throw in diced avocado.
- Throw in some sprouts.
- Throw in some chopped toasted cashews or peanuts.
- Use any other kind of seaweed—nori, kelp, wakame, arame, etc.
- Throw in some cooked lentils, brown rice, thawed frozen corn kernels, or any grain you have on hand and turn it into a complete main course.

Kale, Beet, and Seaweed Salad

JAPANESE EGGPLANT SALAD GF

In this dish, as in every dish that involves eggplant, I keep the oil-gobbling monster away from frying with a vengeance. I refuse to submit to its tyranny, so roasting is the answer, and it delivers a great reward besides the lean result—the wonderful resulting added layer of smoky flavor.

2 medium eggplant, cut in half lengthwise
¼ cup toasted sesame oil
6 large cloves garlic
1 2-inch ginger, grated
3–4 tablespoons brown rice vinegar
2–3 tablespoons bottled hot sauce
3–4 tablespoons soy sauce
4 scallions, sliced very thin
¼ cup minced cilantro

Preheat the oven to 450°F. Line a cookie sheet with foil or parchment paper. Spray the paper with vegetable spray. Add the eggplant cut side down in one layer, and spray it generously with vegetable spray. Roast 30 to 40 minutes, or until very soft and brown. When it is cool enough to handle, dice the eggplant using a sharp knife. Transfer to a mixing bowl, with all remaining ingredients. Mix thoroughly. Store refrigerated in a glass jar. Makes about 4 cups. Serve at room temperature.

Variation: Moroccan eggplant salad GF

Roast and dice the eggplant exactly as above, ignoring all the remaining ingredients in the recipe. Instead, add ⅓ cup olive oil, ¼ cup fresh lemon juice, 2 tablespoons cumin, 2 tablespoons paprika, 4 cloves minced garlic cloves, salt and pepper, and mix thoroughly.

MOROCCAN GRATED CARROT SALAD GF

I never understood why this salad smells exactly like salami, which makes it even more funky. My son packs it in avocado or cheese sandwiches. Try it sometime!

4 cups grated carrots (thin shredder of a food processor), packed
4 large cloves garlic
1 small bunch flat-leaf parsley
Juice of 2 lemons
½ cup olive oil
Salt and pepper to taste

Place the carrots in a bowl. Mince the garlic and parsley in a food processor, and add them to the bowl. Whisk the juice, oil, salt, and pepper in a little bowl, and pour over the carrots, tossing thoroughly to combine. Store refrigerated in a glass jar. Serve at room temperature. Makes 8 servings.

HARICOTS VERTS, ASPARAGUS, AND ARTICHOKE SALAD GF

You will love to serve this gorgeous salad as a side dish too. Haricots verts are French string beans, much denser, crisper and tastier, slender, and bright. Green asparagus, please, not their elegant and expensive but insipid sun-deprived white cousins.

1 bunch thin asparagus, tough ends discarded, cut in half
1 pound haricots verts (frozen perfect too)
1 pound frozen artichoke hearts (they are small: leave them whole), or frozen artichoke bottoms, thawed and sliced thin
3 roasted peppers (page 92) (settle for bottled), sliced thin
½ cup very good olive oil
Sea salt to taste, gray salt if you see it at an affordable price

Bring water to boil in a large pot. Add the asparagus and haricots verts and cook just 3 to 4 minutes, even less if you are using frozen. Drain and rinse under cold water, working quickly so the vegetables retain their bright color.

Place all the vegetables in a bowl or platter and toss them with the oil and salt. Makes 8 servings.

TOMATO WEDGES WITH SEA SALT GF

Hardly a recipe at all. When tomatoes are gorgeous, or if you find affordable (affordably expensive, to be exact) heirloom tomatoes, cut them in wedges and toss them with a very good olive oil and some coarse sea salt. To this simple and outrageous treat, you can add any of the following: shredded fresh basil, sun-dried tomatoes, good pitted olives, capers, mozzarella, a few grinds of pepper.

Heirloom Tomatoes

PANZANELLA GF

The cute name comes from the Italian word pan, *which means "bread." The ideal leftover dish, as it is made from 2- to 3-day-old bread. Gluten-free bread will work perfectly here. The bread cubes soak up all the flavors, so it will get better as it sits a few hours. Panzanella is versatile and will lend itself perfectly to the addition of some white beans, shredded lettuce or spinach, roasted pepper, even diced cooked fish or sliced smoked salmon (in this case, no cheese). When you make the dressing, consider skipping the anchovies, as the salad includes a few salty ingredients.*

1 pound loaf whole-grain bread, gluten-free OK, cut into small cubes
1 seedless cucumber, sliced very thin
½ medium red onion, sliced very thin
3 large tomatoes, or 6 plum tomatoes, halved, seeds squeezed out, diced
1 cup Niçoise or oil-cured olives
½ cup mint leaves, packed, cut in ribbons
½ cup basil leaves, packed, cut in ribbons

Optional: 1 cup tiny cubes strong cheese, such as feta, cheddar or kashkaval
1 cup Caesar's dressing (page 26), a drop more if necessary (skip the anchovies so you can feel free to include more of the salty salad additions)

Place all salad ingredients in a salad bowl. Pour the dressing over the salad and toss, preferably 2 to 3 hours before serving. Serve as is or on a bed of shredded romaine (add this just before serving). Makes 8 servings.

ISRAELI SALAD GF, P

A little more time-consuming than I like my dishes to be, with all the dicing, but you will be rewarded with a fun and delicious salad. I will start with the most basic mixture, which you will recognize as a good Israeli salad (as distinct from the inevitable undressed cucumber-toma-to-onion hash that accompanies many orders of falafel and burgers), and then take it places.

3 romaine hearts, sliced very thin
1 seedless cucumber, diced half-inch
2 beefsteak tomatoes, or 4–5 plum tomatoes, diced half inch
1 cup radishes, diced small
1 bunch scallions, sliced very thin
½ cup olive oil
⅓ cup fresh lemon juice
Salt and pepper to taste

Place all the salad ingredients in a shallow bowl or platter. Whisk the oil, lemon, salt, and pepper and toss into the salad just before serving. Makes 8 servings. Delicious with burgers and kebabs and falafel sandwiches.

Delicious additions: Only if you are not getting too impatient with all the dicing (yes, I use people's time as judiciously as I use their money!). Choose from chopped flat-leaf parsley, diced red pepper, sliced good pitted green olives, diced avocado, even finely chopped raw cauliflower.

RUSSIAN SALAD GF, P

We grew up eating this hearty "salade russe" as we called it. The name signals the presence of a few Russian staples: beets, dill, pickles. The authentic way includes chopped hard-boiled eggs into it, about 3 to 4 for the amounts given below: Add only if you intend to make a main course out of it, or serve them in a little bowl on the side. Delightful with cold fish, poultry, or meat dishes.

1 large beet
2 large Yukon potatoes, or 1 medium rutabaga (yellow wax turnip)
2 large carrots
½ small red onion
1 half-sour pickle
1 small bunch dill
2 ribs celery, peeled
¼ cup olive oil
¼ cup unfiltered apple cider vinegar (health food stores)
Salt and pepper to taste

Peel and dice all the vegetables small ½ inch. Cook the beets separately (so as not to turn the whole dish an unpleasant red) in a wide-bottom pot or a large skillet, with water just to cover, until tender and the water cooks out. Cook the turnip and carrots the exact same way in another pot. Transfer all the vegetables to a bowl. Cut the onion, pickle, dill, and celery in large chunks and place in the food processor. Pulse the mixture until minced. Add the oil, vinegar, salt, and pepper and pulse 2 to 3 more times, until just combined. *While the vegetable mixture is still warm*, pour the ground mixture over them and mix thoroughly. Store refrigerated in glass jars. Makes about 8 cups. Serve at room temperature.

SARDINE SALAD GF

Sardines are to Mediterraneans what tuna is to most Americans. They are so underrated in America! Is it their fault that they look so homely and smell so pungent? Have you tried them in a sandwich or panini with some lettuce and tomato? Try them in this recipe and let me know if they are beginning to grow on you! Don't recoil from the sardines with skin and bones on, and don't discard any of it: You won't see them in the finished dish—plus, that's where all the flavor and nutrition are. You will love this salad in a sandwich as well.

2 cans sardines, skin and bones on, oil and all
¼ cup tahini (sesame paste)
4 scallions, sliced very thin
Juice of 2 lemon, or a little more to taste
Ground pepper to taste
Splash of bottled hot sauce
4 cups very finely chopped romaine, watercress, or sprouts, or a combination (I recommend it, so it can absorb some of the excess saltiness of the sardines)

Mash the sardines with their oil and the tahini with a fork in a bowl. Add the scallions, lemon juice, pepper, and hot sauce and combine thoroughly. Fold in the greens and mix. Makes 8 servings.

MOROCCAN SWISS CHARD CARROT SALAD GF, P

Wonderful match, spicy and colorful!

6 thin long carrots, peeled
⅓ cup olive oil
4 large cloves garlic
2 ribs celery, peeled and cut in large chunks
1 large bunch Swiss chard, ribs and leaves, sliced thin (spinach OK, or a mixture)
Dressing:
Juice of 2 lemons, or a little more to taste
2 tablespoons paprika
1 tablespoon cumin
Bottled hot sauce to taste
Salt and pepper to taste
Boil the carrots in a little water until tender, then slice them ½ inch thick.

Meanwhile heat the oil in a large skillet. In a food processor, mince the garlic. Add the celery and grind coarse, using the pulse button. Add to the skillet and sauté until just fragrant. Add the Swiss chard and cook about 10 minutes, until very reduced and very tender. Transfer the mixture to a bowl and add the cooked sliced carrots. Whisk the dressing ingredients in a small bowl and pour over the vegetables, mixing thoroughly. Store refrigerated in a glass jar. Makes about 6 cups. Serve at room temperature.

VEGETABLE TUNA SALAD GF, P

Folding in other veggies makes the salad leaner, crunchier, less salty, and much more interesting. Tuna has enough flavor to pull it off. Why throw away the oil and use mayo? This will make you the best sandwiches, with lettuce and sliced tomato if you like.

2 6-ounce tuna packed in oil, undrained
1 medium carrot
1 medium zucchini or cucumber
3 ribs celery
1 small red onion
Ground pepper and bottled hot sauce to taste, optional

Place the tuna in a mixing bowl, oil and all. In a food processor, using the shredding disk, grate the carrot, zucchini, celery, and onion. Transfer the mixture to the bowl and add the pepper and hot sauce. Mash thoroughly until the mixture comes together, adding a few drops of oil if necessary. Store refrigerated in a glass jar. Makes about 4 cups. Serve at room temperature.

> **LISA'S TIP**
>
> **Celery** can provide volume and crunch to a variety of dishes for a low price and a low caloric content, with only 6 kilocalories in one medium stalk. The health benefits of celery include contributing to bowel health and lowering blood pressure and cancer risks.

Variations: White fish salad GF, P

Substitute 2 cups flaked smoked white fish–or even store-bought white fish salad if fish bones intimidate you–for the tuna, and proceed as above, adding a finely diced green apple to absorb excess salt

Pickled herring salad: drain it thoroughly, dice it and any included onions small, and add a couple diced boiled potatoes and green apples.

TOFU EGG SALAD GF

Egg salad, another treat I and many of us cholesterol-watching diners must use very sparingly and often forgo altogether, but wait till you taste this: You will never miss the original it got its inspiration from. Delicious enough to serve to everyone! Needless to say, if you are one of those lucky ones who can afford eggs, proceed exactly as in the recipe, using eggs instead of tofu.

2 pounds firm tofu, drained, squeezed thoroughly dry (if eggs are no problem: 12 hard-boiled eggs)
1 small red onion
½ bunch dill, fronds and stems
½ medium pickle, or 2–3 gherkins
1 rib celery, peeled
½ red bell pepper
½ Granny Smith (green) apple, unpeeled
⅓ cup mayonnaise, low-fat OK
Juice of 1 lemon, or a little more to taste
3–4 tablespoons Dijon-style mustard
1 teaspoon turmeric
1 tablespoon curry, optional, if you want curried "egg salad"
Salt and pepper to taste

Mash the tofu in a bowl with a fork. In a food processor, using the metal blade and the pulse button, mince the onion, dill, pickle, celery, pepper, and apple. Add the mixture to the bowl. Whisk the mayonnaise, lemon, mustard, turmeric, curry if using, salt, and pepper and stir into the bowl, mixing thoroughly but gently so as not to make the mixture mushy. Serve alone as a dip or sandwich spread, or as a salad on a bed of lettuce. Store refrigerated in a glass jar. Makes about 6 cups. Serve at room temperature.

Spices

Cooking with spices adds flavor to your favorite dish while also packing in plenty of nutrition. Here are some superstars.

Ginger, often used in cooking and herbal medicines around the world, offers a pungent flavor and unique zest to any dish. Some research also supports numerous benefits of ginger, including anti-nausea, anti-cancer, and anti-inflammatory properties.

Turmeric, responsible for the yellow color of curry powder, contains powerful anti-inflammatory and antioxidant properties that may offer protection against diabetes, arthritis, diabetes, and Alzheimer's disease.

Garlic may protect against heart disease by lowering cholesterol levels, reducing blood pressure, and providing anti-clotting activity.

Cinnamon has been shown to play a role in lowering blood sugar in diabetics as well as containing antimicrobial effects.

MINTED WATERMELON FETA CHEESE SALAD GF, P

Wacky combo? I admit this is quite a stretch from the way watermelon is usually enjoyed: only one small good problem—it's fabulous, so go for it! You must have noticed as I did that seeded watermelon is much tastier than the "convenient" and bland seedless hybrid. Just spit out the seeds discreetly, OK?

8 cups watermelon, cut into ½-inch cubes
¾ cup crumbled feta cheese
2 cups cherry or grape tomatoes halved
1 cup fresh mint, packed, sliced very thin
6 scallions sliced thin

Dressing:

¼ cup fresh lemon or lime juice
¼ cup olive oil
salt and pepper to taste (you might need no salt at all)
pinch of red pepper flakes

Place all salad ingredients in a platter. Whisk the dressing ingredients in a little bowl and pour over the salad. Mix very gently so as not to extract moisture. Makes 8 servings.

WHITE BEAN SALAD WITH ARTICHOKES AND SWISS CHARD GF

This delightful and rustic salad wears several hats—all Italian! Deliziosi!

⅓ cup olive oil
6 large garlic cloves
1 large bunch flat parsley
Good pinch red pepper flakes
1 large sprig rosemary, leaves only
1 large bunch Swiss chard, leaves and stems, thinly sliced
2 cups frozen artichoke hearts or bottoms, halved, quartered if larger
3 cups canned white beans, drained and rinsed
Juice and zest of 2 lemons
Ground pepper to taste

Heat the oil in a large skillet. In a food processor, finely grind the garlic and parsley and add to the skillet. Sauté until just fragrant, about 1 minute. Add the red pepper flakes, rosemary, and Swiss chard and sauté 2 to 3 minutes. Add the artichokes, reduce the flame to medium and cook covered for 3 more minutes. Let the mixture cool, transfer to a platter, and combine with all remaining ingredients. Serve at room temperature.

Variations

- Throw in some flaked cooked salmon or smoked salmon.
- Throw in some diced cooked or smoked chicken or both.
- Throw in some sun-dried tomatoes, good olives, diced tomatoes, sliced basil.

TABBOULEH GF

Although the recipe is in my first cookbook, Levana's Table, *I don't have the heart to leave this great favorite out of this book, especially in light of the fact I have found ways to make it with several other quick-or-no-cooking grains, which is great news for us and all our gluten-free friends.*

I promise you will never go back to those half-pint containers at the supermarket once you have tried this homemade version.

1 cup bulgur (wheat, spelt, barley, or brown rice bulgur are all ideally calibrated and perfectly suitable, the latter perfect for gluten-free diners)
1 cup boiling water
4 whole scallions, sliced very thin
1 bunch flat-leaf parsley, chopped fine
1 bunch fresh mint (no substitutions), leaves only, chopped fine
4 plum tomatoes, halved, seeded and cut in small dice, optional
½ cup extra-virgin olive oil
Juice of two lemons
1 tablespoon ground cumin
Salt and pepper to taste

Mix the bulgur and the boiling water in a stainless steel bowl or pot. Immediately cover very tightly to prevent any heat from escaping. Let rest 10 to 15 minutes. Meanwhile, cut the scallions, parsley, mint, and tomatoes, if using. Transfer to a bowl. Add the oil, lemon juice, cumin, salt, and pepper to taste.

Fluff the bulgur thoroughly with two forks and add it to the mixture. Serve at room temperature. The leftovers will keep well for a day, and up to 3 days if you are not including the tomatoes. Makes about 8 servings.

Note: Quinoa (page 238) is perfect for tabbouleh (great choice for Passover). Only, you need to cook it first as it won't lend itself to soaking in boiling water.

Quinoa tabbouleh

FISH

orn and raised in the port city of Casablanca, I had no fish aversions whatsoever to overcome. Au contraire! I grew up eating fish almost every day, prepared in every way imaginable, even for breakfast. With the eclectic selection of fish dishes I am including, I intend to make a fish lover out of you, as I have done for hundreds of guests, students, and customers. Many home cooks have only recently (and timidly) started experimenting with fish. In the past, unsure how to discern its freshness or prepare it, let alone how and where to buy it, most cooks avoided unfamiliar fish and stuck with the old standbys: salmon, sole, and flounder (or frozen fish fillets). They further limited themselves by cooking these few varieties in the same repetitive ways—poached salmon, broiled sole, fried flounder.

Although increasingly unusual types of fish are available at local grocery stores, the big change these days is in consumers' consciousness. Fish is delicious, nutritious, and low in fat and takes just a few minutes to prepare. Don't be afraid to branch out when shopping and keep in mind these few important guidelines:

Where to buy fish: Fish markets and good supermarkets regularly receive a wide variety of good fresh fish. Fish is fresh when it is firm to the touch and its eyes are wide open. Fish should be resting on plenty of ice, with good drainage to eliminate stagnant melting ice. It should look bright, clear, unspotted, and unmarred. It should smell briny, not "fishy."

Frozen fish: If you have a fish market near you, or a good fish department at your supermarket, do not bother with frozen fish. However, if you can't buy fresh, there are a couple of facts you should know. Fish captured at the peak of its freshness and immediately frozen will be nearly perfect when thawed. I love frozen vacuum-packed and find it just about as good as fresh at a better price. Good frozen fish is packed tightly to prevent the icy air from causing freezer burns. It is frozen quickly, to prevent ice from accumulating on the flesh and draining away its moisture during the thawing process. When you buy frozen fish, use the same guidelines as when buying fresh fish: Look for firm, bright, unmarred fish that appears free of freezer burns or bruises. Above all, do not refreeze thawed fish.

How to cut fish: Do you recoil at the sight of scales, guts, bones, gills, and heads, even if they are those of a poor harmless dead fish? Ask your fishmonger to make salmon and striped bass steaks for you—to clean and fillet whole sides of salmon, mahimahi, bass, and tile; to thoroughly bone fish such as shad and white fish; to remove the skin of delicate fillets such as sole, flounder, and tilapia; to cut tuna steaks to the desired size and rid them of that unappealing and bitter-tasting black-red border (blood line). Once you establish a relationship with your fishmonger, you can make requests. Do not be afraid of being imposing: Every honest merchant loves a polite, informed consumer!

How to clean fish: Thoroughly remove all gills and scale the fish thoroughly (chances are, you almost always have your fishmonger do this). Throw it in plenty of cold water mixed with salt and lemon juice or vinegar: This will ensure perfectly cleaned fish.

How to cook fish: Dark varieties, such as bluefish and mackerel, are best briefly broiled so they remain moist and robust. Tuna, both the dark and the light albacore variety, should be quickly seared or grilled, leaving the inside barely cooked. Thick white fillets such as mahimahi, grouper, bass, and halibut lend themselves well to pan-frying, steaming, baking, broiling, and even stewing. Salmon is delicious baked, seared, stuffed, poached, marinated, and grilled. Thin flatfish fillets such as sole and flounder are too delicate for prolonged cooking or marinating and are best pan-fried, grilled, or "en papillotte" (more about this later), with a sauce or lemon wedges on the side. Whole small fish such as whiting or trout can be broiled, baked, or stewed with quick-cooking vegetables such as onions, garlic, and tomatoes. All fish share one crucial characteristic: they toughen and lose moisture when overcooked. So take out that fish just in time!

Before we get in earnest into the real recipes, here are some delicious foolproof no-recipe fish recipes for when you are in the mood for an off-the-cuff dinner:

I am sorry to say fish dishes don't freeze well, so either divide the recipe or make another meal out of it the next day, or even two days later. All you need to do is, as always, ensure proper sealing and no double-dipping.

How to have dinner ready in no time flat: Take whole small fish or fish fillets, squeeze lots of lemon juice on them, drizzle on olive oil and soy sauce, and bake at 400 degrees for 10 to 12 minutes.

No-recipe fish dinner: Great place to mix and match and enjoy a different dish each time at no extra labor cost! Bake salmon steaks or fillets at 425°F with absolutely nothing on for about 15 minutes, or steam (in a little water) or sear (in a little olive oil) fillets of bass, tuna, scrod, mahimahi, blue fish, branzino—any nice firm fish you find on your shopping day. Then have fun with all the condiments I have included in the pantry chapter (page 19): chutney, Thai sauce, cocktail sauce, olive spread, harissa, to name just a few. It's all here!

STOVE-TOP FISH VARIATIONS

(Please see Stovetop Chicken variations, starting on page 138)

SALMON TERIYAKI GF

Nothing to it, and delicious. Homemade teriyaki, not takeout—now you're talking! Experiment with other types of fish as well: bass, mahimahi, halibut, etc.

1 whole side salmon, about 3½ pounds, skin off, bones out, trimmed
¾ cup teriyaki sauce (page 37)
6 scallions, sliced very thin

Preheat the oven to 400°F. Place the fish in a baking pan just large enough to fit it snugly in one layer (if you have empty spaces, the liquids will burn). Pour the sauce evenly over it and bake 20 minutes. Transfer to a platter with its juices and sprinkle with the scallions. Serve hot. Room temperature OK too. Makes 8 main course servings, or a dozen ample first course servings.

ROASTED SALMON WITH MAPLE GLAZE GF

The short and dazzling favor lineup does its magic with practically no work. You will never say you are bored of salmon again! Bluefish will be suitable here, as well as any thick white fish (bass, mahimahi, halibut, etc.).

Trimming salmon sides

You will notice on the outermost side of each salmon half a flat, opaque strip, which runs the whole length of the fish: It is very fatty and not meaty and contributes nothing but a greasy, fishy taste. Have no mercy, cut it all off and discard it: You are not wasting it, you are saving the salmon. PS: Sushi restaurants use that part of the salmon to great advantage, but you are not a sushi restaurant and are not equipped with their knowledge and quality control, so please don't go there and order it in a good sushi restaurant!

⅓ cup maple syrup
2 tablespoons soy sauce
3 tablespoons Dijon-style mustard
3 tablespoons roasted sesame oil
1 tablespoon cracked pepper, or less to taste
1 whole side salmon, about 3½ pounds, skin off, bones out, trimmed

Preheat the oven to 500°F. Mix all but last ingredient in a bowl. Place the salmon skin side up in a baking pan just large enough to fit it snugly in one layer (if you have empty spaces, the liquids will burn). Pour the sauce evenly over the fish. Bake 15 to 18 minutes. Transfer to a platter and pour the cooking juices over the fish. Serve hot, or at room temperature. Makes 8 main course servings, or a dozen ample first course servings.

Roasted Salmon with Maple Glaze

TILAPIA FILLETS WITH MISO SAUCE AND SHIITAKE MUSHROOMS GF

I love cooking with tilapia as it is delicious, inexpensive, resilient, and reliable. Ready in minutes! When you are in a more luxurious mood, substitute bass or scrod for the tilapia. In a pinch, you can make this dish even without the mushrooms.

8 tilapia fillets, about 6–7 ounces each, thoroughly dried with paper towels
⅓ cup dark miso paste
3 tablespoons toasted sesame oil
2 tablespoons rice vinegar
¼ cup sake
Ground pepper to taste
8 scallions, sliced very thin
1 pound shiitake mushrooms, caps only, sliced very thin
Vegetable or olive oil

Preheat the oven to 450°F. Place the fillets in a baking pan just large enough to fit in one layer. Whisk the miso paste, sesame oil, rice vinegar, sake, and pepper in a bowl and spread evenly on top of the fillets. Scatter the scallions and mushrooms on top of the fillets.

Bake for fifteen minutes. Serve warm or at room temperature, topping each serving with the cooking juices and mushrooms.

SALMON IN POMEGRANATE SWEET-AND-SOUR SAUCE GF, P

Sweet-and-sour combinations work beautifully with salmon. The onions caramelize and contribute a sweet counterpoint to the vinegar. Another quick and delicious dish, just the way I like it—one pan, one step.

1 whole side salmon, no skin, no bones, about 3½ pounds, trimmed
1 large red onion, sliced very thin (use the food processor)
¼ cup olive oil
1 cup pomegranate juice
¼ cup unfiltered apple cider vinegar
2 tablespoons tomato paste
Salt and pepper to taste
1 teaspoon turmeric

Preheat the oven to 425°F. Place the salmon in a pan just large enough to accommodate the fish in one layer. Scatter the onions on top and on the sides of the fish. Mix the oil, juice, vinegar, tomato paste, salt, pepper, and turmeric in a bowl, and pour over the fish. Cook about 20 minutes, or a tiny bit more until the fish flakes easily and the liquids thicken. Serve hot or at room temperature. Makes 8 main course servings or a dozen or more first course servings.

HERB-ROASTED SALMON GF, P

Your house will fill with the heady fragrance of the lemons and herbs. This is a snap to make: even the individual roll variation I am including is much simpler than it looks and will make you look like a pro with just a few more minutes' work!

3 tablespoons olive oil
Juice and peel of 2 lemons
1 bunch flat parsley
Sea salt and freshly cracked pepper to taste
A handful of fresh herbs of your choice: thyme, basil, rosemary, tarragon, chervil, etc. (no more than 2 kinds), leaves only
6 large cloves garlic
1 side salmon, skinless and boneless, about 4 pounds, trimmed

Preheat the oven to 500°F. Place all but last ingredient in a food processor and grind until you obtain a smooth paste. Rub the salmon in this paste, using it all up. Place the salmon in a pan just large enough to contain it (if you have empty spaces, the liquids will burn). Roast 20 minutes. Serve warm or at room temperature. Garnish with lemon slices and chopped herbs.

Herb-Roasted Salmon Medallions

Variation: Herbed salmon medallions GF, P

Preheat the oven to 425°F. Cut the salmon into 10 strips, reserving the tail end for another use. Cut each strip through their thickness, leaving them attached at one end: You will get long thin strips. Rub each strip in the paste, then roll tightly and secure with toothpicks. You will get neat little cylinders (medallions). Place the medallions in a pan just large enough to contain them. Roast 20 minutes. Serve warm or at room temperature. Garnish with lemon slices and chopped herbs.

ALMOND-STUFFED SALMON GF, P

Save this beautiful dish for festive occasions. The Sephardi answer to poached salmon. I often serve it at the Seder table. More labored than my other dishes, yes, but not nearly as complicated as the finished dish would suggest. My mother likes to joke that the gauze-wrapped fish looks like it just came out of the operating room, but there will be no hint of this alarming association at the table, as you will have removed all the patient's bandages first!

For a more dramatic presentation, bring the whole unwrapped fish surrounded in its gelled broth and garnished with large sprigs of lemon and parsley.

You might want to make this fish with a large trout or bass too.

Apple corer

I love this nifty little gismo: it costs pennies and takes hardly any room in your kitchen drawer. It goes right through the center of the whole apple, and cores the whole fruit in one neat strike.

Stuffing:

1 medium onion
1 bunch flat parsley
Peel of 2 lemons
1 cup whole unblanched almonds
2 Granny Smith (green) apples, cored, and quartered
2 eggs
¼ cup olive oil, plus a little more for rubbing the stuffed fish
2 tablespoons sugar
¼ teaspoon nutmeg
Salt and pepper to taste

1 salmon, thoroughly cleaned, boned, and butterflied (net weight 6½ to 7 pounds); ask your fishmonger to do this for you
Cheesecloth, in one layer

Cooking liquid:

1 cup water

1 cup dry white wine
¼ cup olive oil
1 teaspoon turmeric
2 good pinches saffron
4 bay leaves, or 1 teaspoon ground
¼ teaspoon ground cloves
1 large onion, halved across then finely sliced (use a food processor)
2 lemons, unpeeled, finely sliced (use a food processor)

Preheat oven to 375°F. In a food processor, finely grind the onion, parsley, lemon peel, and almonds. Add the remaining stuffing ingredients and pulse 2 to 3 times until only just combined. Stuff the fish with the ground mixture. Rub the whole fish with a little olive oil (just a precaution to prevent the cheesecloth from sticking to the fish and bruising the skin). Wrap the whole stuffed fish tightly in cheesecloth, tucking the ends under the fish. Place the fish in a baking pan only large enough to hold it.

Mix all the cooking liquid ingredients and pour over the fish. Cover the pan loosely with foil. Bake 1¼ hours. Let the fish come to room temperature, then chill. The liquid will thicken. Unwrap the fish, saving all the surrounding liquids. Slice the fish neatly with a sharp serrated knife and serve with some of the gelled broth, garnished with lemon and parsley. Makes 8 main course servings, or 12 to 16 first course servings (simply cut each main course slice right across).

BAKED SNAPPER WITH RAISINS AND PINE NUTS GF, P

Overlaid with wonderful Mediterranean flavors. You might also want to consider another firm and thick type of fish fillets such as bass, salmon, or scrod.

¼ cup olive oil
1 large onion, chopped
1 large tomato, diced small
¼ cup wine vinegar
⅓ cup black or golden raisins
2 tablespoons Sucanat or honey
1 small bunch flat-leaf parsley, minced
1 teaspoon turmeric
Salt and pepper to taste
⅓ cup pine nuts, toasted (300°F about 12 minutes)
8 snapper or tilapia fillets, about 6 ounces each

Preheat oven to 425°F. Heat the oil in a skillet. Add the onion and sauté until translucent. Add the tomato and sauté 3 more minutes. Add vinegar, raisins, Sucanat, parsley, turmeric, salt, and pepper and sauté 3 more minutes. Place the fish fillets in an ovenproof pan just large enough to hold them. Pour the sauce over them. Bake for 20 minutes. Sprinkle the pine nuts on the fish and serve hot or at room temperature.

FISH COOKED MOROCCAN-STYLE (CHRAIMI) GF, P

Israelis affectionately called this dish Chraime, insisting that's what Moroccans call it. (Hello! Never heard of the word in Morocco! It probably got lost in translation . . .) This is precisely the kind of dish where preserved lemon makes all the difference: You should always have them on hand, as they are heavenly in this and many other dishes. Please note the dish has no added salt as the preserved lemon is enough to season it. No preserved lemon: Substitute 1 thinly sliced lemon, and be prepared for a dish 90 percent as good.

Any thick firm fish will be suitable in this dish. My daughter Bella asked me to make sure I don't forget to recommend using diced mock shrimp too, her favorite.

1 cup water
¼ cup olive oil
2 large tomatoes, diced small
½ teaspoon red pepper flakes, or to taste
Good pinch ground cloves
3 bay leaves, or ½ teaspoon ground
1 tablespoon paprika
8 cloves garlic
1 bunch flat parsley
1 small bunch cilantro
½ preserved lemon (page 33), skin only, rinsed
1 red pepper, sliced thin lengthwise

8 serving pieces salmon fillet, or any other thick fish (or 2 pounds mock shrimp, cut across in thirds)

Fish Chraimi

In a large wide-bottom pot, bring the water, oil, tomatoes, red pepper flakes, cloves, bay leaves, and paprika to a boil. Meanwhile, coarsely grind the garlic, parsley, cilantro, and preserved lemon in a food processor using the pulse button. Add the ground mixture to the pot and stir. Add the red pepper and the fish and bring to a boil. Reduce the temperature to medium and cook covered for 20 minutes. Serve hot or at room temperature, topping each serving with the sauce. Makes 8 servings.

TUNA, WILD MUSHROOMS, AND ASPARAGUS RAGOUT GF, P

Don't substitute any other kind of fish for the tuna in this wonderful dish: Nothing will replace its assertive flavor, just like eating a steak.

The recipe can easily be doubled.

3 tablespoons extra virgin olive oil

4 tuna steaks, about 1 inch thick, weighing 6 ounces each, thoroughly dry

2 medium shallots, minced

2 large cloves garlic, minced

1 pound wild mushrooms, in any combination, sliced (if you are using shiitake, discard the stems)

½ cup dry white wine or sake

1 sprig fresh tarragon, leaves only, or 1 teaspoon dry

Salt and pepper to taste

A dozen thin asparagus, tough ends discarded, cut in 2-inch pieces

½ cup water

Heat the oil in a heavy skillet until very hot and smoking. Add the tuna steaks and sear, 1 minute on each side. Remove from the pan and set aside. Add the shallot and garlic to the skillet and sauté until translucent. Add the mushrooms and sauté until most of the liquid evaporates. Add the wine, tarragon, salt and pepper, asparagus, and water and cook covered for about 10 minutes. Add the reserved tuna and heat through, 1 to 2 more minutes. Slice the tuna thick across the grain and transfer to a platter with all the veggies and sauce. Serve hot or at room temperature. Makes 4 servings.

FISH NIÇOISE EN PAPILLOTTE GF, P

A packaged meal. Only, not that kind of a package! Enclosing the fish and its toppings in parchment paper seals in all its flavors. Papillotte *is a cute French word that means curl, flutter, blink. In the food world, it refers to the frill that tented paper forms around an enclosed ingredient, which remains moist and succulent throughout the cooking process.*

Niçoise signals the presence of tomatoes and olives, but you can play with other vegetables (sliced zucchini, mushrooms, peppers, etc.); it is important to always use very-quick-cooking vegetables to top the fish and slice them all very thin so they are ready at the same time the fish is.

Try this recipe with any firm-fleshed fish such as tilapia, snapper, striped bass, ocean perch, branzino, or mahimahi.

6 black bass fillets, about 7–8 ounces each, thoroughly dried with paper towels
4 rectangles parchment paper, about 3 times the size of the fillets
2 tablespoons olive oil
Ground pepper to taste
3 plum tomatoes, sliced very thin
4 cloves garlic, sliced very thin
¼ cup basil leaves, packed, sliced very thin
⅓ cup pitted Niçoise or oil-cured olives, halved
Vegetable spray

Preheat the oven to 425°F. Place each fillet near the center of a paper square. Drizzle each fillet with the oil. Sprinkle ground pepper over each. Top with tomato slices, garlic, basil, and olives. Fold the paper squares to enclose the fish loosely but completely, crimping the paper as you go, forming packets. Leave enough room when shaping the packets to provide an outlet for steam. Spray the top of each closed packet with vegetable spray.

Bake for about fifteen minutes. Transfer the packets to individual dishes. Let each guest slit open his own bag and eat out of it. Makes 6 servings.

Fish Niçoise En Papillotte

MOCK CRAB SUMMER ROLLS WITH THAI DIPPING SAUCE GF

Summer rolls are those delightful paper-thin rice disks that you dip in warm water to soften (no cooking!), fill with virtually anything you like, roll and dip in the sauce of your choice: I love the suggested Thai dipping sauce, but you could use teriyaki sauce, or even a mixture of toasted sesame oil and soy sauce and nothing more. Seeing the filling through the translucent skins makes it even more fun. It would be all right to make them earlier in the day, maybe even a day before, keep them refrigerated and bring them to room temperature at serving time, just as long as you don't let the rolls touch, or they might get stuck.

Use your imagination and personal preference and use any filling you like, always keeping the selection short and to the point: rice noodles (soak in hot water, drain and cut smaller with scissors), diced cooked or smoked chicken, grated carrots, julienned snow peas, thinly sliced nappa cabbage, finely shredded kale, seaweed presoaked in hot water, chopped peanuts, etc.

Don't let the fragile-looking disks daunt you: You might ruin and have to discard a couple before you get the hang of it, but you will have fun learning and rolling, right on the job!

Summer Rolls with Thai Dipping Sauce

1 romaine heart, shredded thin
2 cups shiitake mushrooms, caps only, sliced thin
1 pound mock crab, finely flaked (use your hands)
2 ribs celery, peeled and sliced very thin
4 scallions, sliced very thin
20 rice paper leaves

Keep a pot of water barely simmering on a low flame. Mix all but last ingredient in a bowl.

Dip one rice paper leaf in the simmering water just a few seconds, turning it on all sides, until it is pliable, not a second longer. Place the leaf on a cutting board. Spoon a heaping tablespoon of the mixture in the center. Roll the leaf tightly, bringing the sides into the center and rolling tightly all the way up. Place on a platter seam side down. Repeat with the remaining leaves and mixture. Be sure the rolls are not touching. (Spray the finished rolls with vegetable spray as an extra precaution.) Serve at room temperature with Thai dipping sauce (page 38) or teriyaki sauce (page 37). Makes about 20 rolls. About 2 rolls per guest.

CURRIED FISH WITH TOMATOES AND POTATOES GF, P

Consider this a complete meal. Once you master the delightful gamut of Indian flavors in your own kitchen, it will be kind of hard to have an appreciation for them in a restaurant, as you will do better each time at home. For a vegetarian dish, substitute 2 pounds of extra-firm tofu cut into inch cubes or unflavored seitan for the fish. Passover: Skip the hard-to-get ingredients such as curry and tamarind.

¼ cup olive oil
1 large onion, quartered
1 2-inch piece ginger
5–6 sprigs cilantro, tough stems removed
1 jalapeño pepper
1 tablespoon curry, or more to taste
1 tablespoon cumin
1 teaspoon tamarind powder (settle for 1 tablespoon lemon zest)
2 large tomatoes, or 5 plum tomatoes, diced small
3 large potatoes, peeled and cut into 1-inch cubes
Salt to taste
1 cup water
1 cup coconut milk
3 pounds thick fish fillet (scrod, sea trout, Chilean sea bass, halibut, salmon, etc.), cut into 2-inch cubes

Heat the oil in a heavy, wide-bottom pan. In a food processor, finely grind the onion, ginger, cilantro, and jalapeño and add to the hot oil. Sauté until just translucent. Add the curry, cumin, and tamarind and cook one more minute, until just fragrant. Add the tomatoes, potatoes, salt, water, coconut milk, and fish, or tofu, and bring to a boil. Reduce to medium and cook covered for 15 minutes or a little longer until the potatoes are tender. Serve hot. Makes 8 servings.

MOCK CRAB CAKES WITH RED PEPPER COULIS GF

I don't think you will find more than a handful of fried dishes in this whole book, only those very few dishes whose flavor or texture would be compromised by cooking them any other way, and this is one of them.

Mock crab

Crab cakes and other seafood goodies were always verboten in the world of kosher dining as well as that of all diners who frown at eating seafood, until some inspired professional foodie recreated the texture and flavor with a plain-vanilla-type fish called pollock. It is processed minimally, so I have no trouble using it. Mock shrimp, I'm told, is not nearly as good as its genuine cousin, but it still does a pretty good job when combined with other ingredients for a soup, salad, or stew.

---

1 small onion, quartered
1 small bunch flat parsley
1½ pounds mock crab, thawed
½ cup fresh bread crumbs (from any plain loaf, including gluten-free)
½ cup flour, any flour
2 eggs (only if you are restricted: use ½ cup flax mixture, page 224)
2 tablespoons dashi powder (settle for salt to taste)
Ground pepper to taste
1 tablespoon paprika
Zest of 1 lemon
Vegetable oil for frying

Heat the oil in a large skillet, to come up about ½ inch. Keep the temperature at medium, not smoking, hot.

In a food processor, finely grind the onion and parsley. Add the fish and pulse until you obtain a minced mixture. Don't process longer, or you might lose the texture. Transfer to a bowl and add all remaining ingredients. Combine thoroughly. Add a little more bread crumbs if necessary to make the batter adhere. Form round patties about 1 inch thick and throw them in the skillet without crowding. Fry about three minutes on each side until golden. Transfer to a platter lined with paper towels to absorb excess oil. Serve hot with the red pepper coulis (page 41). Makes 8 servings.

MOCK CRAB SALAD GF

I can't tell you how often I make this treat, and at the drop of a hat. I always notice with pleasure it's a huge hit with the young crowd. If I don't have time to thaw the fish, I simply dip the sealed container in warm water for a few minutes. I trust you will welcome the serving suggestions I have included, but most often I serve it by itself: It's that good!

1 pound frozen mock crab chunks, thawed and thinly crumbled
3 ribs celery, peeled and sliced very thin
1 long seedless cucumber, halved and sliced very thin
1 bunch scallions, sliced very thin
¼ cup toasted sesame oil
2 tablespoons soy sauce
2 tablespoons bottled hot sauce

Mix all ingredients together in a bowl. Serve at room temperature in any of the following ways:

- Alone
- Tossed with 8 ounces cellophane noodles, soaked in hot water, drained and cut up (adjust the seasonings to accommodate the bulkier salad)
- On top of salad greens
- As hors d'oeuvres on endive leaves or cucumber rounds

Mock Crab Salad

QUICK SALMON MOUSSE GF

I played with a few funky ingredients and ended up with this fabulous mousse. This is such a fun dish to use as a spread or thinly sliced over good bread or crackers. Be sure to use canned (yes, canned) red salmon, and don't remove the skin or bones: They will mercifully lose their objectionable look and disappear in the blending process, leaving only their lovely gelatinous texture (PS: It's good for you too!).

1 15-ounce can red salmon, liquid and all
1 envelope unflavored gelatin
½ cup boiling water
1 small bunch dill, fronds and stems
Juice and grated zest of one lemon
1 small onion, halved
1 cup dairy-free cream cheese (8-ounce container)
1 tablespoon paprika
Good pinch cayenne
Good pinch nutmeg
Ground pepper to taste
¼ chopped chives

Pour the liquid from the salmon can in a bowl and stir in the gelatin. Let the mixture stand a few minutes, then stir in the boiling water, mixing thoroughly. Reserve the mixture. Place all the remaining ingredients except chives in a food processor and process until perfectly smooth. Add the reserved gelatin mixture and process a full minute, scraping the sides of the bowl to ensure everything is combined. Stir in the chives with a spoon. Pour the mixture into a 6-cup bowl or loaf pan and refrigerate a few hours until the mixture is set. Serve chilled. To unmold, stand the bowl in warm water for just a few seconds then invert onto a plate. Makes a dozen servings.

SASHIMI SALAD GF

Tartare with a nice Japanese twist. I love to play with all Asian flavors: They are so intense they "cook" the fish practically on contact. A little goes a long way, making the finished dish a smart lean choice. It's nice to see sushi ingredients easily and casually recombined in a salad. The seaweed gives it a delightfully briny kick. Be sure to use the highest-quality fish.

1¼ pounds boneless salmon or tuna fillet, or a combination
1 cup grated daikon (shredding disk of the food processor)
1 cup grated carrots (shredding disk of the food processor)
¼ cup hijiki (or other seaweed: wakame, arame, etc.), soaked in just enough hot water to cover for 10 minutes (the water will be absorbed)
4 scallions, sliced very thin
¾ cup Chinese green tea dressing (page 24)

Place the fish fillet in the freezer for 30 minutes. Slice paper thin with a sharp knife. Combine with the vegetables in a platter. Pour the dressing over the mixture and toss gently. Serve at room temperature. Makes 8 servings.

SEA BASS POACHED IN DASHI-SAKE BROTH GF

The bad news is bass is an expensive treat, but the good news is there is very little you need to do: It's the best. Asian minimalism at its best. The cooking broth is incredibly flavorful and fragrant, and is mild enough not to overpower the delicate flavors of the fish.

3 cups water
1 cup sake
2 tablespoons dashi powder (dashi would be best; settle for ⅓ cup white miso paste)
¼ cup toasted sesame oil
Bottled hot sauce to taste
A dozen basil leaves, thinly sliced
2 pounds Chilean sea bass (or any other good thick white firm fish), cut into inch cubes
6 baby bok choy, halved lengthwise

In a wide pot, bring the water, sake, miso, oil, and hot sauce to a boil. Add the fish and bok choy and cook covered for 5 minutes. Turn off the heat and keep the pot tightly covered another 10 minutes. Serve the fish, bok choy, and broth in soup bowls. Makes 8 servings.

SEVICHE GF, P

A great Latin favorite: a super combination of flavors and textures. The dish doesn't cook in the classical sense, but rather "cooks" on contact with the acid, oil, and seasonings; and the end result is not raw and risky, as you might fear, but delightfully cured, fragrant, and spicy. Go for it! It goes without saying you should start with the highest-quality fish.

1 jalapeño pepper
4 large cloves garlic
1 small red onion
5-6 sprigs cilantro, tough ends cut off
1½ pounds of firm flesh fish: (cod, scrod, halibut, tilapia, salmon, etc.), cut in half-inch cubes
½ cup olive oil
¾ cup lime or lemon juice
1 tablespoon cumin
1 tablespoon oregano
1 large tomato, seeded and diced small
½ cup oil-cured black olives
Salt and pepper to taste
1 medium-ripe avocado, diced small (optional)

In a food processor, mince the pepper, garlic, onion, and cilantro using the pulse button. Transfer the mixture to a bowl and add all but last ingredient, tossing gently so as not to bruise the fish. Marinate 2 to 6 hours. Strain and discard the liquid (or use it in another batch). Toss in the avocado, if using, just before serving. Makes 8 servings. Delicious the next day or two as well.

SLICED SEARED TUNA WITH MANGO-PINEAPPLE SALSA GF, P

The tropical flavors of the fruit salsa is a perfect foil to the hearty tuna flavor. If you get urges for a steak a little too often, try giving tuna equal time. Don't be afraid of muffing it. Just two golden rules: super fresh and rare!

2 tablespoons olive oil
4 tuna fillet steaks, 1 inch thick, no skin and no black particles, thoroughly dried with paper towels
Salt and coarsely ground pepper to taste

Heat the olive oil in a heavy skillet until smoky. Sprinkle the fish with salt and pepper, making sure the pepper grounds adhere to the tuna, and add to the skillet. Cook only about 2 minutes on each side. Fish must remain rare.

Let the fish rest a few minutes. Slice thinly against the grain. Serve with mango-pineapple salsa (page 40) or any other condiment in the pantry chapter (page 19). Makes 4 main course servings.

TRICOLOR FISH TERRINE GF, P

You will create a sensation with this dish! It will make you look like a chef without too much hard work. You will like the freedom it gives you on party day, as you can make it a day or two ahead of time and keep it chilled. Passover winner too! If you get ambitious, layer the mixture in a dozen greased muffin tins and invert them at serving time

Fish mixture:

2 pounds salmon or tilapia filets
½ cup olive oil
4 eggs
⅓ cup tapioca flour or arrowroot (Passover: potato starch)
½ cup dairy-free milk, low-fat OK, (Passover: dry white wine)
1 medium onion, quartered
Zest of 1 lemon
Pinch nutmeg
Salt and pepper to taste
1 cup frozen spinach, squeezed thoroughly dry
¼ cup basil leaves
1 cup sun-dry tomatoes, briefly soaked in warm water and squeezed thoroughly dry (Passover: if they're hard to find, use ¼ cup tomato paste)

Preheat oven to 375°F. Grease a 1½ quart rectangle mold and line in with plastic, letting the sides overhang.

Grind the fish mixture ingredients in a food processor until perfectly smooth. Divide the mixture in three.

Process one-third in the food processor with the spinach and the basil. Scrape thoroughly so you won't have to wash it to mix the red layer. Pack tightly and neatly in the mold. Tightly pack the second (white) third on top on the green layer in the mold. Process the last third with the sun-dried tomatoes or tomato paste until perfectly smooth. Pack on top of the white layer in the mold, gently so as not to disturb the layers beneath.

Fold the overhanging plastic over the top of the mold. Place the mold in a pan two-thirds full with hot water. Bake for 1 hour or until the top is firm. Serve chilled, with pesto (page 43) or watercress wasabi sauce (page 42).

Makes a dozen servings.

Variation: Tricolor white bean terrine

Substitute 6 cups canned and thoroughly drained white beans for the fish and proceed just as above.

Tricolor Fish Terrine

SPINACH- AND MUSHROOM-STUFFED FISH FILLETS GF, P

Beautiful enough to use as main course. The stuffing takes only a few minutes to make and freezes very well, so you might consider doubling the amounts and freezing the unused part for another meal. It will be suitable to stuff thinly pounded chicken cutlets too, using the same instructions as in this recipe.

¼ cup olive oil
4 large cloves garlic
½ cup basil leaves, packed
½ cup parsley leaves
1 large onion, quartered
½ pound mushrooms
1 10-ounce box frozen chopped spinach, thawed, and squeezed thoroughly dry
1 cup canned crushed tomatoes
Salt and pepper to taste
Good pinch red pepper flakes
¼ cup arrowroot or tapioca (Passover: potato starch)
Optional: ¼ cup pine nuts, toasted (300°F oven, 10–12 minutes)
8 tilapia, sole or flounder fillets, patted dry
Vegetable spray
Paprika

Preheat oven to 375°F. Heat the oil in a heavy pan. In a food processor, finely grind the garlic, basil, and parsley. Add the onion and mushrooms and pulse to get a coarse grind. Add to the hot oil and sauté until all liquids evaporate. Stir in all remaining ingredients and cook 2 to 3 more minutes until the mixture thickens. Place a little of the stuffing on the center of the fillet. Fold the sides tightly over stuffing and place seam side down in a pan big enough to just fit the fillets. Repeat with remaining fillets and stuffing. Spray the fillets with vegetable spray and sprinkle with paprika. Bake about 30 minutes. Serve hot or at room temperature, spooning the cooking liquids over the fish. Makes 8 servings.

LISA'S TIP

Spinach is available year-round in grocery stores around the country, offering a readily-available source of many vitamins and minerals. Spinach contains the minerals iron and potassium, and vitamins A, K, C, and the B vitamin folate. Spinach also contains phytochemicals, which may boost your immune system and help keep your hair and skin healthy, and flavonoids, which may have antioxidant properties that may be preventative against certain kinds of cancer.

BAKED FISH STICKS GF

We never knew, or have forgotten, that fish sticks used to be fresh fish, used as we are to encountering them only in the frozen section of processed foods. Rather than zap the infamous fish sticks off the list of healthy foods, why not recast them in a healthy way, prepare them at home in no time, and let children big and small enjoy them? Baked and crisp, these bear only a passing resemblance to their greasy and soggy cousins, sticks and nuggets of all persuasions. Incidentally, this will work perfectly with chicken breasts, exactly as in this recipe!

2 pounds fish fillets (tilapia, cod, scrod, grouper, salmon, etc., cut into long 1-inch strips)

Flour, any flour

Salt and pepper to taste

2 eggs (only if you are restricted: use ½ cup flax mixture, page 224)

2 cups fresh bread crumbs, from any plain bread loaf (gluten-free OK too)

Preheat the oven to 425°F. Mix the flour with salt and pepper in a plate. Beat the eggs in a separate plate. Place the bread crumbs in a third plate.

Dredge each fillet in the flour mixture, shaking off the excess. Roll it in egg, shaking off the excess, then press it into the crumbs. Spray the fillets on both sides with vegetable spray and place in a baking sheet lined with foil or parchment paper. Repeat with all fillets. Bake about 10 minutes or until crisp. Serve hot, alone, or with cocktail sauce (page 34) or any sauce of your choice (see The Pantry, page 19). Makes 8 servings.

POULTRY AND MEAT

You will find many wonderful meat and poultry dishes in my previous cookbooks, and since so many of you already have them, I wouldn't like to duplicate those treats here. You will hardly be deprived. Only one thing I am spreading on really thick: What I call my one-two-three chicken dishes. You will be amazed just how many fabulous dishes you can make using only chicken, turmeric, and one (just one) vegetable. This is what my mom fed us all our childhood, and as you see, I have never gotten tired of it. Who would believe you just threw three things in a pot with some water, cooked it in an hour, and ended up with such a great treat? Lowest maintenance imaginable! I am including directions for substituting meat or fish for the chicken.

Levana Restaurant, which we ran for twenty-five years until it closed two years ago (we still run several Passover programs in prestigious locations all over the world and cater corporate meals out of our commissary), was the first kosher restaurant to serve bison. I hope and pray it is tomorrow's meat: To think that such an imposing-looking animal yields such tender and lean meat, with very low cholesterol! We eat very little red meat at home, and I try my best to make it bison.

The kosher connection: "Don't get mad, get kosher!" This is a cute but very telling sign we often see on kosher butcher storefronts. Kosher animals cannot be diseased or suffer from any lesions, or they will be unfit for ritual slaughtering; in other words, only perfectly healthy animals are suitable for kosher consumption. Also, the way they are ritually slaughtered, which consist in running an extremely sharp knife across their jugular vein, makes them die practically on contact, and as painlessly as possible. A Christian friend I was describing this to once told me, "So you people are the original animal rights activists!"

We entertained many non-kosher-observant customers at our restaurant, and almost all of them would ask how come our steaks were so much more tender and more delicious than the ones they were accustomed to eating. And the answer is that the salting process acts as a natural tenderizer to the meat. I often see in food magazines instructions for getting a tender turkey and priming it for roasting. One of those articles made me chuckle. It went something like, "Remove 2 shelves from your refrigerator, fill a very large square tub with very cold water, add 2 pounds kosher salt, leave the turkey in this brine 2 days, turning it over twice a day, etc." Is it any wonder the public consumes turkey so rarely, if at all, besides during the compulsory Thanksgiving Day? My own comment about this utterly impractical little adventure is, simply, get a kosher turkey—end of story! My non-kosher food spies assure me: The difference in flavor and texture is like the difference between night and day. And the main reason is the salting process that follows the slaughtering.

All the following recipes have been prepared with kosher meat and poultry, and therefore do not list salt as one of the ingredients. Those of you using non-kosher poultry and meat should add salt to taste in all the following dishes in this chapter.

I have made each dish to serve several portions. As always, don't divide: Freeze! Or seal the unused portions and refrigerate a couple days, and make another dinner out of the other half of the dish.

POACHED CHICKEN BREASTS GF, P

Hardly a recipe, but it will be a great building block for many dishes: Place 6 chicken cutlets (no thinning) in a skillet with 1½ cups water. If dark chicken meat is what you prefer, go ahead and use boneless chicken thighs and shape them into rolls before placing them in the skillet, open side down (just a precaution to ensure they don't dry up). Bring to a boil, then reduce the flame to medium. Cover and cook 15 minutes. Turn off the flame and leave the skillet covered 10 more minutes. Eat with any of your favorite sauces listed in this book, or dice or slice and use in one of the salads listed in this book.

STOVE-TOP CHICKEN VARIATIONS: ONE, TWO, AND TURMERIC!

I am starting this chapter with these no-brainer cooking-without-cooking dishes. It illustrates perfectly how a finished dish can be so much more than the sum of its parts, however modest, and what wonderful things happen when you let each ingredient shine on its own, without any competition whatsoever, even if you are not a cook! The ingredient list in these dishes is so short (three—two plus turmeric, to be exact) and the prep work so minimal it just can't get any simpler, or more delicious. Talk about minimalism! Simplicity and elegance all rolled into one.

Only one great piece of advice, which will bring you to the best and most reasonable investment you ever made in your kitchen: Buy yourself a large, broad-bottom stainless steel pot with a lid, and enjoy all those moist and succulent stove-top preparations.

Please do not remove the chicken skins until serving time, or you will end up with a dry and unappealing dish. You will note that the recipes have no added fat.

Turmeric

We grew up with "yellow food" and were practicing good nutrition without even knowing it. Those of you who saw the wonderful Indian movie *Water* will remember the wedding scene where all the dinner guests got their foreheads smeared with turmeric—a symbol, as it was explained, of good health and immunity. The health community is finally paying great attention to turmeric, the greatest antioxidant and anti-inflammatory of all: I can't praise it highly enough. I throw it in as many dishes as I possibly can: While it does its magic, it hardly affects the flavor of the food, if at all—it just imparts a yellow color and a slight bulk to the texture of the finished sauce.

Fish lovers: Follow the recipes below using 8 6-ounce servings of firm-flesh fish such as tilapia, salmon, scrod, bass, etc., instead of chicken, but add ¼ cup olive oil to the pot. Transfer the fish with a slotted spoon onto a platter after 20 minutes of cooking and let everything else in the pot cook as below.

Meat lovers: Follow the recipes below using cubed beef, lamb, or bison instead of chicken. Cook the meat (about 4 pounds) alone in 6 cups of water for 2 hours and then add the other ingredient of your choice plus turmeric to the pot and cook as below. Here the water used is the meat's cooking liquid. Add some water if necessary when adding the vegetable if you ran out of liquid.

CHICKEN AND CELERY GF, P

8 serving pieces chicken (I count 2 pieces per person, for example: 6 thighs, 6 drumsticks, 4 half breasts—16 pieces total for 8 people), with skin on

2 teaspoons turmeric
2 whole bunches celery, ribs peeled and cut into 2-inch chunks, or 2 large heads celery root, peeled and cut into inch cubes
3 cups water

Place all ingredients in a wide heavy pot. Bring to a boil, then reduce the flame to medium and cook covered for about 1 hour. Transfer the chicken pieces onto a platter. If the sauce is not thick enough, reduce it on a high flame, uncovered, just a few minutes until it reaches the consistency of maple syrup. Pour the sauce over the chicken. Serve hot. Makes 8 servings

CHICKEN AND ONIONS GF, P

Same as chicken and celery, substituting 3 large onions, very thinly sliced, for the celery.

CHICKEN AND MUSHROOMS GF, P

Same as chicken and celery, substituting 2 pounds whole domestic or cremini mushrooms—the smaller the better—for the celery.

CHICKEN AND POTATOES GF, P

Same as chicken and celery, substituting 2 pounds unpeeled organic new potatoes (only organic potatoes are safe with their skin on)—the smaller the better—for the celery.

CHICKEN AND FENNEL GF, P

Same as chicken and celery, substituting 2 heads of fennel—hard core discarded, very thinly sliced—for the celery.

CHICKEN AND SWEET POTATOES GF, P

Same as chicken and celery, substituting 2–3 large sweet potatoes, cut into inch chunks, for the celery.

CHICKEN AND SWISS CHARD GF, P

Same as chicken and celery, substituting 2 large bunches Swiss chard (or kale, or collard greens, or mustard greens) leaves and ribs, sliced thin, for the celery.

CHICKEN AND CARROTS GF, P

Same as chicken and celery, using 2 pounds thin (not baby!) carrots, cut into 2-inch segments.

CHICKEN AND TURNIPS GF, P

Same as chicken and celery, substituting a large rutabaga (yellow wax turnip), cut into inch cubes, for the celery.

CHICKEN AND PLANTAINS GF, P

Same as chicken and celery, substituting 6 medium-ripe plantains, cut into 2-inch segments, for the celery.

CHICKEN AND TOMATOES GF, P

Same as chicken and celery, substituting 4 large beefsteak tomatoes or 12 plum tomatoes, diced small, for the celery.

CHICKEN AND OLIVES GF, P

Same as chicken and celery, substituting 2 cups good-quality pitted green olives, thoroughly rinsed, for the celery.

Chicken and Mushrooms

CHICKEN AND GARLIC GF, P

Same as chicken and celery, substituting 3 heads of garlic, all cloves separated and peeled, for the celery. When reducing the sauce at the end of cooking, mash the garlic cloves thoroughly with a fork, then pour over the chicken.

CHICKEN AND ARTICHOKES GF, P

Cook the chicken with the turmeric and water and add 2 pounds quartered frozen artichoke bottoms or whole frozen artichoke hearts in the last 15 minutes of cooking.

CHICKEN AND CORN GF

Cook the chicken with the turmeric and water and add 2 pounds frozen corn kernels in the last 15 minutes of cooking.

ROAST CHICKEN FIVE WAYS— MAKE THAT SIX

For all roast chicken lovers out there, here are very simple ways to treat yourself, getting a different and delicious dish each time. Make sure you never run out of my dry spice rub—it's fabulous and so versatile. A whole roast chicken makes for a more dramatic presentation, but pieces will work just as well. Just remember the golden rule for roast chicken and every bird: Breast side down! Turn it over to get its final beautiful amber color only in the last quarter of cooking time.

BASIC ROAST CHICKEN GF, P

The nothing chicken. That's right, I am not forgetting anything! Just the chicken, ma'am! Still my children's favorite!

8 serving pieces chicken (2 per person, 16 pieces total: legs, thighs, half breasts), or 2 whole chickens

Preheat the oven to 425°F.

If you are using chicken pieces: Place the pieces *skin side down* in a baking dish in one layer. Bake uncovered for 40 minutes. Take out the breasts, they should be done. Turn the dark pieces over and bake another 15 minutes. Serve hot. Delicious at room temperature too.

If you are using whole chicken: Bake *breast side down* for 1 hour, turn over, and bake 15 more minutes. Makes 8 servings.

MOROCCAN-ROASTED GF, P

8 serving pieces chicken (2 per person, 16 pieces total: legs, thighs, half breasts), or 2 whole chickens

⅓ cup dry spice rub (page 31)

Smear the chickens or pieces all over with the mixture. Proceed exactly as for basic roast chicken. Makes 8 servings.

HERB-ROASTED GF, P

2 medium onions, sliced very thin
Juice of two lemons
6 large cloves garlic
3 sprigs tarragon
3 sprigs thyme
2 sprigs rosemary
Coarsely ground pepper to taste
2 tablespoons paprika

8 servings chicken: legs, thighs, breast halves (allow 2 pieces per serving, 16 total), or 2 whole chickens

Mix all ingredients and rub all over the chicken. Proceed exactly as for basic roast chicken. Makes 8 servings.

IN TERIYAKI SAUCE GF

Use ½ cup teriyaki sauce (page 37) and rub all over the chicken. Proceed exactly as for basic roast chicken. Makes 8 servings.

MAPLE-ROASTED GF

½ cup maple syrup
⅓ cup Dijon-style mustard
1 cup dry white wine
Cracked pepper to taste

8 servings chicken: legs, thighs, breast halves (allow 2 pieces per serving, 16 total), or 2 whole chickens

Mix all ingredients and rub all over the chicken. Proceed exactly as for basic roast chicken. Makes 8 servings.

IN BARBECUE SAUCE GF, P

1 cup good natural-brand ketchup
1 cup pineapple or orange juice
¼ cup lemon or lime juice
2-inch piece ginger, peeled
6 large cloves garlic
1 tablespoon bottled hot sauce, or more to taste

8 servings chicken: legs, thighs, breast halves (allow 2 pieces per serving, 16 total), or
2 whole chickens

Process all but last ingredient in a food processor until smooth.

Rub all over the chicken. Proceed exactly as for basic roast chicken.

Makes 8 servings.

Barbecued Chicken

ROAST TURKEY GF, P

Choose a nice 12- to 14-pound turkey—preferably fresh, or frozen and completely thawed. Use any of the roast chicken recipes, using twice the amounts of listed ingredients for each respective recipe, plus 6 cups liquid (water, juice, wine, or a combination). Proceed just as for basic chicken. Bake 2½ hours breast side down, 1 hour breast side up. Check for doneness by inserting a knife in the thick part of the breast: If it doesn't run clear, bake a little longer. While you slice the turkey, reduce the cooking liquids (no starches whatsoever please) in a saucepan on a high flame to 3 to 4 cups and strain over the sliced turkey.

CHICKEN WITH APPLES GF, P

The modest apple is the star of this rustic and delicious dish. Hard cider gives the dish its originality and is easy to find, but just in case you can't secure it, use 3 cups natural apple cider.

LISA'S TIP

Green apples

The magic of green apples is that besides being a nutritional treasure, they are equally at home as a fruit—to eat out of hand or use in baking—or as a vegetable.

3 tablespoons olive oil
4 Granny Smith (green) apples, peeled and cut in wedges
2 tablespoons sugar or Sucanat
Zest of 2 lemons
3 leeks, sliced
8 serving pieces chicken—16 pieces total: legs, thigh, half breasts, skins on
2 teaspoons turmeric
1 bottle hard cider
2 tablespoons cinnamon
Freshly ground pepper to taste
3 tablespoons calvados, applejack, or slivovitz

Heat the oil in a heavy, wide-bottom pot. Add the apples and sauté until golden. Add the sugar and lemon peel, and cook 2 more minutes until caramelized. Remove the apples and set aside. Place the leeks, chicken, turmeric, cider, and cinnamon in the pot and bring to a boil. Reduce the flame to medium and cook covered for 1 hour. Add the reserved apples, ground pepper, and calvados and cook a few minutes more until just heated through. Transfer the chicken and apples to a platter and check the sauce. If it is too thin, reduce on a high flame 2 to 3 minutes until syrupy. Pour over the chicken and serve hot, with rice, puréed vegetables, or noodles.

MOROCCAN CHICKEN WITH STRING BEANS GF

The demure string bean gets elevated to star status in our Moroccan way of cooking. Side dish? Never heard of it! The string beans will be past the al dente stage here—they are integral part of the dish. I love to use haricots verts, string beans' slender and elegant French cousin (aren't all French cousins slender and elegant? Not fair!). I find haricots verts increasingly easy to find: They are a little more expensive but well worth it, and perfect frozen as well. If not, of course string beans will do, but in this case, use only fresh, as frozen string beans won't stand up to the cooking time.

8 servings chicken (drumsticks, thighs, half chicken breasts: 16 pieces total)
2 good pinches saffron
1 teaspoon turmeric
1 large, or 3 plum tomatoes, cut into small dice
6 large cloves garlic, minced
2 dozen pitted green olives, rinsed and sliced
2 cups water
2 pounds haricots verts, fresh or frozen (settle for fresh string beans)
½ preserved lemon (page 33), skin only, thoroughly rinsed and minced (settle for the juice and zest of 1 lemon)
¼ cup minced flat-leaf parsley
3 tablespoons minced cilantro

Place chicken, saffron, turmeric, tomatoes, garlic, olives, and water in a wide, heavy pot. Bring to a boil. Reduce the heat to medium high, cover, and cook for 40 minutes. Add the haricots verts and cook for 20 more minutes. Add the preserved lemon, parsley, and cilantro and cook for 10 minutes more. Transfer the chicken and vegetables to a serving platter. Check the liquids left in the pot. If they look too thin, reduce over high flame until thickened, 2 to 3 minutes. Pour the sauce over chicken. Serve hot. Makes 8 servings.

BALSAMIC ROASTED CHICKEN BREASTS GF, P

You will never say your chicken breasts come out dry ever again. The marinating step is important here, so please do not skip it—the reward is a fabulous dish. Smile: This is one of only a handful of recipes in my book that do need an extra step, so, not too bad! Don't bother reheating the leftover sliced breasts: Serve them at room temperature, or dice them into a salad or a pasta dish.

1 bunch basil, leaves only (about 1 cup packed)
½ cup olive oil
6 large cloves garlic
Coarsely ground pepper to taste
1 cup dry white wine
6 whole chicken breasts, medium size, skin off, bones out
¼ cup balsamic vinegar

In a food processor, form a paste with the basil, oil and garlic, pepper, and wine. Rub the chicken with this mixture in a bowl and marinate overnight.

Preheat the oven to 450°F. Arrange the chicken in one layer, marinade and all. Bake 15 minutes. Add the vinegar and bake 10 more minutes. Let the breasts rest just a few minutes, then slice each breast across—you will get 3 to 4 thick slices per breast. Serve hot with all the cooking juices. Room temperature will be OK too. Makes 8 servings.

CAPON WITH MAPLE GLAZE GF, P

Quite often, for a group of up to a dozen, I like to use capon instead of the larger turkey. Available year-round, succulent, festive, and hardly more expensive than a turkey. A very frequent treat at my table. If you can't find it, use a small turkey and proceed exactly as directed.

2 large red onions, sliced very thin
¼ cup olive oil
2 cups strong Earl Grey tea, decaf OK (4 tea bags steeped in 2 cups boiling water)
2 cups unsweetened pomegranate juice
½ cup Dijon-style mustard (omit on Passover)
1cup maple syrup
1 tablespoon coarsely ground pepper
6 sprigs rosemary
6 sprigs thyme
1 8- to 10-pound capon

Preheat oven to 325°F. Mix all the sauce ingredients. Place the capon breast side down in a baking pan just large enough to fit the bird and pour the sauce over. Cover loosely with foil. Bake for 2 hours. Turn the bird over and bake another hour, or until the juices run clear and the breast is a nice amber color. Transfer the capon to a platter and let rest 15 minutes before carving. Reduce the sauce at high temperature in a saucepan until thick and syrupy and strain, pressing hard on the solids. Pour the sauce over the sliced bird. Makes a dozen ample servings.

CHICKEN CURRY WITH TOMATOES AND PLANTAINS GF

Fresh tomatoes are the star of this wonderful dish: Please do not substitute canned tomatoes—there will be a huge difference! To seed them, simply halve them and squeeze the seeds gently out. Plantains come in two varieties: green to medium ripe and even riper. The former are used as vegetables in stews while the latter are sweeter and less starchy, reserved for sweet side dishes and desserts. In this dish, they are quite a match for the tomatoes. Consider this dish a complete main course.

3 tablespoons olive oil
1 large onion, quartered
1 jalapeño pepper
1 strip lemon grass, chopped, or 2 tablespoons powder
2 tablespoons curry, or more to taste
1 tablespoon cardamom
1 tablespoon mustard seeds
8 serving pieces chicken (drumsticks, thighs, thick cutlets: 2 pieces per person, 16 total)
2 cups water
2 large tomatoes, or 4 large plum tomatoes, seeded, and diced
3 large medium-ripe plantains, sliced 1 inch thick

Heat the oil in a heavy pot. In a food processor, coarsely chop the onion, pepper, and lemongrass. Add the ground mixture to the hot oil and sauté until translucent. Add the curry, cardamom, and mustard seeds and fry one more minute, until fragrant. Add all remaining ingredients and bring to a boil. Reduce the flame to medium and cook covered for 1 hour. Make sure there is enough cooking liquid in the pot. Add a little if necessary. The sauce should be nice and thick. Serve hot. Makes 8 servings.

CREOLE CHICKEN WITH RICE GF

There is no cuisine that doesn't boast a wonderful rice-and-chicken dish: paella, jamba-laya, gumbo, arroz con pollo—all close relatives of the happy chicken-and-rice dinner family. It is often prepared with fish as well. It does sound like a long list of ingredients, but the good news is, it's a whole meal, and it's quite simple. It is often served in the same skillet it was prepared in, which makes it even simpler. Perfect for buffets, as it reheats very well.

Sofrito:

3 tablespoons olive oil
2 medium onion, quartered
2 ribs celery, peeled and cut in thirds
4 large cloves garlic
1 bunch flat-leaf parsley
1 small bunch cilantro, stems discarded
1 red bell pepper, seeded and cut in chunks

1 small can tomato paste
2 cups canned crushed tomatoes
1 teaspoon cayenne, or more to taste
Good pinch ground cloves
6 bay leaves, or 1 teaspoon ground
1 tablespoon paprika
Generous pinch saffron
Salt and pepper to taste
8 serving portions chicken, dark and white meat, or all dark (16 pieces in all)
8 ounces natural (no nitrites) smoked turkey, diced small
3 cups basmati rice, white or brown
2 cups sliced okra, frozen OK

Heat the oil in a wide, heavy pot. Make the sofrito: Coarsely grind in a food processor the onion, celery, garlic, parsley, cilantro, and red pepper and add the ground mixture. Sauté until translucent. (If you have sofrito in your refrigerator or freezer, page 41, use 1 cup, thawed, and skip this whole first sautéing step; proceed with the recipe from this point on.) Add the tomato paste and sauté 1 more minute, stirring. Add the tomatoes, cayenne, cloves, bay leaves, paprika, saffron, salt, pepper, chicken and turkey, and 6 cups of water. Bring to a boil. Reduce the heat to medium and cook covered for 45 minutes. Add the rice and okra and cook for 15 more minutes, or a little longer until the rice and chicken are tender. Serve hot. Makes 8 servings.

CHICKEN BREASTS MOLE SAUCE GF, P

I can't tell you how many times I have knocked my guests' socks off with this dish, both the chicken and the turkey variation: Improbable ingredient combo, simple preparation, amazing dish!

⅓ cup olive oil
1 large red onion, chopped fine
8 chicken cutlets (do not pound thinner)
1½ cups strong jasmine tea, decaf OK
Good pinch saffron
Good pinch cayenne
6 bay leaves, or 1 teaspoon ground
3 tablespoons tomato paste
½ cup semisweet chocolate chips

Heat the oil in a large skillet. Add the onion and sauté until translucent. Add the cutlets, juice, saffron, cayenne, and bay leaves and bring to a boil. Reduce the heat to medium and cook covered for 20 minutes. Transfer the cutlets to a platter. Whisk in the tomato paste and chocolate chips and cook one more minute. Pour the sauce over the cutlets and serve hot with rice.

Variation:

Roast turkey mole sauce. Double the ingredients above, and add 3 cups water. Preheat oven to 325°F. Mix all the sauce ingredients except the chocolate. Place a 12- to 14-pound turkey or capon breast side down in a baking pan just large enough to fit the bird and pour the sauce over. Cover loosely with foil. Bake for 2 hours. Turn the bird over and bake another hour, or until the juices run clear and the breast is a nice amber color. Transfer the capon to a platter and let rest 15 minutes before carving. Reduce the sauce at high temperature in a saucepan until thick and syrupy and strain, pressing hard on the solids. Stir in the chocolate chips, mixing until smooth. Pour the sauce over the sliced bird. Makes a dozen ample servings.

JAPANESE CHICKEN STEW WITH ROOTS AND SEAWEED GF

A little trip to a health food store will do the trick—you will get all the ingredients you might not be able to find at your supermarket. Each one is a real powerhouse, and the dish is as delicious as it is funky.

¼ cup toasted sesame oil
2 tablespoons minced or grated ginger
1 stalk lemongrass, minced, or 1 tablespoon dry
8 chicken cutlets, cut in strips
1 cup sake (liquor stores), or mirin (health food stores)
¼ cup soy sauce
1 teaspoon red pepper flakes
1 cup burdock, very thinly sliced
¼ cup hijiki (or other seaweed: wakame, arame, etc.)
3 cups sliced shiitake, caps only
½ small head nappa cabbage, sliced thin
3 medium carrots, sliced ½ inch thick
4 cups water
2 cups soybean sprouts
6 scallions, sliced thinly
6 sprigs cilantro, stems cut off, minced

Heat the oil in a wide heavy pot. Add the ginger and lemongrass and sauté just one minute. Add the chicken and cook, stirring, 2 to 3 minutes. Transfer the mixture to a platter and reserve. In the same skillet, bring the sake, soy sauce, pepper flakes, burdock, hijiki, shiitake, nappa cabbage, carrots, and water to boil. Reduce to medium and cook covered for 20 minutes. Add the reserved chicken mixture and cook 10 more minutes. Add the sprouts and cook just one more minute, until heated through. Serve hot with the cooking broth, sprinkled with the scallions and cilantro.

SCHNITZEL GFA

Too many diners complain that they love schnitzel but are disappointed that they are so easily dried out. My daughter-in-law Ruthie makes the best schnitzels but always keeps insisting she does nothing in particular, so I decided to spy on her once when she made the dish, from beginning to end. The result is some friendly troubleshooting for everyone.

- *Dry them thoroughly with paper towels so they don't get soggy.*
- *Pound them evenly so they cook evenly.*
- *Don't pound them thinner than ⅓ inch.*
- *Don't cook them over very high heat, as chicken breasts are sensitive to excessive heat and might scorch.*
- *Cook them until* almost, not completely, *cooked. Keeping them in a very low temperature oven will do the rest of the job until serving time, and get them cooked to perfection. Gluten-free: There are lots of gluten-free breads you can make crumbs out of.*

Bread crumbs

We all have little chunks of bread we hate to throw away. Don't hesitate to make your own bread crumbs; they will taste much better than store-bought. Put a few pieces of stale bread in a food processor and grind for a few seconds—that's the whole story!

Vegetable oil for frying
8 chicken cutlets, thoroughly dried with paper towels and pounded about ⅓ inch thick
Flour, any flour
Spices and herbs of your choice: ground pepper, minced parsley flakes, nutmeg, minced fresh garlic, oregano
2 eggs
2 cups fresh bread crumbs, gluten-free OK

Put oil to heat in a heavy large skillet to come up about ⅓ inch deep. While the oil is heating, get everything ready: Mix the flour with the seasonings and place in a plate. Beat the eggs in a bowl. Place the bread crumbs in a separate plate. When the oil is hot, reduce to medium high. Dredge each cutlet in the flour mixture, shaking off the excess, then dip in the egg, shaking off the excess, then press into the bread crumbs. Repeat with all cutlets. Fry about 2 minutes on each side until just golden. Do not overcook. Transfer onto a plate lined with paper towels to absorb any excess moisture. When you are done frying, remove the paper towels, cover the cutlets with foil, and let them rest a few minutes in a low-temperature oven before uncovering. Serve warm or at room temperature.

MOROCCAN TURKEY PATTIES
IN LEMON SAUCE GF, P

I never wait for Thanksgiving to use turkey: It is lean and nutritious, and ideally suited to countless preparations. This dish will be just as delicious made with ground beef, lamb or bison, or fish. Another wonderful Sephardi dish.

Cooking liquid:

2 tablespoons oil
Good pinch saffron threads
1 teaspoon turmeric
3 cups water

Turkey mixture:

1 small onion, quartered
1 small bunch parsley
1 egg, or egg substitute (page 224)
2 tablespoons oil
1 small bread roll
1 tablespoon grated lemon peel
Salt and pepper to taste
Pinch nutmeg
1½ pounds ground turkey or chicken

Sauce ingredients:

¼ cup fresh lemon juice
2 tablespoons Dijon-style mustard (omit on Passover)
1 egg yolk (skip if you are restricted)
¼ cup parsley, minced

Bring all cooking liquid ingredients to boil in a wide heavy pot. Meanwhile, in a food processor, grind all but last turkey mixture ingredient to a smooth paste. Transfer to a bowl with the ground meat and mix thoroughly by hand. Form oval patties and throw them gently in the pot as you go. Reduce the flame to medium and cook covered for 30 minutes. Carefully take out the patties with a slotted spoon and transfer onto a platter. Reduce the cooking liquid to about 1 cup. Remove from the fire; add the sauce ingredients and stir vigorously with a whisk, just a few seconds. Pour the sauce over the patties. Serve warm or at room temperature.

Note: Fish patties GF, P

Substitute fish for the turkey or other meat and proceed exactly as above.

STEAMED CHICKEN BREASTS WITH BABY BOK CHOY AND SHIITAKE MUSHROOMS GF

Steaming is an easy and super-nutritious way to cook, and bamboo steamers are a wonderful thing: They sit snugly in a skillet and have compartments that pile on top of one another, which allows you to place the longest-cooking item (tofu, fish, chicken, beef) in the bottom layer and the quicker-cooking items (snow peas, baby bok choy, nappa, sprouts, etc.) on the topmost layer, with everything in between (medium layers for carrots, string beans, mushrooms, celery, squash, etc.). I have built my steamer "real estate" to several stories, piling those layers nice and high. It's such a fun and quick way to cook. My trick is, at the end of cooking, I reduce the bottom cooking liquids and add some miso paste, and get a wonderful sauce.

2 cups water
½ cup sake
1 tablespoon grated fresh ginger
1 stalk lemongrass, minced, or 2 tablespoons powder (skip if you can't find it)
2 tablespoons bottled hot sauce
¼ cup toasted sesame oil
8 chicken cutlets
1 pound shiitake, caps only, sliced
8 baby bok choy, split lengthwise
1 bunch scallions, sliced very thin
⅓ cup white miso paste (dark if you prefer a more intense flavor)

Put the water, sake, ginger, lemongrass, hot sauce, and oil in a wok or pan large enough to accommodate your steamer and bring to a boil. Reduce the flame to medium. Line the first part of the steamer with the cutlets and place it in the pan. Place another steamer layer on top of the first and place the mushrooms. Place a third steamer layer on top of the second, place the bok choy in, and cover. Cook 15 minutes. Transfer the vegetables and cutlets to a platter. Add the miso paste to the cooking liquids in the bottom pan, whisking until smooth, and cook just 2 to 3 more minutes, and then pour all over the dish. Serve hot.

Note: Substitute firm fish fillets (such as tilapia, bass, or salmon), tofu, or thin beef strips for the chicken and proceed as above.

Steamed Chicken Breasts
with Baby Bok Choy and
Shiitake

UNBAKED TRICOLOR TURKEY TERRINE GF

"Stuck" with leftover turkey or chicken? Sounds like a very good problem to me. Recycle, and get a wonderful terrine: No cooking, no baking! Perfect for sandwiches, or as a first course or main course with a salad.

4 cups cooked turkey or chicken
1 small red onion
1 cup natural (no nitrites) smoked turkey (optional, but I recommend it)
¼ cup brandy or rum
¼ cup dairy-free milk, low-fat OK
¼ cup soy or rice milk powder
¼ cup olive oil
3 tablespoons brandy or bourbon
Ground pepper to taste
Good pinch each allspice and nutmeg
¼ cup tomato paste
½ cup frozen spinach, squeezed perfectly dry

In a food processor, process the first set of ingredients until perfectly smooth. Spread one-third of the mixture in a greased loaf pan. Mix the second third of the mixture with the tomato paste in a mixing bowl and spread gently and evenly over the white layer. Add the spinach to the remaining mixture (last third) in the food processor and process until smooth. Spread gently and evenly over the red layer. Cover the loaf in plastic wrap and chill. Unmold and slice.

CHICKEN IN WALNUT SAUCE (SATSIVI) GF, P

Richer than I like my dishes to be, but well worth it for an occasional splurge. It is served cold, with the thick sauce served almost as a side dish with the chicken. My special nod to the Russian part of my family: who knew a Moroccan girl could cook Georgian? You bet I can!

8 servings chicken (drumsticks, thighs, half breasts: 16 pieces in all)
2 large onions, sliced very thin
6 large cloves garlic, minced
2 good pinches saffron
1 teaspoon turmeric
2 cups water
1½ cups ground walnuts
¼ cup unfiltered apple cider vinegar
1 teaspoon each: paprika, cinnamon, ground coriander
1–2 good pinches cayenne

Bring the chicken, onions, garlic, saffron, turmeric, and water to a boil. Reduce to medium and cook for 1 hour. Remove the chicken to a platter with a slotted spoon. Stir into the pot the walnuts, vinegar, and spices and cook another 10 minutes until the sauce thickens. Pour over the chicken. Chill the dish before serving. Makes 8 servings.

Nuts and Seeds

While you may have been told to avoid nuts and seeds due to their high fat and caloric content, these tasty gems contain heart-healthy unsaturated fats and are truly terrific to include in your diet. They contain protein, fiber, and plant stanols, which may help lower cholesterol, and antioxidants including vitamin E.

Research has found that including a serving of nuts (approximately a handful) in your diet may actually prevent weight gain and possibly even promote weight loss, as long as you control total calories. The protein, fiber, and fat in nuts aid in satiety and help you feel full longer, so you may actually end up eating less during the day. Nut eaters have also been shown to have a lower incidence of diabetes when compared to those who rarely ate nuts.

Here are a few **"nut"-rition** points:

NUTS

Almonds are packed with nutrients and are a filling and flavorful snack. They contain protein, vitamin E, healthy fats, along with the minerals calcium and magnesium.

Pistachios contain healthy fats, protein, fiber, and the minerals phosphorus, copper, manganese. They are also rich in plant stanols; research found that substituting these jade gems for fatty meats can actually lower your LDL (bad) cholesterol.

Walnuts not only taste great but also provide a heart-healthy addition to your diet. Rich in the plant based omega-3 fatty acid, alpha-linolenic acid, and antioxidants such as selenium, walnuts also provide protein, fiber, magnesium, and phosphorus to the diet.

SEEDS

Flaxseeds are high protein and rich in the omega-3 fatty acid alpha-linolenic acid. Its high fiber content (2 tablespoons contain nearly 5 grams fiber) can help to reduce cholesterol and regulate bowels. They are also rich in B vitamins, the minerals magnesium and manganese, and plant lignans that may prevent certain types of cancer and diabetes.

Sunflower seeds contain the antioxidant vitamins E, and C, protein, and fiber. They make for a great heart-healthy snack, eaten by themselves, or sprinkled onto a salad or vegetable dish. When eating them as a snack, try "deshelling" them yourself, since a small portion goes a long way, both in terms of calories and flavor.

Chia seeds are rich in the omega-3 fatty acid alpha-linolenic acid, antioxidants, vitamins, and minerals. Research found that that chia seeds may lower blood pressure and reduce an individual's risk of heart problems.

Hemp seeds contain both omega-3 and omega-6 fatty acids that may offer protective benefits against inflammatory conditions, atherosclerosis, and certain

ROAST TURKEY WITH JUNIPER WINE GRAVY GF, P

*If only you would follow these very simple rules, you would enjoy turkey all year round,
without any trepidation or wariness whatsoever—and as importantly, without thinking
about it as a daylong project:*

1. *Start with a very tender turkey: It is my solemn duty to tell you that no turkey (or any
    poultry for that matter) will come anywhere close to a kosher turkey, as the salting step in
    the koshering process makes it ideally tender. Dear non-kosher readers, let me allay any
    fears that any danger of getting inducted into some mysterious order might be lurking
    just from buying a kosher turkey! The greatest danger it might get you into is a fabulous
    dinner!*

2. *Get yourself a real, not disposable, pan. There is no possible comparison between the two.
    Food made in disposable containers tastes and looks hopelessly, well, disposable: Need I
    say more?*

3. *Bake the turkey breast side down so as to keep it very moist throughout the baking time,
    and turn it over only in the last hour of baking, to give the breast a deep amber color.*

4. *Bake the turkey in a liquid: No baking rack. In one fell swoop, the bird is super moist,
    and your gravy is all there. Reduce the cooking liquid and strain. (No thickeners, heaven
    forbid! What could be better than a sauce reduction?) That's the whole story!*

5. *PS: Did you know turkey bones make the best chicken soup?*

*Don't lose your head on a busy Thanksgiving Day and throw all those scrumptious turkey
bones as you are slicing, thinking you are all maxed out: Throw them all in a zipper bag and
freeze—they will make you the best chicken soup! If I might even push my luck a drop further, I
would recommend that you put a large pot of water to boil and right there and then, even as you
slice your turkey, throw all your bones and scraps into the pot, with some onions, carrots, celery,
dill, parsnips (just peel and throw in whole), and a couple teaspoons turmeric. Before you know
it, you will have yourself a gallon of delicious chicken (all right, turkey: the best) soup.*

*I must tell you I don't like stuffing turkey, so I will suggest plenty of side dishes that will go
beautifully with the turkey: Pour a little turkey gravy over your side dish and you got yourself
stuffing.*

I love juniper berries—they are the spice that give gin its unmistakable flavor. They are easy to find in health food stores. Put them in a plastic bag, and crush them with a rolling pin or with a hammer or meat mallet so they give off their full flavor. This is one of my favorite turkey recipes, but there is no reason why you can't make it with your favorite herbs, seasonings, and cooking liquids, just as long as you follow the simple rules I have provided, and get different results each time.

¼ cup juniper berries, slightly crushed (place them in a zipper bag, and crush them with a rolling pin; they might be hard to find on Passover: in this case, just skip them)

3 tablespoon black peppercorns

4 sprigs sage

6 to 8 bay leaves

A dozen whole cloves

1 tablespoon turmeric

2 large red onions, skins reserved, sliced very thin

4 cups dry white wine (if you would rather not use alcohol: substitute cranberry or pomegranate juice, or natural apple cider)

1 12- to 14-pound turkey, preferably fresh, or frozen and completely thawed

Preheat oven to 325°F. Place all ingredients except the turkey in a roasting pan. Throw in the onion skins and combine. Place the turkey in the pan, breast side down. Cover the pan loosely with foil and bake for about 2½ hours. Turn the turkey over, discard the foil, and bake uncovered about 1 hour more, until the breast gets a deep amber color and the juices run clear when you pierce the breast with a knife. Transfer the turkey onto a slicing board.

Let the turkey rest about 15 minutes before slicing. While the turkey rests and gets sliced, reduce the liquid in the pan on a high flame to about 3 to 4 cups (if that's all you have left, then don't reduce), and strain—pressing hard on the solids to extract the most flavor—over the sliced turkey.

CHICKEN SALAD GF, P

A great favorite in my house. You might have leftover cooked chicken, in this case, go ahead and use it. If you are thinking of serving this salad as a main dish, consider serving it over cooked wild rice, as I often do. On Passover, adjust the dressing with the ingredients you have on hand.

6 chicken cutlets, left thick (no pounding)
2 Granny Smith (green) apples, unpeeled, diced small
3 ribs celery, peeled, diced small
½ medium red onion, minced
8 ounces natural (no nitrites) smoked turkey, diced small
1 cup remoulade dressing (page 29), a little more if necessary
½ cup chopped toasted cashews or peanuts, optional

Place the cutlets in a skillet just large enough to fit them in one layer. Add about 1 cup water and bring to a boil. Reduce the flame to medium and cook covered for 15 minutes, no more. (If you are starting out with cooked chicken or turkey, skip this step.) When the chicken is cool enough to handle, dice it small. Place it in a bowl with the remaining salad ingredients. Pour the dressing and toss. Stir in the nuts, if using, just before serving. Serve at room temperature. Makes 8 ample servings.

Variations:

- **Curried chicken salad GF**
  Add 2–3 tablespoons curry to the basic recipe.
- **Chicken salad with celery root GF, P**
  Add 1 medium celery root, grated, to the basic recipe.
- **Chinese chicken salad GF**
  No apples. Add 2 cups very finely chopped nappa cabbage and 2 cups soybean sprouts for the celery root. Substitute Chinese green tea dressing (page 24) for the remoulade dressing.

BURGERS AND KEBABS GF, P

No need for a recipe. Form patties about 1 inch thick with lean ground meat (turkey, beef, bison, lamb) or ground fresh tuna. Broil or grill 2 to 3 minutes, indoors or outdoors, and serve with sliced tomatoes, a good natural-brand ketchup, with whole-grain hamburger buns.

If you like your burgers spicy (kebabs), choose from your favorite seasonings and add to the meat before cooking: bottled hot sauce, cumin, oregano, chopped mint, chopped parsley, chopped cilantro, ground coriander, etc. Make the burgers smaller and cook only 1 to 2 minutes on each side, and serve them with Israeli salad (page 107) and hummus (page 98).

BEEF CHICKEN NORI ROULADE GF

Don't let the multiple steps daunt you: They are quick and simple, and the end result is a fun and professional-looking coil, perfect for a first course or as hors d'oeuvre.

2 eggs
¼ cup olive oil
1 medium onion, cut in chunks
Peel of 2 lemons
Ground pepper to taste
¼ teaspoon nutmeg
1½ pounds ground beef or bison
1½ pounds ground chicken or turkey
12 sheets nori, you might need a couple more

Put water to boil in a large pot, then keep the flame on medium.

In a food processor, grind the first set of ingredients to a very smooth paste. Divide the mixture in two. Mix the first half with the beef in a bowl, and the second half with the chicken in another bowl, combining each mixture thoroughly by hand.

Lay out a large rectangle of plastic wrap over a bamboo mat. Place a sheet of nori on top, right over the nori sheet below. Spread a thin layer of the chicken mixture neatly over the whole surface of the nori. Top with a second nori leaf. Top with a thin layer of the beef mixture. Roll tightly, using the mat as a guide. Secure the rolls with twisters. Repeat with the remaining sheets and meat mixtures. Lower the logs gently in the water and poach about 15 minutes. Take them out with tongs and let them cool. Chill the rolls completely. Slice and serve chilled, alone or with watercress wasabi sauce (page 42). Makes 8 to 10 servings.

Variation: Salmon tilapia roulade GF

Substitute salmon and tilapia for the beef and chicken, respectively, and proceed exactly as above.

CHOLENT AND ALL VARIATIONS

This is the food we observant Jews love to hate, and simply won't give up anytime soon. I get countless requests for a "totally gasless" cholent recipe, and my answer always is, while I think this would be pure utopia (come on, guys, get real!), I have many ideas for a cholent that is "environmentally safe," as my son Yakov calls it with a wink. Take a look at all I do with cholent: low carb, low starch, gluten-free, vegetarian, Passover, you name it!

3 pounds very small organic potatoes, unpeeled (only organic potatoes are safe with their peel on)
2 cups whole spelt berries (health food stores)
1 cup chickpeas
2 lamb shanks or two pounds lamb necks
1 turkey thigh
2 pounds beef neck bones
2 good pinches saffron threads
2 teaspoons turmeric

Place the ingredients in a Crock-Pot or in another heavy pot. Add about 10 cups water. Plug in the Crock-Pot just before Shabbos (if you are using a regular pot, bring it to a boil just before Shabbos). Leave the cholent on a low-temperature setting. Makes 8 to 10 servings.

Variations

I am highlighting all the variations that will work for Passover: Who knows, you might get even more attached to that week's cholent than to the one you eat year-round!

- **Other bean and grain choices, GF:** Substitute other grains for the spelt and chickpeas, in any combination: wheat berries, barley, wild rice, mung, azuki, oats, etc. All excellent choices, and many gluten-free. The other beans you are used to (you know who they are): The long cooking time takes out the worst in them, whereas they might be perfectly OK in a bean soup, or in a dish of rice and beans, or a bean salad. Your cholent will be delicious and more digestible without them, I assure you!
- **If you want to use all turkey parts**, **GF, P:** Use 2 to 3 turkey thighs, plus ¼ cup olive oil. Turkey parts are a much better choice than chicken parts, thighs being the best choice as they take better to the long, slow cooking. You can also use all lamb, or all beef or all bison chunks in any combination you like, but no added oil.
- **For a delicious gelatinous texture, GF, P:** Throw in a calf's foot.
- **Make a vegetable mixture, GF, P** (affectionately called "kishka"): 2 grated sweet potatoes, ½ cup raisins, 1 small chopped onion, 2 tablespoons oil, ½ cup ground almonds, cinnamon, and salt and pepper to taste. Shape into a log, wrap in cheesecloth, tie the ends, and throw in the pot. Perfect for Passover!
- **Add a few unpeeled eggs, GF, P:** They will get brown and will develop a deep flavor.
- **Add a couple of heads of garlic, GF, P:** The cloves will get incredibly sweet and tasty during cooking.

- **Make the following ground meat mixture, GF, P:**
  1 pound lean ground meat (turkey, bison, beef, or lamb), 6 large cloves of chopped garlic, 1 small bunch of minced parsley, ¼ cup of raw brown rice or other grain (Passover: use quinoa), 1 egg, ground pepper, and a pinch of nutmeg. Shape into a log, wrap in cheesecloth, tie the ends, and throw in the pot.
- **Low carb, GF, P:** Omit the wheat and potatoes. Add 2 bunches of celery—ribs separated, peeled, and cut in 3-inch chunks. Place in the bottom of the pan with the meat and seasonings on top. Do not add any water. Perfect for Passover.
- **GF, P:** Throw in a couple sweet potatoes cut in large chunks.
- **GF, P:** Throw in a dozen pitted dates.
- **Replace some of the water with a couple cans of beer.**
- **No-grain Cholent, GF, P:** Perfect for Passover! Leave the meat in and choose vegetables that stand up to the long cooking time: organic small potatoes left whole and unpeeled, mushrooms, garlic, onions, carrots, turnips, celery root, all cut in large chunks, canned or fresh crushed tomatoes, herbs of your choice, dry red wine.
- **All-vegetarian cholent, GF, P:** Any of the above selections with no meat, or with the addition of seitan (skip on Passover), unflavored.
- **Cholent as soup, GF, P:** Any of the above selections, with 6 to 8 cups more water. Serve in soup bowls.
- **What to do with leftover cholent, GF, P:** Don't throw it out, and don't leave it as is—what looked enticing on Saturday might look drab and unappealing on Monday, unless, of course, you give it a little makeover! Add to it some water, crushed tomatoes, red wine, oregano, cumin, paprika, even a handful chocolate chips, and you have yourself a delicious bean soup. Who would guess this is a recycled dish—and if they do, if you can recycle in such style, then more power to you!

BEEF STEW WITH GREEN TEA AND ROOT VEGETABLES GF

Green tea is a staple in my cooking, baking, and marinating. It imparts great depth without any need for added alcohol, which makes the end dish less caloric but no less delicious.

For any stew, I always ask the butcher to cut the meat chunks larger than they usually cut them: This way, I can control the cooking better, and the dish looks much more presentable. This dish is delicious made on the stove top or in a Crock-Pot: Great to know when we need to find dinner ready. Put it on and forget about it—it will be ready when you are!

4 pounds beef or bison shoulder, cut into two-inch cubes for stew
3 tablespoons olive oil
6 cups water
1 large sweet potato
1 large parsnip
1 large red onion
1 large celery root
1 large carrot
2 cups strong green tea, decaf OK
1 teaspoon turmeric
3 tablespoons olive oil
2 tablespoons grated ginger

Stove top: In a wide-bottom, heavy pot, bring the beef, water, and olive oil to boil. Reduce to medium and cook covered for 2 hours.

Cut all the vegetables into 1-inch cubes (remember to use a hammer, it will go one-two-three). Add them to the pot with all the remaining ingredients. Give the mixture a good stir. Bring to a boil. Reduce to medium and cook covered about 45 minutes. Uncover and check if all vegetables are tender. If you are left with too much liquid, reduce it by turning up the flame to high and cooking 2 to 3 minutes longer, until the liquids have reduced, leaving a thick sauce. Serve hot. Makes 8 to 10 servings.

With a Crock-Pot: Place all the ingredients except the water *(no water)* in a 6-quart Crock-Pot. Give the mixture a good stir. Set the Crock-Pot on low in the morning. It will be ready for dinner (10 to 12 hours total cooking time).

Variation: Substitute dark beer for the tea.

BLACKENED LONDON BROIL GF, P

London broil is a wonderful choice for those times you would like to indulge your occasional red meat craving, being so lean and tender. This is hardly a recipe; it is so simple you can make it in minutes. This is where all your pantry's goodies come in handy: Rub a 3-pound London broil, beef or bison, with 3 to 4 tablespoons dry spice rub (page 31) and broil in your oven broiler or on a barbecue, 7 minutes on each side for medium rare. Slice thin, serve hot or at room temperature. In a pinch, broil it exactly as above without any spices and serve it with Dijon-style mustard on the side: Yum! Throw any leftover slices in a salad or a sandwich.

ROAST BEEF WITH WILD MUSHROOM SAUCE GF, P

Only for festive occasions, as it is more expensive than I like my dishes to be, but it will be the best roast you will ever have, and the sauce is to die for. I find that starting the roast at such high temperature sears it right in the baking pan, right in the oven (in other words, without the extra step of searing it in a skillet first, transferring to a roasting pan, etc.) and ensures a wonderful crust and a rare center—the way we love a roast to be! Use a real, not disposable, pan please: You will see the difference at dinnertime!

1 6–7 pound shoulder roast, tied, at room temperature
2 large onions, thinly sliced (food processor)
8 cloves garlic
6 bay leaves, or 1 teaspoon ground
2 good pinches saffron
2 teaspoons turmeric
2 tablespoons coarsely ground pepper
¼ cup olive oil
1 cup dry red wine (variation: 1 can dark stout beer)
4–5 sprigs rosemary
7–8 sprigs thyme

Preheat the oven to 500°F. Place the roast in a pan just large enough to contain it. Mix all remaining ingredients in a bowl. Pour over the roast. Bake, loosely covered with foil, for half an hour. Uncover and reduce the oven temperature to 350°F. Bake 1½ hours longer. The roast will be medium rare. Transfer the roast to a cutting board. Strain the contents of the pan, pressing hard on the solids, and reserve for the sauce (recipe follows).

Discard the solids. Let stand about 10 minutes before slicing. Slice thin and serve with the sauce. Makes 8 to 10 servings.

Wild mushroom sauce

Get whatever wild mushrooms are available and affordable. Reducing the sauce takes only a few minutes. Sauce reduction is the ultimate cooking secret, across the board: Do not neglect this reducing step by trying to thicken the liquids with some starch. You will lose the integrity and intensity of the flavors—it won't be nearly as good!

¼ cup olive oil
1½ pounds wild mushrooms total—in any combination: shiitake caps, cremini, portobello, chanterelles—sliced
Reserved cooking liquid

Heat the oil in a large skillet. Add the mushrooms and sauté. Add the reserved cooking liquid and cook until the liquids reduce to about 2 cups and thicken slightly. Serve with the sliced roast.

BOEUF BOURGUIGNON GF, P

Spend a wonderful evening with a few French classics and some wine to go with dinner! By the way, my bourguignon has been included in Joan Schwartz's charming book, deceptively innocent, called Meat and Potatoes. *My secret ingredient here is crème de cassis, the wonderful black currant liqueur.*

This dish reheats very well and improves with age, so go ahead and make it a day or two ahead.

4 pounds beef or bison shoulder, cut into 2-inch cubes for stew

6 cups water

3 tablespoons extra-virgin olive oil

6 cloves garlic, peeled

2 cups dry red wine

¼ cup crème de cassis (liquor stores; Passover: use a nice berry liqueur)

2 large tomatoes, diced small

1 tablespoon coarsely ground black pepper

6 bay leaves, or 1 teaspoon ground

4 sprigs fresh thyme, leaves only (or throw the sprigs in whole, but don't forget to discard them at the end of cooking)

2 pounds very thin long carrots, peeled (about 20)

20 very small organic potatoes, scrubbed (only organic potatoes are safe with skins on)

2 dozen tiny onions, peeled and left whole (frozen OK: they are already peeled)

On a stove top: Place beef, water, and oil in a heavy, wide-bottom pot. Bring to a boil. Reduce to medium and cook covered for 2 hours. Add the garlic, wine, cassis, tomatoes, pepper, and bay leaves and cook 30 more minutes. Add thyme, carrots, potatoes, and onions and cook 30 more minutes. The meat should be fork-tender. Transfer meat and all vegetables on platter with a slotted spoon. If the liquid left in the pot is too thin, reduce it on a high flame until it is thickened, the consistency of maple syrup. Pour the reduced liquid over the whole dish and serve hot. Will make 8 to 10 servings.

With a Crock-Pot: Layer all the ingredients except the water *(no water)* in a 6-quart Crock-Pot, in the order they were given. Set the Crock-Pot on low in the morning. It will be ready for dinner (10 to 12 hours total cooking time).

Variation: Try the dish using dark stout beer instead of wine, as my daughter-in-law Ruthie does.

Beef Bourguignon

UNSTUFFED CABBAGE GF

You can find recipes for stuffed cabbage anywhere. What I would like to share here is a recipe for a dish that was earnestly meant as stuffed cabbage I made in my early bridal days, when I attempted to duplicate some of my mother-in-law's wonderful Eastern European dishes, in a great desire to reassure her that her son will get his usual native dinner treats with his Moroccan-born wife. My rolls all came undone, cabbage leaves hanging on for dear life above the meat layer. I was mortified, but my unflappable mother-in-law lifted the pot's lid, took a couple whiffs, steering the steam toward her with an expert hand, and said, "This is going to be delicious, I can tell: Who cares how it looks, as long as it has taam *[cute little word for 'flavor']?" Serendipity had upstaged skill once and for all, and I just continued to make this dish the lazy way—good-bye rolls! So here comes: Sort of like sloppy Joes with a healthy twist. Perfect choice for buffets.*

¼ cup olive oil
1 large onion, quartered
4 ribs celery, peeled
2 Granny Smith (green) apples, unpeeled, quartered
1 large bunch dill, fronds and stems
3 pounds lean ground beef, turkey or bison (lamb will work perfectly too)
1 large head white cabbage, center cores discarded, sliced very thin (food processor)
1 cup golden or black raisins
2 cups short grain brown rice
6 cups canned crushed tomatoes
6 cups cranberry or pomegranate juice
¼ cup tomato paste
2 tablespoons cinnamon
2 tablespoons paprika
4–5 bay leaves, or 1 teaspoon ground
Salt (just a drop if at all) and pepper to taste

Heat the oil in a wide-bottom pot. In a food processor, coarsely grind the onion, celery, apples, and dill. Add the ground mixture to the pot and sauté until translucent. Add the meat and sauté a few more minutes, stirring, until no longer pink. Add all remaining ingredients and bring to a boil. Reduce the flame to medium low and cook covered for 1½ hours, stirring occasionally to avoid scorching, or a little longer until the cabbage and the rice are very tender and the liquid in the pot is nice and thick. Transfer to a platter and serve hot. Makes a dozen ample servings.

CHINESE MEAT LOAF GF

The easiest and tastiest ever! The meat is extended by several vegetables—so you end up with a leaner and lighter meat loaf—and the potato flakes make it particularly smooth. Children love it! It will be delicious served cold in sandwiches as well as hot. If you decide to use ground turkey, try your best for dark turkey, go a little heavier on the seasonings, and add 2 tablespoons paprika for color.

2½ pounds lean ground lean beef, bison, or turkey

3 tablespoons toasted sesame oil

1 cup grated carrots, packed

1 cup natural potato flakes (health food stores)

1 cup coconut milk, light OK

1 bunch cilantro, all tough stems removed, minced

1 bunch scallions, sliced very thin

2 tablespoons grated fresh ginger

2–3 tablespoons chili sauce

2 eggs

Preheat the oven to 375°F. Mix all ingredients thoroughly by hand. Pour the mixture into a loaf pan. Bake about 1 hour, or a little longer until the top is just firm to the touch. Makes 8 to 10 servings.

ALL-AMERICAN MEAT LOAF GF

If the classic is what you would prefer, replace sesame oil with olive oil, coconut milk with good natural brand ketchup, ginger, and chili sauce with your favorite seasonings: oregano, cumin, minced garlic, etc. Proceed exactly as above.

BEEF STEW WITH LEMON OREGANO SAUCE GF, P

If this book is endowed with so many wonderful recipes, you have my daughter Bella to thank almost as well as me: While I was writing this book, she would call me regularly and ask me with great urgency if I thought of including this or that dish. ("Mommy, how could you leave it out?") This dish was on top of her must-have repertoire.

8 lamb shanks, or 4 pounds lean lamb, bison, or beef in 2-inch cubes
6 cups water
2 good pinches saffron
1 teaspoon turmeric
2 large onions, sliced very thin
3 tablespoons dry oregano
⅓ cup fresh lemon juice

Put the meat and water in a heavy wide-bottom pot and bring to a boil. Reduce the flame to medium, cover, and cook for 2 hours. Add saffron, turmeric, and onions and stir. Cook covered for 45 minutes longer. Gently stir in the oregano and lemon juice and cook 15 more minutes. If the liquid in the pot is not thick enough (we want the consistency of maple syrup), reduce on a high flame, uncovered, a few more minutes. Makes 8 to 10 servings.

Variation: Chicken stew with lemon oregano sauce GF, P

Same ingredients, using 16 pieces chicken total (legs, thighs, half breasts, skins on) and only 2 cups water. Bring the chicken, water, saffron, turmeric, and onions to a boil and give the mixture a good stir. Cook covered for 45 minutes. Gently stir in the oregano and lemon juice and cook 15 more minutes. If the liquid in the pot is not thick enough (we want the consistency of maple syrup), reduce on a high flame, uncovered, a few more minutes.

SPAGHETTI AND MEATBALLS GFA

We all used to pile into my mother-in-law's small apartment for her famed dish and always lied to her that somehow ours didn't come out as good as hers: Anything to have her make a vat of it, which would disappear in minutes. All the children in our family still clamor for it and feed it to their own children. So what was my mother-in-law's secret ingredient besides being so lovely and fun that we used to invade her house regularly? Cranberry sauce, that's what! You will find very good brands in health food stores, minimally processed, with none of the offending corn syrup.

Do not hesitate to experiment with low- or no-gluten noodles such as rice, soba, quinoa noodles, as I do: delicious and much gentler on your system! You will be able to have pasta more often. It's been years since I last had wheat noodles, and I don't miss anything about them one bit, least of all the bloating and discomfort that used to follow each white pasta meal as surely as night follows day.

Sauce:

  2 cups water
  2 large cans crushed tomatoes
  1 small can tomato paste
  1 15-ounce can natural jellied cranberry sauce
  2 tablespoons oregano
  ½ teaspoon red pepper flakes
  2 tablespoons cinnamon

Meatballs:

  1 medium onion
  1 bunch parsley
  ¼ cup olive oil
  Salt and pepper to taste
  ½ cup warm water
  2 pounds ground turkey, chicken, or lean beef
  2 eggs (or flax egg substitute, page 224)
  1 pound cooked spaghetti or rice noodles (these need only be soaked in hot water and drained)

In a wide-bottom, heavy pot, bring all the sauce ingredients to a boil. Meanwhile, grind the onion and parsley in a food processor until smooth. Transfer to a bowl with all remaining meatball ingredients and mix thoroughly by hand. Form balls with the mixture and throw them in the hot sauce liquid as you go. When you have used up all the meat mixture, reduce the flame to medium low and cook covered for about 1½ hours. Serve hot over the noodles. Makes 8 to 10 servings.

Rice Spaghetti and Meatballs

VEGETABLE DISHES

As always, the thrill of cooking without cooking and getting delicious results is too hard for me to resist, so this is where I'll start this chapter. To illustrate, let me share a vegetable dish I grew up with and make regularly at my home: rutabaga (yellow wax turnip), diced small, cooked in a little water, olive oil, salt, and turmeric until tender and all the water cooks out, and served at room temperature: That's the whole story! Likewise, chop up lettuce, watercress, Swiss chard, arugala, or spinach and sauté it in a little olive oil with a little salt added. Sounds too good to be true, doesn't it? Well, just try it! I might just have started a good problem for you! Stick a whole kabocha, acorn, or butternut squash in a preheated 375°F oven. Bake an hour or a little longer, until a knife goes through it without resistance. Split the squash, remove the seeds, and eat it as is or add a little cinnamon, olive oil, and salt. Oh, I nearly forgot: Spray some fresh or frozen cauliflower florets, or fresh or frozen halved brussels sprouts with vegetable spray and sprinkle them with salt, place them on a foil-lined cookie sheet in one layer, and roast them at 400°F for about 45 minutes, or a little longer until dark and tender. In my house this is snack food!

Roasted garlic

So many wonderful things you can do with roasted garlic. Roast several heads, and freeze them. Slice about ¼ inch off the pointed end of the head of garlic, leaving the cloves exposed. Smear lightly with olive oil, wrap in foil, and roast about 45 minutes, until the cloves are soft and squeezable

ROASTED VEGETABLES GF, P

Everyone loves a plate of grilled veggies, to eat as is or to use as a filling for sandwiches. I have chosen to share the most ridiculously simple way. First of all, my "grilled" veggies are roasted, requiring no turning over and no maintenance. Second, the trick is to combine your veggies according to their cooking time. To the selection below, you can add string beans, asparagus, endives, radishes, brussels sprouts, and fennel; but you will roast carrots, sweet potatoes, parsnips, potatoes separately because they have a longer cooking time. Roast beets all by themselves so they don't bleed into your other veggies, or use the wonderful golden beets now available at all good produce stores. For all roasting, remember, one layer, no piling! Lining the baking sheet with foil reduces, or sometimes even eliminates, cleaning.

When the vegetables are roasted, go ahead and get a little fancier if you wish: toss in a little olive oil, chopped fresh basil, a few drops of balsamic vinegar, and a little ground pepper. Most often, I add nothing at all!

2 large zucchini, cut in sticks
2 large red onions, sliced thick
3 large red peppers, cut in large sections
1 large eggplant, cut in sticks
2 large portobello mushrooms, caps and stems separated, stems cut in half
Sea salt to taste

Preheat the oven to 450°F. Line a large cookie sheet (you might need 2) with foil. Spray heavily with vegetable spray. Place the vegetables snuggly and in one layer on the cookie sheet.

Spray heavily again with vegetable spray. Sprinkle with sea salt to taste. Bake for about 30 minutes, or until the vegetables look lightly charred. The mushrooms (or string beans or asparagus) might be ready first. Slice the mushrooms on a bias when they are cool enough to handle.

Roasted Vegetables

SPINACH FRITTATA GF, P

A frittata is the Latin answer to our classic omelets: It is an open-faced omelet, about an inch high, with other ingredients mixed into the egg mixture rather than used as a filling. The batter is poured into a large skillet and placed on a stove top, just a few minutes until the bottom is set, then baked a few minutes in a hot oven until just set. It is then cut into wedges. Frittatas are great fun as you can use any filling you like, they are ready in minutes, and can be served hot or at room temperature. Also, one serving of frittata will include just about one egg, making it a good choice for all of us watching their egg intake.

I will make a few suggestions, and you will have fun playing with the fillings and getting different results each time. A good-quality oven-proof large skillet is all you need to make a frittata for 8 to 10 servings in one shot. Frittata is good at room temperature too, so don't worry about leftovers.

¼ cup olive oil
6 large cloves garlic
1 medium onion, quartered
2 large bunches spinach or Swiss chard, or 1 bunch kale, leaves only (settle for 2 10-ounce box frozen chopped spinach or kale, thawed and squeezed dry)
½ cup basil leaves, packed
½ cup parsley, leaves and stems, packed
10 eggs
2 cups milk or dairy-free milk, low-fat OK
Salt and pepper to taste
Good pinch nutmeg

Preheat oven to 450°F. Start by selecting a large oven-proof skillet. Heat the oil in the skillet. In a food processor, mince the garlic and onion using the pulse button, add to the hot oil and sauté just a minute or two. Coarsely chop the spinach, basil, and parsley in a food processor and add to the skillet. Sauté until all liquids evaporate, just a minute or 2. In a mixing bowl, beat the eggs with the milk and seasonings and pour slowly and evenly on top of the spinach mixture. Cook about 5 minutes on a medium flame until the bottom looks firm. Transfer to the oven and cook another 5 minutes or a little longer until the top looks barely set. Cut in wedges and serve hot or at room temperature. Makes 8 to 10 servings.

Variations (Be generous with the veggies you are including and make a short and sweet selection.)

- Add some freshly grated Parmesan.
- Sauté other vegetables: diced zucchini, sliced mushrooms, diced tomatoes, cut-up asparagus, diced red pepper, grated carrots, etc.
- Add diced cooked potatoes, frozen corn, small frozen or fresh cauliflower or broccoli florets, diced frozen artichoke hearts, diced cooked or smoked chicken, or diced cooked fish.
- Use other seasonings: thyme, rosemary, tarragon, etc.

COOKED TOMATO SALAD: MATBUKHA GF, P

This is one of our Moroccan favorite dishes, a sort of comfort food for ex-pats and honorary Sephardis alike: See how they mop that sauce with their bread! Shakshuka is nothing more than Matbukha with eggs scrambled into it and served as a main course, and gets its funny name from the Arabic word for "scramble."

1 whole head garlic
2 red bell peppers, washed, cored, and seeded
2–3 jalapeño peppers
2 tablespoons olive oil
3 large beefsteak tomatoes, or 8 plum tomatoes, diced small (settle for 1 28-ounce can *diced* tomatoes, liquid and all)
½ cup olive oil
2 tablespoons paprika
3 garlic cloves, minced
Salt and pepper to taste

Preheat the oven to 425°F.

Slice about ¼ inch off the pointed end of the head of garlic, leaving the cloves exposed. Drizzle the olive oil onto the garlic and the peppers, place them on a cookie sheet, and roast for 30 minutes, or until the garlic is soft and the peppers are charred (the peppers might be ready a few minutes before the garlic). Press the cloves out of their skins while still warm and mash with a fork. Peel the peppers and cut them into thin strips.

In a heavy, wide-bottom pot, bring the tomatoes, oil, and paprika to a boil. Reduce the heat to medium, add the roasted garlic and peppers, and cook covered for about 30 minutes, stirring frequently. All of the water should evaporate, and the oil will resurface (if you neglect this step, you will not get the desired look and texture but a glorified tomato sauce). Add the freshly minced garlic and the salt and pepper to taste. Let cool and store in a glass jar in the refrigerator: it will keep for up to two weeks. Use a slotted spoon to serve so the oil stays behind.

Variation: Shakshuka GF, P

Stir 8 eggs into the Matbukha on a medium flame, mixing thoroughly with a wooden spoon, and cook just a few more minutes until the eggs are barely set. If you would rather end up with a more pristine look, leave the eggs whole, break them one by one, and set them over the mixture, close but not touching, and cook covered on a low flame until they look barely set.

Serve hot, alone, or with a good whole-grain bread, or on a bed of cooked (canned OK) white beans (except on Passover). Makes 8 servings.

Shakshuka

BROCCOLI CAULIFLOWER KUGEL GF, P

I love to play the "move-over-potatoes" game: not because I don't love them, but more because I can enjoy them only occasionally. I am confident you will concur: This recipe will move effortlessly from your stepchild "restricted" list to your A-list, just because it's perfectly delicious! Wait till you see all the variations you can play with! I love to use frozen veggies because they are all ready to go, clean, and full of flavor and with all their nutrition intact, but of course you can use fresh: No need to cook anything before baking, unless otherwise noted.

3 cups frozen broccoli florets
3 cups frozen cauliflower florets
1 medium onion, quartered
6 eggs
1 cup dairy-free milk, low-fat OK (Passover: white wine or water or a combination)
½ cup flour, any flour (Passover: potato starch)
⅓ cup olive oil
Salt and pepper to taste
Good pinch nutmeg
½ teaspoon dry thyme or ground bay leaves
1 teaspoon turmeric

Preheat oven to 375°F. In a food processor, coarsely grind the vegetables. Transfer the mixture to a bowl and add all remaining ingredients, combining thoroughly. Pour the mixture into a greased 11-by-14-inch baking pan. Bake about 40 minutes, or a little longer until the top is barely firm. Serve hot. Room temperature will be good too. Makes 8 servings.

Variations: Short and sweet selections.

In addition to—or instead of—part or all of the cauliflower and broccoli, consider these possibilities, in equal parts—all equally good and exciting.

- Frozen chopped spinach, kale, or collard greens, thawed and squeezed dry.
- Frozen corn kernels or peas (no need to thaw).
- Frozen artichoke hearts, chopped.
- Grated carrots, sweet potatoes, kabocha, potatoes, zucchini, parsnips, celery root, etc.
- Canned pumpkin, good quality, unflavored.
- Vary the seasonings according to the selection you go with: cinnamon, ginger, dill, oregano, etc.
- Sautéed mushrooms (only these must be sautéed first, or they will release much too much moisture and throw off the good liquid-solid balance).
- Use 1 cup of cooked grain, anything you might have. No need to cook it just for the recipe, only if you have it on hand.
- Make it into a dairy main course: Use milk instead of dairy-free milk, low-fat OK, add 1 cup freshly grated Parmesan to the batter, and top with buttered bread crumbs, gluten-free OK, before baking (toss 1 cup fresh bread crumbs with 2 tablespoons butter).

- Make it into individual servings: Pour the batter into greased muffin molds and bake 30 minutes or a little longer, until the tops are set.
- Make it into a quiche (anytime except on Passover). Make a pie crust (recipe below). Pour your batter over the crust and bake, same temperature, same time as above.

Savory pie crust

½ cup margarine spread
½ teaspoon salt
2½ cups flour, any flour
3–4 tablespoons very cold water

Work the margarine, salt and flour until the mixture resembles coarse meal. Mix in the water and work by hand only until the mixture forms a smooth dough. Working quickly, line a 12-inch pie dish with it, going from the center toward the sides, all the way up the sides. Pour your selected filling and bake according to your recipe's baking time.

MOROCCAN POTATO PIE GF, P

We grew up with this delightful dish my mom used to whip up in no time each time someone called to tell us they were in town and on their way to our house. (That's right, that's an apt description of our social life: "Hello! And surprise! I am at your door! It's been so long!") That and a few other goodies seemed to hit the spot each time. This is one of the numerous times you will find that having a jar of preserved lemons on hand will be most welcome, with their incomparable taste and heady aroma. Of course you can still make it without, but it won't be as exciting! Never run out of them: They take minutes and last months!

⅓ cup olive oil
10 eggs
1 bunch flat-leaf parsley, chopped fine
2 good pinches saffron
1 teaspoon turmeric
½ preserved lemon (page 33), skin only, rinsed and minced (settle for 2 tablespoons lemon zest)
1 teaspoon ground pepper, or less to taste
Salt to taste
Good pinch nutmeg
1 cup total frozen corn, carrots, and peas, optional
3 large potatoes, peeled

Preheat oven to 375°F. Grease a 10-inch ovenproof skillet with straight sides. Mix all but last remaining ingredients in a bowl and combine thoroughly. Only then, grate the potatoes and immediately stir them in the mixture, so as not to give them any time to oxidize. Pour the batter into the skillet and bake 30 to 40 minutes, or until golden and puffy, but not longer so the egg mixture doesn't toughen. Makes 8 main course servings.

Variation: Moroccan chicken pie GF, P

No potatoes: 2–3 cups cooked chicken, minced, and 1 large slice bread, gluten-free OK, soaked in water, broth, or dairy-free milk (Passover: replace the slice bread with ⅓ cup potato starch). Proceed exactly as above.

ARTICHOKE AND LIMA BEAN TAJINE GF, P

Tajine is the name of the earthenware pot that gave its name to all dishes cooked in it. In our native Moroccan cooking, there is no such thing as a "side dish." Equal time for veggies and meat or fish—this is where our respect for veggies comes from. Vegetables cook, either alone or along with the fish or the chicken or the meat and various seasonings, according to their respective cooking times: *This* is what makes our cooking so flavorful and exciting, and makes us *eat our vegetables* without any begging or urging.

¼ cup olive oil
4 large cloves garlic
1 bunch flat parsley
2 boxes frozen artichoke hearts
3 cups frozen lima beans or edamame (Passover: substitute 2 large potatoes, diced)
1½ cups water
3 bay leaves, or ½ teaspoon ground
1 teaspoon turmeric
Good pinch red pepper flakes
Juice and zest of 2 lemons
Salt and pepper to taste

Artichoke and Lima Bean Tajine

Heat the oil in a large skillet. In a food processor, finely grind the garlic and parsley. Add the ground mixture to the oil and sauté until just fragrant. Add all remaining ingredients and bring to a boil. Reduce the flame to medium and cook about 10 minutes. Serve warm with your favorite grain. Makes 8 servings.

BEER-BRAISED MUSHROOM TEMPEH STEW

I am afraid tempeh looks as uninspiring as it sounds. But if you do go past its appearance and unromantic name, you are in for a real treat: Tempeh is made from cooked and slightly fermented soybeans and compressed into patties; it is then diced and used in stir-fries, soups, and stews. Because of its low-fat and high-protein content, it is an ideal choice in vegetarian diets. Tempeh can be found in the refrigerated section of most health food stores and in the natural foods aisle of well-stocked grocery stores. In the finished dish, tempeh will have soaked up all the good cooking juices and lost its objectionable drab color and spongy texture. So, have I used my modest powers of persuasion enough for you to try it? I hope I have. It's delicious! You might want to consider throwing everything in a Crock-Pot and set on a low temperature in the morning for that night's dinner, or at night for the following day's lunch.

2 12-ounce cans beer
⅓ cup olive oil
1 large red onion, sliced very thin
6 large cloves garlic, minced
1 pound shiitake mushrooms, caps only
½ pound any other wild mushrooms you can afford, cubed
¼ cup hijiki (or other seaweed: wakame, arame, etc.)
2–3 tablespoons maple syrup
2 sprigs tarragon
1 bunch chives, sliced thin
2 pounds tempeh, cut in inch cubes
1 teaspoon turmeric
Ground pepper to taste
½ cup dark miso paste

In a wide-bottom pot, bring all but two last ingredients to a boil. Reduce to medium and cook covered for 1 hour. Gently stir in the ground pepper and miso, until the miso breaks up and is evenly incorporated. Serve hot with brown rice or any other grain. Makes 8 servings.

PLANTAINS, SQUASH, AND APPLE BAKE GF, P

Almost too good to be a savory dish, so feel free to let it double as dessert. I notice many produce markets now offer diced butternut squash, simplifying the preparation work. You might want to use kabocha squash (my favorite member of the whole squash family).

4 large plantains, firm-ripe
1 medium butternut or kabocha squash, no peeling necessary, cut into 2-inch chunks
4 Mackintosh apples, unpeeled, cut into large wedges
1 cup coconut milk, light OK
¼ cup rum or brandy
2 tablespoons cinnamon
1 tablespoon vanilla extract
½ cup agave or Sucanat
Salt and pepper to taste

Preheat the oven to 375°F. Peel the plantains and cut lengthwise, then in thirds. Mix all ingredients gently in a bowl then place in a baking sheet. Roast 30 minutes, or a little longer until the vegetables are tender. Transfer to a serving platter and pour all the cooking liquids over them. Serve warm or at room temperature. Makes 8 servings.

CABBAGE, FENNEL, AND APPLE COMPOTE GF, P

This trio is a real winner, besides being a real nutritional powerhouse. It will do excellently, alone or as a side dish with poultry or sliced steak. The food processor will do all your slicing and grating in a wink of an eye!

¼ cup olive oil
1 large onion, chopped
2 Granny Smith (green) apples, unpeeled and coarsely grated
3 tablespoons sugar
1 small head cabbage, sliced very thin
2 large heads fennel, heads sliced very thin, fronds chopped
1 cup dry white wine (or natural apple cider, if you would rather not use alcohol)
1 cup water
Salt and pepper to taste
1 sprig sage, leaves only, chopped

Heat the oil in a heavy pan. Add onion and apples and sauté until translucent. Add the sugar and fry 2 to 3 more minutes. Add all remaining ingredients. Bring to a boil. Reduce to medium low. Cover and cook about 30 minutes, stirring occasionally, until very soft and most liquids evaporate. Serve warm or at room temperature. Makes 8 servings.

CABBAGE CORN STRUDEL

Another treat using cabbage as the star. I have always enjoyed the numerous cabbage dishes my Russian mother-in-law inspired me to make. My son Maimon, on a trip to Russia as a teenage school counselor, came back swearing he will never again get anywhere near a beet, a cabbage, or a potato, which were coming out of his ears after a month. How long did he keep that promise? A few weeks, at the most! I should tell you I make the filling quite often, sans phyllo or bread crumbs (my daughter-in-law Ruthie always does), and it looks less elegant but tastes just as delicious, for those times you can't fuss and don't need as dramatic a presentation. This dish makes a stunning first course or hors d'oeuvre. You can jazz it up by dicing a little smoked salmon in it. The crumbs are sprinkled on the phyllo to absorb any forming moisture so the phyllo stays crisp, so be sure not to skip that simple and important step. The strudels will freeze very well: Reheat uncovered at 300°F for 15 to 20 minutes until crisp. I periodically check to see if gluten-free phyllo becomes commercially available: I doubt you will want to make it from scratch, but believe it or not, you can find the recipe online!

¼ cup olive oil
1 large onion, quartered
6 cloves garlic
Small bunch dill, fronds and stems
3 cups very thinly sliced nappa cabbage or white cabbage, packed
2 cups grated carrots, packed
1 cup frozen corn kernels
Salt and pepper to taste
12 leaves phyllo (have the whole box on hand in case of "accidents")
⅓ cup fresh bread crumbs
½ cup vegetable oil

Preheat oven to 375°F. Make the filling: Heat the olive oil in a skillet. In a food processor, coarsely grind the onion, garlic, and dill. Add the mixture to the skillet and sauté until wilted. Add the remaining filling ingredients and sauté until all the liquids evaporate.

Take 2 piled phyllo leaves, short side facing you. Brush lightly with oil. Add 2 more piled leaves and brush again lightly. Sprinkle with ⅓ of the bread crumbs. Spread ⅓ of the filling on the bottom side of the phyllo (the side facing you). Roll tightly all the way up. Repeat with the remaining leaves, crumbs, and filling. You will get 3 rolls total. Score the rolls by cutting the top layers only with a sharp serrated knife, about 3 inches apart (closer apart if you intend to use them for hors d'oeuvres). Place the phyllo rolls on cookie sheet. Brush the tops of the rolls lightly with oil. Bake 30 to 40 minutes or until lightly brown and very crisp. To serve, slice all the way down along the scored lines. Serve hot. Makes 8 servings.

EGGPLANT ROULADES GF

Fun and delicious. As always, I ignore the eggplant's insatiable appetite for oil, skip the frying and roast the slices, just enough to make them pliable and ready to roll! These roulades will reheat very well in a 300°F oven for just a few minutes.

2 medium eggplant, with peels on, sliced evenly lengthwise ¼ inch thick, about 16 slices total
Vegetable spray
Stuffing:
¼ cup olive oil
1 medium onion, quartered
4 cloves garlic
2 medium zucchini, grated (use a food processor)
¼ cup fresh basil leaves, packed
1 small bunch flat parsley
1 large tomato, or 2 plum tomatoes, diced small (settle for 1 cup crushed canned tomatoes)
½ cup dry white wine
¾ cup fresh bread crumbs, from any plain bread, gluten-free OK
Salt and pepper to taste
1 tablespoon oregano
Paprika for dusting the finished rolls

Preheat the oven to 425°F. Line a cookie sheet with foil or parchment paper and spray with vegetable spray. Arrange the eggplant slices on top and spray again. Bake about 20 minutes. Reserve the slices and leave the foil lining on the cookie sheet. Reduce the oven temperature to 375°F.

Meanwhile, make the stuffing: Heat the oil in a skillet. In a food processor, coarsely grind the onion and garlic and add to the hot oil. Sauté until translucent. Add the zucchini and sauté until the liquids evaporate. Finely grind the basil and parsley and add to the skillet. Add the tomatoes and wine. Cook until most liquids evaporate. Add the bread crumbs, salt, and pepper and combine.

Place a little filling in the center of a slice and close the flaps toward the center. You will get a neat roll. Place the roll seam side down on the same cookie sheet. Repeat with the remaining slices and filling. Dust the finished rolls with paprika for a nice color. Bake 20 minutes. Serve hot. Makes 8 servings.

Dairy: Stir about 1 cup freshly grated Parmesan (Swiss cheese for a milder flavor) into the filling and proceed as above.

Stuffed mushrooms: GF Select large mushrooms, and finely chop the stems, using them instead of the grated zucchini. Fill the caps generously (no need to roast them first), packing the stuffing in, and bake just as above.

Stuffed zucchini: GF Proceed just as above, substituting large sliced zucchini for the sliced eggplant.

KABOCHA, KALE, AND SEAWEED STEW GF

It doesn't get healthier than this! This is a complete meal in one pot. Macrobiotic food lovers will enjoy this no end as well. The green tea imparts a clean taste and added nutrition.

¼ cup toasted sesame oil
2 tablespoons olive oil
4 leeks, sliced
4 large cloves garlic
2 inch piece fresh ginger, peeled
2 tablespoons curry powder
1 teaspoon turmeric
½ medium kabocha squash, unpeeled, seeded and cut in inch cubes (use a hammer)
¼ cup hijiki (or other seaweed: wakame, arame, etc.)
1 bunch kale, stems and all, thinly sliced
2 cups strong green tea, decaf OK
1 cup water
Salt and pepper to taste
2 cups soybean sprouts, optional
6 scallions, sliced thinly
6 sprigs cilantro, stems cut off, minced

Heat the oils in a wide heavy pot. In a food processor, mince the leeks, garlic, and ginger using the pulse button. Add the mixture to the skillet, and sauté for 2 to 3 minutes. Add the curry and turmeric and sauté just a few seconds more. Add the squash, seaweed, kale, tea, water, salt and pepper to taste, and bring to a boil. Reduce the flame to medium and cook covered for 30 minutes. Add all remaining ingredients and toss, cooking 1 to 2 more minutes, just until heated through. Transfer to a platter and serve hot, alone or with rice or noodles. Makes 8 servings.

Kabocha, Kale, and
Seaweed Stew

VEGETABLE LATKAS AND BURGERS GF

Forget about those insipid and processed patties in the frozen section of your supermarket or health food store: processed is processed, organic or otherwise! Rather, make your own delicious vegetable latkas and burgers on Channukah and anytime with any ingredients you like. And if frying is a deterrent, here's how to bake them as well!

Oil for frying
1 cup flour, any flour
4 eggs, or 1 cup egg substitute (page 224)
1 large onion, grated very fine (use a food processor)
Salt and pepper to taste
8 cups grated vegetables: carrots, sweet potatoes, zucchini, celery root, turnips, parsnips; or minced frozen vegetables: cauliflower, broccoli, spinach, etc., in any combination you like (the shorter the selection the better; use the food processor).

Your favorite seasonings (no garlic powder ever): oregano, thyme, cinnamon, etc.

Heat the oil in a heavy skillet, about ⅓ inch high, until very hot. Mix all ingredients thoroughly in a bowl. Form patties and throw them in the hot oil. Fry until golden, about 3 minutes on each side. Take out with a slotted spoon and transfer onto a plate lined with paper towels. You will get about 16 patties total. Serve hot, alone, or with your favorite sauce (see The Pantry, page 19). Makes 8 servings.

Variations

- Potato latkas: proceed as above, using no other vegetables than 8 large grated potatoes; work quickly so they don't have any time to oxidize. Potato kugel: add ⅓ cup oil to the potato mixture and bake in an 11-inch x 14-inch baking pan in a preheated 375 degrees oven for about 1 hour until the top is firm
- Bake instead of frying. Add ¼ cup olive, flax, or other oil to your mixture; form your patties; place them on a cookie sheet; spray them with vegetable spray; and bake in a preheated 375°F oven for about 30 minutes.
- Grain-based: Substitute 2 cups cooked rice, millet, quinoa, lentils, chickpeas, any cooked grain you might have on hand for the flour, and proceed as above.

NAPPA CABBAGE, MUSTARD GREENS, AND MUSHROOM STIR-FRY GF

All the flavors in this dish are so intense and assertive I never worry about what tempera-ture they should be served at. Ideally, I would stir-fry them and serve them hot, but if I need to make them in advance or serve them at a buffet, or at a Shabbos lunch, no trouble serving them at room temperature.

2 tablespoons olive oil
2 tablespoons toasted sesame oil
1 2-inch piece ginger, grated
1 small nappa cabbage, sliced very thin
1 bunch mustard greens (or kale, spinach, Swiss chard), leaves only, sliced very thin
1 large carrot, grated
1 pound shiitake caps, sliced
3–4 tablespoons soy sauce

Heat both oils in a large skillet. Add the ginger and sauté for just one minute until fragrant. Add all the leaves and stir-fry until wilted. Add the carrot and mushrooms and stir-fry 2 to 3 more minutes until all liquids evaporate. Add the soy sauce and toss.

Serve hot or at room temperature. Makes 8 servings.

Variation: If you would like to turn this dish into a main course, scramble some eggs or some soft tofu into it at the end of cooking and heat through.

SUSHI ROLLS GF

As we all learn often at our own expense, sushi is good only if served the minute it is assem-bled, which is why sushi recipes are so scant and why we eat sushi mostly in restaurants. A closer look will tell you not only why this is so but also what you can do to make it go a longer way.

- *The rice must be freshly made and the temperature controlled. Refrigerating it toughens it, and no amount of bringing it back to room temperature restores it to that ideal texture that is so prized in sushi rolls.*
- *The fish must be . . . well, you have heard the expression, sushi quality. This means super duper fresh since it is served absolutely raw. So no fooling around with the caliber and the quality of the fish, or we have a serious safety hazard on our hands.*

Anytime I am not serving sushi exactly the minute I make it, I simply make it—without rice—and end up with a pretty good problem: less rice, more veggies and fish. Also, anytime I am not a thousand percent sure of the freshness or can't leave my fish to firm up in the freezer for a couple hours, I simply use cooked mock crab, smoked salmon, or no fish at all.

The following is a roll I love to make, as it gives me very little trouble, but I skip the rice each time I need to make the rolls on a day I can't cook (Shabbos lunch, outdoors, etc.). You can choose from many other exciting veggies: minced shiitake, grated daikon, thin asparagus, etc. Fresh fish: only the best fresh tuna or salmon, chilled in the freezer for an hour or two and cut into thin strips. Have fun mixing and matching!

Rice: Only if you are serving the rolls within 2 hours

2 cups plus 2 tablespoons water
2 cups sushi rice (brown rice great too, even though it won't look as perfect as white)
¼ cup rice vinegar
2 tablespoons sugar
Salt to taste

8 sheets nori
1 bamboo mat
6 scallions, sliced very thin
1 avocado, cut in thin strips
1 seedless cucumber, cut in thin strips
1 red pepper, cut in thin strips
1 cup minced mock crab

Put water to a boil in a pot. Place the rice in a large strainer and run cold water over it, swishing it with your hand until the water runs clear. Add the rice to the boiling water, reduce the heat to low and cook covered for 15 minutes (if using brown rice: 4 cups water, 2 cups short-grain brown rice—cooking time 40 minutes). Turn off the heat, cover the rice with a towel, cover the pot again, and let rest 15 minutes. Gently stir in the vinegar, sugar, and salt.

Place half a sheet of nori on top of the bamboo mat. Use thin rubber gloves: it will make your work easier. Take a small handful of the rice, if using, and spread neatly over the whole surface of the nori in a thin layer. Add some of the vegetable-fish mixture on the front of the rice rectangle, along the whole length (if not using rice, put in more veggies). Roll tightly, using the bamboo mat as your guide. Repeat with the remaining rice, nori, and vegetables. With a very sharp knife, make six slices with each roll.

Serve with pickled ginger (easy to find), soy sauce, and wasabi paste (wasabi powder mixed with a little water).

HOT AND SWEET PARSNIPS GF, P

Those of you who have my first book, Levana's Table, *make this dish quite often, I am always told: It fits so nicely in this book I must include it here as well! Poor parsnips too often serve as crowd actor, and then get discarded (as in chicken soup), but here they are* it: *Who knew they could be so fabulous?*

1½ dozen very thin parsnips, peeled and left whole (settle for 5–6 larger ones, peeled and quartered lengthwise)

2 cups water

3 tablespoons olive oil

3 tablespoons sugar or Sucanat

1 tablespoon paprika

1 teaspoon turmeric

½ teaspoon cayenne pepper, or less to taste

1 tablespoon ground cinnamon

Salt and pepper to taste

Place all the ingredients in a wide heavy pot and bring to a boil. Reduce the heat to medium, cover, and cook for about 20 minutes, or a drop longer until the parsnips are tender and the liquids in the pot have thickened. Pour the sauce over the parsnips. Serve hot or at room temperature. Makes 8 servings.

Hot and Sweet Parsnips

HERB-ROASTED POTATOES AND ASPARAGUS GF, P

I love to roast them together and end up with two side dishes, with a minimal amount of labor. The new potatoes' skins are very thin, so no need to peel, and they are melt-in-your-mouth tender. If you can't find asparagus, skip them and go on with the recipe: You will be left with wonderful herb-roasted potatoes.

2 pounds organic whole tiny potatoes (only organic potatoes are safe with their skin on). If you can't find tiny potatoes, settle for small, halved

3 tablespoons olive oil

1 sprig rosemary

3 sprigs thyme

4 large cloves garlic, minced

Sea salt and pepper to taste

1 bunch thin asparagus, tough ends discarded, cut in thirds

Preheat the oven to 450°F. Scrub the potatoes and dry thoroughly. Line a large cookie sheet with foil or parchment paper. Place all but last ingredient on the tray and combine the mixture thoroughly, arranging them in one layer. Bake for 20 minutes. Add the asparagus and toss again. Bake 15 more minutes, or a little longer until all vegetables look soft and roasted (in case you are using all potatoes and no asparagus—potatoes' total baking time: 35–40 minutes). Serve hot. Makes 8 servings.

POTATO, OLIVE, AND TOMATO TAJINE GF, P

Straight from the Moroccan kitchen of my childhood. Ridiculously simple ingredients and hardly any labor. I have included a choice of protein to make it a full one-pot dish, but you can choose to go without and make this a wonderful all-vegetable main course. When you see what magic the preserved lemon does to this dish, you will never ever want to run out!

2 dozen very small organic potatoes, unpeeled, halved potatoes (only organic potatoes are safe with their skin on)

2 dozen green pitted olives, rinsed

2 cups canned crushed tomatoes

Optional: 1 pound extra-firm tofu, tempeh, or seitan cut in inch cubes, or 8 pieces chicken (cutlets, thighs, drumsticks)

1 medium onion, sliced very thin

¼ cup olive oil

1 teaspoon turmeric

1 tablespoon paprika

3 cups water

1 small bunch parsley

¼ preserved lemon (page 33), skin only, rinsed

4 sprigs cilantro, tough stems discarded

Bring the first set of ingredients to boil in a wide heavy pot. Reduce the heat to medium and cook covered for 30 minutes. In a food processor, finely grind the parsley, preserved lemon, and cilantro and stir this mixture gently into the pot. Cook another 15 minutes or until the chicken (if using) is tender. With a slotted spoon, transfer all ingredients to a platter, leaving mostly the cooking liquids. If they are too thin, reduce a few minutes on a high flame until the sauce thickens and pour evenly over the dish. Serve hot. Room temperature OK too. Makes 8 servings.

RATATOUILLE MOROCCAN-STYLE GF, P

A lot of dicing, but I think you will find it well worth it. Plum tomatoes are perfectly suited for cooking, as they have little juice and lots of flesh. I love to serve ratatouille at picnics, as it lends itself perfectly to room temperature serving.

⅓ cup olive oil
6 large cloves garlic
1 large onion, quartered
2 red peppers, cut in large chunks
1 medium-size eggplant, peeled and diced small
3 medium-size zucchini, diced small
4 plum tomatoes, diced small
2 tablespoons paprika
1 teaspoon ground turmeric
2 good pinches red pepper flakes
1 tablespoon cumin
Sea salt and pepper to taste
1 cup water
1 bunch flat-leaf parsley
4–5 sprigs cilantro, tough stems cut off
½ preserved lemon (page 33), skin only, rinsed (settle for 2 tablespoons lemon zest or 1 teaspoon tamarind powder)

Heat the oil in a wide heavy pot. In a food processor, finely grind the garlic. Add the onion and peppers and grind coarsely. Add the mixture to the pot and sauté until translucent. Add the eggplant, zucchini, tomatoes, paprika, turmeric, salt and pepper, and water and stir to combine. Cook covered on a medium flame 30 minutes, or a little longer until the vegetables are tender. In a food processor, mince the parsley, cilantro, and preserved lemon and stir into the pot. Cook 3 to 4 more minutes, stirring occasionally. Serve warm or at room temperature.

Makes 8 servings.

Variation: Classic French ratatouille GF, P

Instead of (not in addition to, please!) the cumin, cilantro, and lemon, add ½ cup chopped fresh basil and 2 tablespoons oregano toward the end of cooking: Voilà!

ROASTED RADDICHIO, ENDIVES, AND FENNEL GF, P

Bitter and sweet face off in this rustic yet elegant dish and emerge best of friends. It will go beautifully with roast chicken, beef, or turkey or on top of polenta wedges, quinoa, or rice for a vegetarian entrée, with a sprinkling of grated cheese if desired.

3 tablespoons olive oil
2 tablespoons balsamic vinegar
¼ cup maple syrup or agave
1 large head raddichio, cut in 6 wedges
3 large endives, cut in quarters
1 large head fennel, cut into thin wedges
⅓ cup basil, leaves only, packed, sliced thin
Salt and pepper to taste

Preheat oven to 450°F. Mix all the ingredients thoroughly in a bowl and arrange in one layer on a cookie sheet lined with foil or parchment paper. Roast for 20 minutes, or a little longer until the vegetables look wilted and charred. Serve hot or at room temperature. Makes 8 servings.

Roasted Raddichio, Endives, and Fennel

BRAISED RED CABBAGE AND APPLES GF, P

Get ready to kiss this huge pile of veggies good-bye: It will be reduced to a shadow of itself at the end of cooking, but what a handful! Talk about what "stuffing" will go with your turkey!

⅓ cup olive oil
1 large onion, chopped
3 Granny Smith (green) or Mackintosh apples, cut in small chunks
½ cup unfiltered apple cider vinegar
⅓ cup sugar
4 bay leaves, or 1 teaspoon ground
½ teaspoon ground cloves
2 cups natural apple cider
1 medium head red cabbage, tough centers discarded, thinly shredded (food processor)
Salt and pepper to taste

Heat the oil in a wide heavy pot. Add the onion and apples and sauté until tender. Add all remaining ingredients and bring to a boil. Reduce the flame to medium low and cook covered for about 1½ hours, stirring occasionally, or a little longer until the cabbage looks very tender and very reduced and all liquid has evaporated. Serve hot. Perfect with baked turkey. Try serving at room temperature as well, as a "condiment" with cold meat, chicken, or fish. Makes 8 servings.

ROASTED LEEKS, ONIONS, AND GARLIC GF, P

If you love all members of the onion family, as I do, here is a simple and inexpensive way to showcase some of them and enjoy them as a side dish or as a spread in a sandwich with your favorite filling.

2 large leeks, tough green leaves discarded, cut across lengthwise, then cut into 2-inch segments
4 shallots, quartered
2 dozen cloves garlic
1 large red onion, sliced about ½ inch thick
¼ cup olive oil
Salt and pepper to taste

Optional: a few drops balsamic vinegar, a little rosemary and thyme
Preheat the oven to 450°F. Line a large cookie sheet with foil. In a mixing bowl, toss all ingredients together. Arrange on the sheet in one layer. Roast 25 to 30 minutes until soft and roasted. Serve warm or at room temperature. Makes 8 servings.

WHITE VEGETABLE PURÉE GF, P

Not nearly as generic as it sounds, although it does sound more intriguing in French: purée blanche. This goes way beyond mashed potatoes and affords you greater, leaner, lower starch, and more nutritious choices when making purée. When he was a little boy, my son Yakov, a mashed potato lover if I ever met one, wiped out a whole plate of it after I told him the usual white lie (pun not intended, or is it?) that was de rigueur every single time I needed to introduce him to a new food: I told him it was mashed potatoes. No, it's not very nice to lie to your children, but if it will make them eat their veggies (a little like with a placebo), it seems that the end justifies the means, and you will need to do it just that once!

It goes without saying that you could use potatoes and proceed exactly as I am instructing you, but wait till you taste this! There are several other white veggies you could include here, in any combination you like, and get another variation each time you experiment: leeks, garlic, cauliflower, fennel, even canned white beans. If you are making roast chicken, use some of the chicken fat that will gather in the baking pan instead of the oil, or butter or clarified butter (page 278) if you are making the dish dairy (in this case, use milk and throw in a little grated cheese if you wish).

3 cups water or dairy-free milk, low-fat OK, or a combination
3 medium turnips, or 1 large rutabaga (yellow wax turnip)
3 medium parsnips
2 medium or 1 large celery root (potato purée: 8 large potatoes and no other vegetable)
¼ cup olive oil
Salt and white pepper to taste
Garnish: 3 tablespoons finely chopped chives (or basil or parsley)
Pinch nutmeg

Heat the water in a wide pot. Peel and cut all the roots into chunks and add to the pot. Add the oil, salt, and pepper and bring to a boil. Reduce the flame to medium, cover, and cook, adding a little liquid if necessary, 20 to 30 minutes or until all vegetables are tender. The mixture should look good and dry: If any liquid remains in the pot, turn up the flame for just a minute or two until the liquids evaporate.

While the mixture is very hot, mash with a potato masher until fluffy. Alternatively, place in small batches in a food processor (please be careful not to overmix, or the mixture will get gummy) and pulse until just blended but still chunky, not mushy. Stir in the nutmeg and chives and serve hot. Makes 8 servings.

SPINACH, TOFU, AND LENTIL CURRY WITH CUCUMBER RAITA GF

I had never much cared for Indian food, having been exposed only to some mediocre commercial offerings that caused more heartburn than pleasure, until I was introduced to it properly by a Trinidadian who worked with me many years and used all the influences of her native cuisines to great advantage. Not only did she teach me how to cook fabulous Indian dishes the quick and natural way, she also showed me the proper serving decorum. Here is one of my favorites: The red lentils disperse in the dish and thicken the sauce naturally. If you would rather make this with another protein, substitute 3 to 4 cups diced chicken breast, seitan, or tempeh for the tofu.

¼ cup olive oil
1 large onion, chopped
1 2 inch piece ginger, grated or minced
1 tablespoon curry, or more to taste
1 teaspoon ground cumin
1 jalapeño pepper, minced (if you don't like it too hot, seed it first)
4 cups water
1 cup coconut milk
2 cups frozen or fresh sliced okra (or cauliflower or peas or broccoli)
2 large tomatoes, chopped, diced
1 stalk lemongrass, tough outer leaves discarded, minced (or 2 tablespoons powder)
1 cup tiny red or yellow lentils
1 pound extra-firm tofu, cut into inch cubes
1 large bunch spinach (or kale or mustard greens), leaves only, sliced
Salt to taste
¼ cup chopped cilantro (skip if you are not fond of it)

Heat the oil in a heavy, wide-bottom pan. Add the onion and ginger and sauté until translucent. Add the curry, cumin, and jalapeño and sauté until fragrant, just one more minute. Add all remaining ingredients, stir gently, and bring to a boil. Reduce to medium and cook covered for 30 minutes, or a little longer until the sauce is thick but runny. Serve hot over rice or other grains, or over diced or mashed white vegetables, with coconut cilantro chutney (page 40) and cucumber raita (recipe follows) on the side. Makes 8 servings.

Cucumber raita GF

2 cup plain low-fat yogurt (soy or coconut yogurt for non-dairy)
Salt and pepper to taste
1 tablespoon cumin
Red pepper flakes to taste (skip if you want an all-mild raita)
¼ cup mint leaves, packed, chopped
1 tablespoon sugar
1 large seedless cucumber, grated coarse

Mix all ingredients gently in a bowl. Serve chilled with curried dishes. Makes about 4 cups.

STEAMED VEGETABLE DUMPLINGS

These cook in no time, and steaming makes them a lean choice. Since everything is minced and cooks almost instantly, you might consider adding or substituting some lean ground turkey, lamb, beef, or bison, even fish, for some of the vegetables and proceed with the recipe just as instructed below. Do all your mincing and shredding in a food processor. You will love working with wonton and all other wrappers once you get the hang of it. Get yourself a bamboo steamer: It is very inexpensive—you will amply amortize it, and then some!

Cabbage leaves for lining the top layer of the steamer
3 tablespoons olive oil
4 scallions, sliced very thin
2 cups finely shredded Chinese or nappa cabbage, packed
1 cup grated carrots, packed
1 cup minced shiitake mushroom caps, packed
Salt and pepper to taste

Steamed Vegetable Dumplings

1 8-ounce package frozen round wonton wrappers, thawed

Put water to boil in the lower part of a steamer. Place the upper part of the steamer on the lower part. Line the bottom of the upper part with some cabbage leaves so you have no trouble removing the finished dumplings.

Mix all the filling ingredients thoroughly. Take one wonton wrapper and moisten all around the edges with water. Place one tablespoon filling in the center. Gather all the edges around the filling and pinch firmly, leaving the filling exposed at the top. Place the filled dumpling on the upper part of the steamer. Repeat with the remaining filling and wrappers, placing them close but not touching. Cover and cook about 15 minutes. Transfer to a platter or serve directly in the steamer layer in which they cooked. Serve hot with sesame dipping sauce (page 43). Makes 8 servings.

STEAMED VEGETABLES WITH FRESH TOMATO COULIS GF, P

This is hardly a recipe. I am just doing my rounds and making sure you have considered this delicious dinner option: Cut some vegetables to about the same size so they are ready at the same time and look pretty—broccoli, cauliflower, mushrooms, string beans, zucchini, red peppers, artichoke hearts, etc., and steam in the steamer part of a pot just a few minutes, until barely tender (carrots, sweet potatoes, kabocha, or butternut squash take a little longer to cook, so steam them separately). Dip in a bowl of your favorite quick sauce: tomato coulis (page 41), or red pepper coulis (page 41).

VEGETARIAN CHOPPED LIVER GF, P

There is nothing more perishable than chopped liver, and I am always dissatisfied with the way it comes out after freezing, so I ended up declaring a complete moratorium on it (much to my chagrin, as I adore it!) and instead decided to perfect a vegetarian version that would approximate my treat. So what do I think? You will be delighted! You can now enjoy it for a few days and share with your vegetarian friends. Also, unlike its unyielding liver cousin, it has no cholesterol and does freeze perfectly. Hint: When I say fry the onions until very dark, I really mean very dark, not burned dark! You wouldn't believe the depth of flavor this step will impart.

3 medium eggplants, peeled and halved lengthwise
⅓ cup olive oil
2 large onions, chopped
3 hard boiled eggs
1 cup toasted walnuts (preheated 325°F oven for 12–15 minutes)
Salt pepper to taste

Preheat oven to 475°F. Line a cookie sheet with foil, spray with vegetable spray. Arrange the eggplant in one layer on a cookie sheet, cut side down, and spray again with vegetable spray. Roast until dark, dry, and very soft, about 30 minutes. Meanwhile heat the oil in a large skillet, reduce the heat to medium, and fry the onions until very dark, stirring occasionally. Set the onions aside. Transfer the eggplant, eggs, walnuts, and seasonings to a food processor and grind until smooth. Transfer the mixture to a bowl and stir in the onions. Store refrigerated in a glass jar. Makes about 4 cups.

ZUCCHINI AND BRUSSELS SPROUTS IN TOMATO SAUCE GF, P

Mediterranean flavors at their best. I find brussels sprouts somewhat underrated and underused in our country. They are much more exciting than they sound, and much less innocent than they look; and their pungent bite provides a nice counterpoint to the mildness of the zucchini.

3 tablespoons olive oil
1 large onion, chopped
3 large garlic cloves
2 large zucchini, diced
1 pint brussels sprouts, the smaller the better, frozen OK, larger ones halved lengthwise
1 cup canned crushed tomatoes
½ cup raisins
1 teaspoon turmeric
2 bay leaves, or ½ teaspoon ground
1 cup water
Salt and pepper to taste
1 tablespoon sugar
2 tablespoons vinegar
¼ cup chopped parsley

Heat the oil in a large skillet. In a food processor, coarsely grind the onion and garlic and add to the skillet. Sauté until translucent. Add the zucchini, brussels sprouts, tomatoes, raisins, turmeric, bay leaves, water, salt, and pepper and bring to a boil. Reduce the flame to medium and cook covered for 10 minutes. Add the sugar, vinegar, and parsley and cook 5 more minutes. Served hot or at room temperature. Makes 8 servings.

Variation: Substitute one pound sliced fresh or frozen okra for the brussels sprouts and proceed exactly as above.

MINTED ZUCCHINI AND PEA PURÉE GF

Mint: another worthwhile partner for the mild and gentle zucchini, with its zippy flavor and exuberant fragrance. I love to serve this as a side dish as well as a spread.

¼ cup olive oil
1 large onion, quartered
4 large cloves garlic
1 small bunch parsley
8 thin zucchini (settle for 2–3 large ones), coarsely grated
2 cups frozen peas, the smaller the better
¼ cup mint leaves, packed, chopped
½ cup plain yogurt or dairy-free yogurt
Salt and pepper to taste
Good pinch nutmeg

Heat the oil in a large skillet. In a food processor, coarsely grind the onion, garlic, and parsley and add to the oil. Sauté until golden. Add the zucchini and sauté a few more minutes, until all liquids evaporate. Gently stir in the peas, mint, yogurt, salt, pepper, and nutmeg and cook just a few more minutes until just cooked through. Mash roughly with a fork or potato masher, leaving it chunky. Serve hot. Delicious at room temperature too. Makes 8 servings.

GRAINS AND PASTA

I have been experimenting with the whole gamut of grains for longer than I care to remember, and not only for my family, but for my guests and my customers too. This was never a hardship to me as I grew up eating an incredible array of whole grains, in every shape and form, in savory and sweet dishes. My extraordinarily resourceful mother never stopped to think of our modest circumstances except to turn them to our collective advantage: There was no room to err on any front (nutrition, fashion, health, school, you name it), so our limited tools just had to be the best tools and be used judiciously. Let me tell you, she ran a tight ship. There was nothing we didn't learn: cooking, sewing, knitting, beading, reading, singing. This must be what earned me the distinguished description of "culinary, literary, millinery" from my dear friend Jonathan. I might add we were often rather recalcitrant students, but somehow our psyche managed to absorb everything and cash in on it when the time came. This is why tinkering is simply second nature to me! If I am benefiting from these skills in adult life, I recognize with great pride that I come by them very honestly, so just in case I haven't said it enough: Thank you, Maman! For the chickpea soup, for the barley couscous, for the baked white beans and eggs, for the lentil salad, for the sweet potato pudding, for the toasted vermicelli with milk and clarified butter, for . . . well, the list is much too long, so let me just add, for giving me a glowing appreciation for glorious whole foods and for the genuine quality of life they engender! Which reminds me, many years ago I knitted a beautiful coat, and my husband joked I should put my label on it, to which my son answered, "Yes, put on your own label: Armommy!"

Any fear that your children won't eat *this*, let me assure you they will happily come around very soon, clamoring for more. Dismal school dining habits die hard, so just hang in there: The rewards are too great to overlook. Tell them eating whole foods is becoming hip too, since this always seems to be the mandate! Hip and here to stay. I recently saw a delightful Italian movie where the maid tearfully urges her beloved dejected mistress to take some nourishment: "Please come and eat. I have just made your favorite dish: sopa di farro." (Spelt soup.)

I have made all the following dishes in this chapter to serve 8. If you are serving a smaller group, rather than divide them (which of course you can do!), why not freeze them? All of them, across the board, keep refrigerated a few days, and freeze perfectly. Seal them, add a date and label, and refrigerate or freeze them. You will be happy to find them when you are pressed for time. Simply leave them to thaw a few hours ahead of the time you need to serve them, then reheat gently (say, 300°F) for 15 to 20 minutes, until heated through.

Just a few pointers for cooking grains and pasta. Just in case the instructions on the box don't include the following:

- Always, *always*, add a few drops of oil and a little salt to your pasta and rice cooking water.
- Wait until the water boils before throwing in your pasta. And don't throw the pasta in one big clump; rather, throw it in gently and gradually, *en pluie* (rain-like), so they remain nice and separated.

- Rinse quinoa thoroughly in a large fine-mesh strainer under plenty of cold running water, until the water runs clear, to get it rid of its soapy saponin. (Sprayed on to keep insects away: What do you know, they love quinoa, as do we!)

- Soak wild rice in water for an hour or so, then strain and rinse it before you proceed to cook it. The brief soaking time encourages the opening of the grains, ensuring full texture and flavor.

- Anytime you are not sure how much cooking water is enough: Err on the side of more for pasta (so it doesn't come to a sticky mess: it will be too late to add more), and err on the side of less for rice (so it doesn't get soggy: you can add more).

ARBORIO RISOTTO WITH SPINACH AND ASPARAGUS GF

Risotto is our high-maintenance kitchen friend, demanding constant attention as the liquids must be added in stages. The good news, though, is it is very versatile and can easily make a complete meal; besides, the cooking doesn't take too long. I am including here several interesting combinations, so feel free to mix and match!

If you are a whole-grain nut, like me, you will have no trouble finding brown arborio rice: It will take a little longer and won't look as pristine as its white cousin, but will be every bit as delicious.

Vegetable mixture:
1 tablespoon olive oil
6 cups baby spinach
1 dozen thin asparagus, tough ends discarded, cut into inch sections
1 cup frozen or fresh green peas
¼ cup olive oil
1 large onion, chopped
4 medium shallots, chopped
2 cups arborio rice
Good pinch saffron
2 cups (inexpensive) champagne, dry white wine or sake
4 cups hot water
Salt and freshly ground pepper to taste
¼ cup chopped parsley

Heat the oil in a wide heavy skillet. Add the spinach, asparagus, and peas and sauté just a minute or two until the leaves are wilted. Reserve.

In the same skillet, heat the oil and add the onion and shallot. Sauté until translucent. Add the arborio and sauté 2 more minutes. Reduce the temperature to medium, add the saffron and wine, and stir until most of the liquid is absorbed. Add the hot water, one cup at a time, adding the next cup only when the first has been absorbed. Total rice cooking time will be about 20 minutes. When the rice is tender, stir in the reserved vegetable mixture, salt, pepper, and parsley and heat through, 2 to 3 more minutes. The mixture will be creamy. Serve hot. Makes 8 servings.

Variations

- Use Swiss chard, kale, mustard greens, watercress, or arugala instead of the spinach. Remove all tough stems, reserving them for another use, and slice the leaves thin.
- Throw in frozen artichoke hearts or bottoms, diced.
- Sauté 1½ pounds mushrooms, any kind you can afford, in any combination you like, and stir into the dish, in addition or instead of the leaves.
- Stir in your favorite herbs—basil, rosemary, thyme, sage—one to two at a time, and get different flavors each time.
- Stir in some freshly grated Parmesan at the end of cooking.
- Throw in some diced natural (no nitrites) smoked turkey or diced cooked chicken.
- Throw in some flaked mock crab or diced mock shrimp.
- Throw in a handful toasted chopped nuts.
- Stir in some crumbled seaweed (nori, hijiki, wakame, arame, kombu, etc.) and/or some sprouts (soy, alfalfa, radish, mung, lentil, etc.).
- Make the dish with another grain: wild rice, brown rice, quinoa, millet, buckwheat, etc. It won't be called risotto, but so what, it will be delicious too and will allow you to play and get different and interesting results each time! Cook the grain as you usually do, using the liquid all at once (as opposed to one cup at a time as you would for arborio), water and wine, or all water, then combine it with your sautéed veggies and other additions, just as suggested in this recipe's variations.
- If you would rather have pasta, proceed just as above, but use your favorite whole-grain pasta instead of rice.

Arborio Risotto with
Spinach and Asparagus

BARLEY, LENTIL, AND KALE PILAF GFA

Brown rice will do just as well in this dish. The tiny lentils cook in no time and disperse to form a thick sauce. Whole foods are no hardship whatsoever when prepared in such interesting ways. Look for black barley in your health food stores, the new grain kid on the block: So elegant!

⅓ cup olive oil
1 large onion, quartered
1 2-inch ginger, peeled
1 stalk lemongrass, though layers removed, or 1 tablespoon ground
1 tablespoon curry, or more to taste
1 teaspoon ground cumin
1 jalapeño pepper, minced (if you don't like it too hot, remove the seeds first)
6 cups water
1 cup pearl barley or brown rice
1 cup tiny red or yellow lentils
Salt to taste
1 can coconut milk
1 large bunch kale, stems and leaves, chopped coarsely
3 tablespoons chopped cilantro

Heat the oil in a heavy, wide-bottom pan. In a food processor, coarsely chop onion, ginger and lemongrass. Add the mixture to the hot oil and sauté until translucent. Add curry, cumin, and jalapeño and sauté until fragrant, just one more minute. Add all remaining ingredients and bring to a boil. Reduce the heat to medium and cook covered for 45 minutes or a little longer until the grain is tender. Serve hot. Makes 8 servings.

Barley, Lentil, and Kale Pilaf

Millet Fritters

MILLET FRITTERS GF

Millet: Not just birdfeed. I sneak it everywhere! It is so full of flavor that it can easily bear being combined with other ingredients for bulk and added crunch and nutrition. Of course you can substitute any other grain, or even beans (3 cups total cooked), and substitute the seasonings of your choice if you want to jazz it up: oregano, cumin, curry, cilantro, scallions, etc. As long as you keep the suggested grain-veggies proportions in mind, everything will work.

3 cups water
1 cup millet
1 large onion
1 large carrot
2 ribs celery
½ cup flour (any flour)
½ cup to 1 cup chopped nuts or seeds (poppy, sesame, chia, hemp, etc.), optional
1 egg (only if you are restricted: use ¼ cup flax mixture, page 224)
1 teaspoon dried thyme
Good pinch cayenne
Good pinch nutmeg
Salt and pepper to taste
1 cup vegetable oil

Bring water to a boil. Reduce the flame to medium, add the millet, and cook covered, about 20 minutes, or a little longer, until tender.

Meanwhile, heat the oil in a large skillet, then keep the temperature at medium hot, not smoking hot. Transfer the cooked millet to a mixing bowl. In a food processor, grate the onion, carrot, and celery and add to the bowl with all remaining ingredients. Mix thoroughly by hand. Form patties with the mixture and throw in the hot oil. Fry 2 minutes on each side, or until just golden. Drain on paper towels and serve hot, alone, or with your choice of a sauce (see The Pantry, page 19). Makes 8 servings.

Note: Millet loaf GF

If you would rather not fry, mix the cooked grain with all remaining ingredients, adding ⅓ cup olive oil to the mix. Pour the mixture into a 6-cup loaf and bake in a preheated 350°F for about 1 hour, or until the top is golden and barely set. Slice and serve hot or at room temperature with your choice of a sauce (see The Pantry, page 19). Makes 8 to 10 servings.

KASHA WITH MUSHROOMS AND ONIONS GF

Kasha, known to much of the world as buckwheat, is a staple in many Eastern European countries. Toasting it gives it a delicious nutty taste, and rolling it in beaten egg keeps every kernel separated and plump. Do not skip either of these very quick steps, or you will get mush.

Experiment with other grains, adjusting the amount of liquid to the grain you are using: quinoa, millet, lentils, rice, etc. In this case, skip the step where you toast the grain and roll it in egg: Only buckwheat requires it (just to be clear: other grains: no toasting, no coating in egg).

2 tablespoons olive oil
1 pound domestic mushrooms, sliced
3 tablespoons olive oil
1 large onion, chopped
2 cups kasha (buckwheat groats), whole granulation
1 egg, or two egg whites
5 cups boiling water
Salt and pepper to taste

Heat 2 tablespoons olive oil in a pot and sauté the mushrooms until all the liquid evaporates. Reserve. Heat 3 tablespoons olive oil and cook the onions over medium heat until very dark, about 20 minutes. Reserve. Place the kasha in the pot over medium heat and toast until fragrant and lightly colored, about 2 minutes. Add the egg and stir quickly until the grains are uniformly coated, about 1 minute more. Add the boiling water and salt and pepper, then reduce the heat to medium and cook covered for about 15 minutes, until the grain is tender. Add the reserved mushrooms and onions and stir. Cook for 2 to 3 more minutes, until heated through. Serve hot. Makes 8 servings.

Variation: Quinoa or rice with chestnuts GF

Omit the mushrooms and add about 10 ounces of vacuum-packed chestnuts, crumbled, in the last few minutes of cooking. Optional: throw in about ½ cup dried cranberries together with the chestnuts, and stir in ½ cup toasted nuts just before serving.

COUSCOUS GFA

Couscous is wonderful and fun, the rock star of Moroccan cuisine. I am including two kinds, with their variations: Boy, you will be happy!

Couscous is native to Morocco, and the word refers to both the grain and the traditional dish made with the grain. It is semolina, or durum (the heart of the wheat kernel), ground to the consistency of coarse cornmeal and mixed with flour and just enough water to make small grains, about the size of millet grains. These plump grains are then dried, preferably in the hot sun. Prepared couscous is very easy to find in bulk at most health food and grocery stores. Let me reassure you, you won't need to do any of this: Beautiful, plump, and no-cooking, ready-to-use couscous is available everywhere.

Sometimes grain sold as couscous is actually a couscous-shaped (usually larger) pasta, affectionately called Israeli couscous, which is not suitable in traditional couscous recipes.

Although the combinations of vegetables and meats vary greatly, the structure of the dish called couscous always remains the same.

Low-gluten and gluten-free couscous

I make couscous with barley couscous for low gluten: Look for it in Indian grocery stores or online. I don't recommend the whole-wheat couscous, as it has an objectionable somewhat-bitter aftertaste. Gluten-free: Try the wonderful brown rice couscous now on the market. You will also find it online. I just love to have couscous on hand, as it needs no cooking and is ready at the drop of a hat (instructions below) to throw in salads or vegetable burgers, or even dessert, sprinkled with a little Sucanat and cinnamon and mixed with a little oil or ghee, with a few golden raisins added.

VEGETABLE COUSCOUS GFA

More plebeian and down-to-earth than the luxurious dried-fruit variety, but every bit as delicious.

2 large onions, cut in thin wedges
3 cups canned crushed tomatoes
⅓ cup olive oil
1 tablespoon turmeric
Salt and pepper to taste
1 small white cabbage, cut in wedges then in slivers
5 thin carrots, peeled and cut in inch dices
4 medium turnips, peeled and cut in inch cubes
2 cups frozen lima or edamame beans
4 thin zucchini, unpeeled and cut in inch cubes
1 small bunch cilantro, tough stems removed, minced
1 small bunch flat-leaf parsley, minced
Couscous grain:
3 cups couscous
3 cups boiling water
¼ cup vegetable oil
Salt and pepper to taste

Make the vegetable mixture. Place the onions, tomatoes, oil, turmeric, salt and pepper, cabbage, carrots, and turnips in a wide, heavy pot with 4 cups water and bring to a boil. Reduce the flame to medium and cook covered for 1 hour. Add the lima beans, zucchini, parsley, and cilantro and cook another 10 minutes.

While the dish is cooking, prepare couscous grain: Place the grain in a stainless steel bowl with the oil, salt and pepper, and water and mix thoroughly. Immediately cover very tightly with 2 layers of foil. Let the mixture rest 15 minutes, then fluff it with 2 forks until the grains are separated.

To serve: pour couscous grain in the bottom of a platter. Pour some of the cooking broth evenly on the grain, only as much as the grain will absorb. Don't allow a mushy or soupy look. Arrange the vegetables over the grain. Pass any remaining broth in a gravy boat. Serve with harissa on the side (page 34). Makes 8 ample servings.

Meat and poultry variations

- **If you would like to include chicken.** Add chicken legs, thighs, and half breasts (about 1 dozen pieces total) at the beginning. Proceed as in the basic recipe.
- **If you would like to include beef or bison or lamb chunks** (about 3½ pounds): Cook the meat in a wide-bottom pot in 6 cups water for 2 hours. Add the onions, tomatoes, etc., and proceed as in the basic recipe.

Passover couscous variation P

Simply substitute quinoa for the other suggested grains and proceed as above for the couscous dish you have selected (no lima beans or edamame).

VEGETABLE AND DRIED-FRUIT COUSCOUS GFA

Naturally sweet and spicy, and so festive!

⅓ cup olive oil
2 large onions, peeled and quartered
2 good pinches saffron threads
1 teaspoon turmeric
2 sticks cinnamon
1 teaspoon black pepper
Salt to taste
2 pounds thin carrots, or butternut squash (unpeeled) cut into 2-inch chunks
3 cups dried fruit: raisins, apricots, prunes, in any combination you like (if you would rather choose just one kind, let it be the apricots)
1 teaspoon ground cinnamon
1 teaspoon ground ginger
½ teaspoon ground cloves
2 tablespoons orange flower water
Couscous grain:

Dried Fruit
Couscous
with Lamb

3 cups couscous
3 cups boiling water
¼ cup vegetable oil
Salt and pepper to taste

1 cup toasted whole or slivered blanched almonds

Heat the oil in a heavy pot. Coarsely grind the onions in a food processor and add to the hot oil. Reduce the flame to medium and fry until dark, stirring occasionally. This step will take about 20 minutes. Add the saffron, turmeric, cinnamon sticks, pepper, salt, carrots, and 2 cups water. Bring to a boil. Reduce to medium and cook covered for 30 minutes. Add all remaining ingredients and cook 15 more minutes.

While the dish is cooking, prepare couscous grain: Place the grain in a stainless steel bowl—with the oil, salt and pepper, and water—and mix thoroughly. Immediately cover very tightly with 2 layers of foil. Let the mixture rest 15 minutes, then fluff it with 2 forks until the grains are separated.

To serve: Pour the couscous grain in the bottom of a platter. Pour some of the cooking broth evenly on the grain, only as much as the grain will absorb. Don't allow a mushy or soupy look. Arrange vegetables and fruit over the grain. Sprinkle the whole dish with the toasted almonds. Pass any remaining broth in a gravy boat. Serve with harissa on the side (page 34). Makes 8 ample servings.

Meat and poultry variations

- **If you would like to include chicken:** Add chicken legs, thighs, and half breasts (about 1 dozen pieces total) at the same time you add the saffron, turmeric, cinnamon sticks, pepper, salt, and carrots and bring the water to 3 cups. Cook covered for 1 hour. Add all remaining ingredients (dried fruit and spices) and cook 15 more minutes.
- **If you would like to include beef, bison, or lamb** (about 3½ pounds): Cook the meat in a separate pot in 6 cups water for 2 hours. Add the meat and its cooking liquids at the same time you add the saffron, turmeric, cinnamon sticks, pepper, salt, and carrots. Make sure you have enough liquids, add a little water if necessary to a total of about 3 cups. Cook covered for 1 hour. Add all remaining ingredients (dried fruit and spices) and cook 15 more minutes.

PASTA WITH BROCCOLI AND SALMON GFA

Nobody will complain about vegetables being boring, as broccoli will disappear and leave in its wake only its bright color and hearty flavor. If you are making this dish for children, or even if you are serving adults and would rather not get too racy, skip the wine and vodka and bring the milk to 3 cups.

1 pound farfalle (bow ties), or any other flat pasta, whole-grain and gluten-free welcome

1 bunch broccoli, stems and florets, cut in large chunks

⅓ cup extra-virgin olive oil

1 large onion, chopped

3 tablespoons flour, any flour

2 cups milk or dairy-free milk, low-fat OK

1 cup dry white wine

¼ cup vodka

3 pounds salmon, cut in inch cubes

1 tablespoon dry tarragon

Good pinch red pepper flakes

Good pinch nutmeg

Salt and freshly cracked pepper to taste

Let the water boil in a pasta pot equipped with a strainer. Add the pasta and boil according to the manufacturer's instructions. Transfer the pasta to a platter and return the strainer to the pot. Add some hot water to the pasta pot if you see you don't have enough. Add the broccoli and cook about 3 minutes. Take out of the pot and grind in the food processor. Reserve.

Heat the oil in a large skillet. Add the onion and sauté until translucent. Reduce the heat to medium. Add the flour and cook, whisking, just 1 to 2 minutes. Very slowly add the milk, the wine, and vodka, whisking constantly. The mixture will thicken. Stir in the salmon, tarragon, red pepper flakes, nutmeg, salt, and pepper and cook covered for 5 minutes. Toss with the pasta and reserved ground broccoli and heat through. Serve hot. Makes 8 ample servings.

PENNE WITH TOMATO SAUCE GFA

There's nothing more versatile than homemade tomato sauce and whatever you might like to throw in. It is guaranteed to leave all (repeat: all) its store-bought counterparts in the dust. So go for it and try all my suggestions! In tomato-based sauces, it's OK to use tubular hollow-shaped pasta and let the sauce go into the holes, which wouldn't do for rich cream-based sauces (for these we need to use flat pasta).

1 pound penne, or other tubular pasta, gluten-free OK
½ cup olive oil
1 large onion, quartered
6 large cloves garlic
2 ribs celery, peeled and cut in big chunks
1 bunch flat parsley
1 large carrot, grated
4 cups canned crushed tomatoes
Good pinch red pepper flakes
2 tablespoons oregano
Salt to taste
Freshly ground pepper to taste

Bring water to boil with a little salt and oil in a large pot, preferably equipped with a strainer insert. Add the pasta and cook accordingly to manufacturer's instructions. Take out the pasta, letting it drain, and reserve ½ cup of the cooking liquid. Heat the oil in a large skillet. Coarsely grind the onion and garlic in a food processor and add to the oil. Sauté until translucent. Coarsely grind the celery and parsley and add to the skillet, and sauté 1 to 2 minutes longer. Add all the remaining sauce ingredients and bring to a boil. Reduce the heat to medium, cover, and cook 30 minutes.

Transfer the pasta to a platter. Toss with the sauce, the reserved cooking liquid and freshly ground pepper. Serve hot.

Variations: Short and sweet selection please!

- Sauté some sliced mushrooms with the onion, garlic, etc.
- Sauté some spinach or Swiss chard leaves or grated zucchini with the onion, garlic, etc.
- Add some pitted, oil-cured olives (watch the added salt).
- Add some capers (watch the added salt).
- Add some dry white wine.
- Add some sliced basil leaves.
- Add some sun-dried tomatoes (watch the added salt).
- Roast 2 to 3 garlic heads and mash the pulp into the sauce.
- Add some sliced roasted red peppers, good-brand bottled OK.
- Throw in some rinsed canned anchovies or dashi powder, but don't add any salt to the sauce.
- Go Tex-Mex and throw in some chopped cilantro, jalapeño, cumin, etc.
- Throw in some grated Parmesan (watch the added salt).

COLD SESAME NOODLES GF

Lapsang Souchong is a Chinese tea with an intriguing pungent, smoky, "tarry" taste. As a drink, you will either love it or hate it, but you will always love it in a dressing or marinade. Settle for Earl Grey if you don't have it on hand.

Children love these noodles: I used to make oodles of them in my catering years. Here is a good place to sneak in a perfectly healthy pasta such as soba or rice noodles: Trust me, the fun sauce will beat any resistance out of the diehard white-pasta eaters out there.

1 pound buckwheat or rice noodles (plain noodles only if you must), cooked according to manufacturer's instructions, and drained

1 cup Thai sauce (page 38), or a little more if needed to coat the noodles

4 scallions, sliced very thin

Toss the noodles with the sauce and the scallions just before serving. Serve chilled or at room temperature.

Variations: Perfect for leftovers

Throw in some thinly sliced cooked or grilled beef, or some diced cooked chicken or natural (no nitrites) smoked turkey and some soybean sprouts or sliced nappa cabbage.

Cold Sesame Noodles

LASAGNA WITH ROASTED VEGETABLES GFA

Lasagna can be made with a variety of fillings (vegetables, tomato sauce, spinach, etc.), all good. Try this, my favorite. Gluten-free: You should have no trouble finding GF lasagna noodles at your health food store.

2 red peppers, diced small
2 large red onions, diced small
3 large portobello mushrooms, or 8 medium, diced small
1 large eggplant, peeled and diced small
2 large zucchini, diced small
1 pound lasagna noodles, boiled until just tender, and drained

Sauce:

⅓ cup olive oil
1 large onion
8 cloves garlic
½ cup flour, any flour
4 cups milk, low-fat OK
1½ cups *freshly* (yes, it makes the whole difference!) grated Parmesan or other strong cheese (such as provolone or kashkaval), plus ½ cup more for sprinkling on the top
1 cup basil leaves, packed, minced
Salt and pepper to taste
Good pinch nutmeg

Preheat oven to 450°F. Line a cookie sheet with foil or parchment paper. Spray with vegetable spray. Place all vegetables on the sheet in one layer (do not pile, use 2-sheet pans). Spray again. Roast for 20 minutes, or a little longer, until dark and roasted. Reduce the temperature to 375°F.

Meanwhile, make the sauce: Heat the oil in a skillet. In a food processor, coarsely grind the onion and garlic and add to the skillet. Sauté until translucent. Add the flour and cook just a few seconds until golden. Add the milk in a slow stream, whisking. Stir in all remaining sauce ingredients.

Spread a thin layer of the sauce in the bottom of an 11-by-14-inch pan. Top with a layer of lasagna noodles, overlapping them slightly. Top with a third of the vegetable mixture. Repeat: sauce, noodles, vegetables, sauce, noodles, vegetables. Sprinkle the top with the reserved Parmesan.

Bake covered for 30 minutes. Uncover and bake another 20 minutes. Do not over-bake, or it will dry. Serve hot.

Variations:

- **For a dairy-free lasagna: GFA** Substitute a dairy-free milk, low-fat OK for the milk, and skip the cheese. Leave the ingredients as is, or throw in some diced cooked fish, or diced cooked chicken if you have any on hand, but there's no need to add another step and cook fish or chicken just for this—it will taste wonderful all by itself.

- **For pasta with roasted vegetables: GFA** If you are in a lazy mood and would rather do away with all the layering and baking, ignore the whole sauce part. Dice and roast the vegetables and toss them with pasta and a good extra-virgin olive oil, salt, and freshly ground pepper to taste.

YERUSHALMI KUGEL GFA

A great Jewish favorite, and a real showcase in Israeli synagogues at Kiddush time: I have seen two burly men flip an enormous pot of it onto a gigantic counter, then slice it across its whole diameter in two or three places with a knife about three feet long (promise!), then cut through the whole stack of disks from top to bottom, in hundreds of cubes. It reminded me of Gulliver's travels. I remember thinking, what a pity it's Shabbos and we can't take pictures of this phenomenon! Then after I watched all the hard work, and inhaled the wonderful whiffs that filled the room, I watched it disappear in minutes, barely getting the time to get a piece of the wonderful stuff for myself.

The trademark of Yerushalmi kugel is the caramelized sugar-oil mixture (high mainte- nance: first hurdle), then combining that mixture with the other ingredients (a real nuisance, as the hot sugar-oil mixture seizes and hardens, and resists combining with the rest of the ingredients: second hurdle). I tried with caramelizing the sugar in water, which is the usual way of making caramel and then combining the caramel with the remaining ingredients, and found it much easier to make the dish this way, and every bit as delicious.

1 pound thin noodles, any noodles
⅔ cup vegetable oil
Salt to taste
1 teaspoon ground pepper, or a little more to taste
1 tablespoon cinnamon
1 tablespoon vanilla extract
4 eggs
1 cup sugar or Sucanat
⅓ cup water

Preheat oven to 350°F. Boil the noodles until just barely tender. If you started with long noodles, cut through the whole pile with scissors until you get smaller pieces. Place in a mixing bowl, and mix in the oil, pepper, cinnamon, vanilla, and eggs. Combine thoroughly. Meanwhile, heat the sugar and water in a small saucepan. Reduce the flame to medium low and cook about 5 minutes, until the mixture turns a nice amber color (watch the cooking, don't let the mixture burn). Immediately add to the noodle mixture and stir to combine. Pour the mixture into a greased 9-by-13-inch pan or a greased tube pan. Bake about 1 hour, or a little longer, until the top looks set. Delicious warm or at room temperature.

LINGUINI WITH FENNEL TUNA SAUCE GFA

If it is true that opposites attract, no dish would bear this out better than this one. Besides, here is a whole new and fun way to eat tuna! Do not be alarmed by the fact that I don't drain it—that's practically all the oil contained in the dish, and that's where all the good flavor is. No added salt, please, as the tuna has amply enough to season the whole dish.

1 pound linguini or other non-tubular pasta, gluten-free OK
3 tablespoons olive oil
1 large head fennel, greens and all, leaves and bulb separated
12 large cloves garlic
1 cup dry white wine
Juice and grated zest of 1 lemon
2 7-ounce cans solid white tuna, oil and all, flaked
Freshly cracked pepper to taste

Boil the pasta in a large pot of boiling water with a little salt and oil added. Drain and reserve ½ cup of the cooking liquid. Set aside.

Heat the oil in a large skillet. In a food processor, coarsely grind the garlic and the fennel leaves and add to the skillet. Sauté 2 to 3 minutes, until wilted and fragrant. Cut the fennel bulb in quarters and cut out and discard the cores. Slice the bulb very thin in a food processor and add to the skillet. Sauté 2 to 3 more minutes. Reduce the flame to medium, add the wine, juice, and zest and cook 5 more minutes. Add the tuna and its oil, the pasta and reserved liquid, and freshly ground pepper and toss thoroughly. Serve hot, room temperature OK.

APPLE NOODLE KUGEL GFA

Kugel is a huge favorite in Jewish cooking. Unfortunately, it often comes too rich and too eggy. I have tinkered with the ingredients, and ended up with a lean, easy eggless and delicious kugel. The noodles used here can be gluten-free, just cut them small after boiling.

1½ cups plain yogurt (dairy-free: soy or coconut plain yogurt are perfect)
1 pound very thin short noodles, boiled until barely tender and thoroughly drained (rice noodles OK too)
4 Granny Smith (green) apples, unpeeled, grated
Salt and pepper to taste
½ cup raisins or currants, a little more if you like it sweeter
1/2 cup maple syrup
½ cup vegetable oil
1 tablespoon cinnamon
1 tablespoon grated lemon zest

Preheat the oven to 350°F. Combine all the ingredients thoroughly in a bowl, making sure not to extract moisture from the apples as you go. Pour the batter into a greased 9-by-13-inch baking pan, or a little larger, and bake for about 1 hour. Serve hot.

Note: For a better presentation and no cutting mess, pour the batter into muffin molds and bake about 40 minutes.

PAD THAI GF

The national dish in Thailand, available at every street corner in every imaginable variation, pad Thai is a delightful stir-fried rice noodle dish including, in any combination, fish or chicken, eggs, vegetables, tofu, peanuts, and the native seasonings—ginger, lemongrass, curry, and coconut: You just can't miss! It's a complete meal, and it's very quick cooking, so don't be daunted by the long list of ingredients. Perfect for buffets too, just as long as you toss in the peanuts just before serving so they don't lose their crunch.

1 pound rice noodles
¼ cup olive oil
1 large onion, quartered
6 large cloves garlic
1 2-inch piece ginger
Choose one of the following proteins: 1 pound mock shrimp sliced thick, 4 chicken cutlets cut in thin strips, 1 pound extra firm tofu, or seitan cut in small cubes
3 cups shredded nappa cabbage
3 cups sliced shiitake mushroom caps
1 tablespoon curry, or more to taste
2 tablespoons minced lemongrass, or 1 tablespoon powder
½ cup coconut milk
3 eggs, beaten in a bowl
⅓ cup sliced scallions
2 tablespoons minced cilantro leaves
2 cups soybean sprouts
2–3 tablespoons bottled hot sauce
Salt to taste
½ cup chopped roasted peanuts

Soak the noodles in hot water just a few minutes and drain. With a scissor, cut through the noodles until fairly small.

Heat the oil in a wide-bottom pot. In a food processor, coarsely grind the onion, garlic, and ginger and add to the pot. Sauté until translucent. Add the protein ingredient of your choice and sauté 2 to 3 more minutes. Add the cabbage and shiitake and sauté 2 to 3 more minutes. Add the curry and lemongrass and sauté just one more minute. Reduce the flame to medium. Add the coconut milk and the noodles and stir. Make a well in the center and pour in the eggs. Stir briskly until the egg has firmed up, just one more minute. Stir in the scallions, cilantro, sprouts, hot sauce, salt, and peanuts and heat through. Serve hot.

STIR-FRIED TOFU, VEGETABLES, AND SEAWEED ON SOBA NOODLES GF

After you taste a good homemade stir-fry, you will never go back to the institutional restaurant variety that uses canned vegetables and globs of bottled stir-fry sauce. Go ahead and substitute whatever nice vegetables you might find: snow peas, asparagus segments, sliced Swiss chard leaves—nothing canned whatsoever please. There's plenty of room to try a different combination each time. You can also add strips of chicken or sliced mock shrimp or substitute either for the tofu or seaweed, but I do love the briny flavor of the seaweed in this dish.

¼ cup each toasted sesame oil and ¼ cup olive oil, mixed
1 pound extra firm tofu, cut in cubes
1 pound shiitake, caps only, cut in strips
1 bunch scallions, sliced thin
1 red pepper, cut in thin strips
2 zucchini, soft center discarded, cut in strips
½ small nappa cabbage, sliced thin
¼ cup hijiki (or other seaweed: wakame, arame, etc.), soaked in 1 cup water
Sauce:
4 large garlic cloves, minced
1 2-inch ginger, peeled and minced
½ cup mirin or sake
Bottled hot sauce to taste, optional
¼ cup soy sauce or more to taste
2 tablespoons arrowroot or kuzu, dissolved in ½ cup cold water
1 pound soba noodles, boiled till just tender and drained

Heat a little of the oil mixture in a large wok or skillet and quickly sauté the tofu cubes, in one layer. Remove with a flat spatula and reserve. Add more oil mixture and quickly sauté the vegetables, in batches if necessary, until crisp tender. Do not overcook, or the vegetables will get limp. Remove and reserve.

Heat the rest of the oil mixture and sauté the garlic and ginger. Add the sherry, the soy sauce, and the hot sauce if using and heat one more minute. Reduce the heat to low and add the starch mixture. Cook one more minute until thickened.

Return everything to the skillet and heat through, stirring to combine, and coat thoroughly. Serve hot.

SOBA NOODLES WITH ROASTED ROOTS GF

Roasting the roots intensifies their flavor and is practically all you have to do to make this delicious dish. The cinnamon is a great match for the root flavors.

1 large turnip
1 large carrot
1 large red onion
1 medium celery root
1 large wedge kabocha squash, unpeeled
12 cloves garlic
½ cup extra-virgin olive oil
2 tablespoons cinnamon
Salt and ground pepper to taste
1 pound soba noodles

Preheat the oven to 425°F. Line a cookie sheet with foil. Dice all the vegetables about ½ inch and combine them with all but last ingredient. Place the mixture in one layer on the cookie sheet (use 2 if necessary) and roast about 20 minutes, or a little longer, until dark and soft. Boil the noodles in a large pot of boiling water with a little added oil and salt. Drain and reserve ½ cup cooking liquid. Toss the pasta and reserved cooking liquid with the roasted vegetable mixture, along with any juice that may have accumulated. Serve hot or at room temperature. Makes 8 servings.

Root vegetables

Would you like to eat them by themselves as well? Go right ahead and snack on them; they are fantastic. Or serve them with roast turkey or chicken. I trust my book amply bears this out: I am crazy about all roots, and why not? Lean, delicious, versatile, incredibly nutritious—how can you miss? I run home with all roots—no matter how misshapen and grimy and odd-looking—I find at the market, the way people bring home cast-off, disheveled animals and by dint of love and attention groom them into perfectly domesticated pets. Roots always make me think of the universal line in Psalm 118:23: "*Even maasu habonim haita lerosh pina,*" which translates as "The stone that the builders discarded has become the cornerstone." Yes, even humble roots are involved in thrilling rags-to-riches stories!

Soba Noodles with Roasted Roots

POLENTA VEGETABLE STRATA GF

A nice take on lasagna, with layered polenta instead of lasagna noodles. Give the food processor your thin slicing, and mincing, to do—everything! Your vegetables will be so thin and even-sized there will be no need to sauté anything before baking. Should you decide to make lasagna, layer your boiled noodles just as you would layer your polenta, and proceed with the recipe.

Play with the seasonings: If you would like to make this a meat dish, like moussaka, go ahead and throw in 1½ pounds ground turkey or lamb, and skip the cheese—it will all cook during baking time. Italian: No cumin and no cilantro, but more oregano and fresh sliced basil.

9 cups water
A few drops olive oil
Salt to taste
3 cups coarse cornmeal
2 medium eggplants, peeled and sliced very thin (use the thinnest slicing disk of the food processor)
2 large zucchini, no peeling necessary, sliced very thin (use the thinnest slicing disk of the food processor)
2 medium purple onions, sliced very thin (use the thinnest slicing disk of the food processor)
⅓ cup olive oil
5 cups canned crushed tomatoes
4 cloves garlic, minced
½ cup minced flat parsley
½ cup minced cilantro
1 tablespoon ground cumin
2 tablespoons dried oregano
½ teaspoon dried pepper flakes, or more to taste
Salt and pepper to taste

Optional: 1 to 2 cups freshly grated Parmesan (in this case, watch the salt—you might not need any)

Boil water, oil, and salt in a large pot. Add the cornmeal and stir until thick. This should take about ten minutes. Pour into a greased cookie sheet, in a layer no more than half an inch thick. You might fill one and a half cookie sheets. Let the polenta cool.

Preheat oven to 425°F.

While the polenta is cooling, thoroughly combine all vegetable ingredients in a bowl. Grease an 11-by-14-inch lasagna pan. Make one layer polenta, making sure you leave no blank spaces. Add half the vegetable mixture. Repeat: one layer polenta, one layer vegetable mixture. Bake the casserole for about 45 minutes, or until the dish looks bubbly and hot and the vegetables look tender. Let cool slightly before cutting into squares. Makes a dozen servings.

PASTA WITH MOCK CRAB, ARTICHOKES, AND OLIVES GF

Several of my favorite summer flavors are in! The only cooking that goes on in this dish is boiling water to soak the pasta. Although it is delicious with rice noodles, if you are a diehard wheat pasta lover, simply substitute your favorite pasta for the rice noodles and proceed with the recipe.

1 pound frozen mock crab chunks, thawed and flaked

4 roasted red peppers, bottled OK, sliced thin

¼ cup oil-cured black olives or Niçoise olives, preferably pitted

2 cups sun-dried tomatoes, briefly soaked in warm water and squeezed dry, sliced thin

1 10-ounce box frozen artichoke hearts, thawed

½ cup basil leaves, packed, sliced thin

1 pound rice noodles, soaked in hot water for 5 minutes and drained, ½ cup liquid reserved

⅔ cup very good olive oil

Salt and pepper to taste

4 garlic cloves, minced

Place all salad ingredients in a shallow bowl or platter and toss thoroughly. Serve at room temperature. Makes 8 servings.

Pasta with Mock Crab, Artichokes, and Olives

BREAKFAST AND BRUNCH DISHES

Too often breakfast consists of lining up at the cart on our way to work or in your office lobby and walking away with a worthless package: A terrible cup of coffee and a fatty, sugary doughnut or a rubbery bagel slathered with butter or cream cheese. I have made my case in full about these food-like substances, to borrow an expression from Michael Pollan, in my chapter on my own diet tools (page 1). Please set aside a moment to read it: You will never again take a single bite out of those mountainous cake-mix muffins or mix instant oatmeal with hot water.

MUFFINS AND QUICKBREADS GF

Because my muffin and quickbread preparations are so versatile, and double perfectly as cakes, I have located the muffin recipes with the cake recipes, page 255. You will be pleased to see that you can whip up a cake as quickly as you can whip up a batch of muffins, with a great variety of the best ingredients, by hand and in no time.

BASIC SAVORY CRÊPE BATTER GF

How will we ever know how wonderful crêpes can be if all we've been doing so far is open a box—and the worst part is, we haven't saved more than a minute or two on the whole thing—and missed out on a great treat, so was it worth it? Of course you know the answer, so I won't rub it in.

My children grew up on crêpes—we just had to have them at least once a week. They are so much fun no one will ever know they are actually eating healthy food. There is only a small ratio principle to keep in mind for perfect, ethereal paper-thin crêpes: 4 eggs or egg substitute (see below), 2 cups flour, 2½ cups liquid. That's the whole thing. Play with this, and get different and exciting results each time.

Crêpes are a wonderful choice when you have company. (Only your kids? That's company, and of the best kind!) Make them while you are talking to your family or guests, and have a good time. You will be amazed at the wonderful selection of flours you will find at health food stores. And the fillings are a great way to recycle leftover chicken or vegetables.

My granddaughter Musia enjoying her crêpes

The crêpe mixture can be made even a couple days in advance. Don't worry if it settles and starts looking somewhat unappealing—just give it a few more turns in the blender before using and it will look and taste like new. If the mixture thickens while it sits, thin it with a little liquid. Passover: If you do find quinoa flour, by all means use it; otherwise, try grinding it as fine as possible in a food processor.

4 eggs (8 egg whites if you can't afford the cholesterol in egg yolks; only if you are restricted: use 1 cup flax mixture, see below)

2 cups flour, *any flour*, alone or in any combination: all-purpose, whole wheat pastry, spelt, corn, quinoa, millet, chickpea, buckwheat, oat, etc.

2½ cups cold liquid, alone or in any combination: seltzer, water, wine, milk, or dairy-free milk, low-fat OK

2 tablespoons vegetable oil

Pinch salt

Blend all ingredients in a blender until smooth.

Make the crêpes: Spray a 9-inch nonstick skillet with cooking spray and let it get really hot. Pour just enough batter to coat the bottom of the pan (use a very small ladle or pour sparingly from a cup equipped with a spout, like a glass measuring cup or the blender itself). Start with the center of the skillet and swirl the batter in the pan all around to ensure that the bottom is very thinly and evenly coated. After a few seconds, the edges will start detaching from the bottom of the pan, and the top will look dry. Turn the crêpe over and cook for a few more seconds. Transfer to a plate and repeat with the remaining batter, spraying the pan each time. Use your favorite filling and roll or fold the crêpe over it, or fold and use the filling as a topping. Eat hot.

Makes a good dozen, enough for 4 servings.

Basic dessert crêpe batter: GF Same as above, plus 2 tablespoons sugar, and 1 tablespoon vanilla extract.

CRÊPE FILLINGS GF, P

Go ahead and make the whole amount even for a small group: It takes the same amount of time and effort, and will refrigerate (2–3 days) or freeze (4–5 weeks) very well.

Creamed spinach filling GF, P

2 tablespoons olive oil
1 small onion, minced
2 tablespoons flour, any flour (Passover: potato starch)
1½ cups milk or dairy-free milk, low-fat OK
1 10-ounce box frozen chopped spinach, thawed and squeezed dry
Salt and pepper to taste
1 teaspoon dried basil
Pinch nutmeg

Heat the oil in a pan. Add the onion and sauté until translucent. Lower the heat and add the flour. Cook 2 minutes, whisking until the flour gets a light brown color. Add the milk in a very slow stream, whisking constantly. The mixture will get thick in about a minute. Add spinach and remaining seasonings and cook 1 more minute.

Chicken filling GF, P

Substitute 2 cups cooked diced chicken for the spinach.

Vegetable filling GF, P

Use 2 cups sautéed mushrooms, onions, broccoli, pepper, zucchini, tomato, etc.

Cheese filling GF, P

I beg you, no store-bought pre-grated packaged cheese. Same calories, no taste. Rather, buy yourself a good-brand grater and grate from a chunk of cheese as you need it in just a few seconds. Grate some intensely flavored cheese such as cheddar, kashkaval, Swiss cheese, or Parmesan (you need much less of it than if you were using a milder-flavored cheese) on the finished crêpe before folding, and add a few grinds of black pepper.

Herb crêpes GF, P

Add your favorite herbs directly into your savory crêpe batter: chopped dill, oregano, parsley, thyme, chives, etc. If all you have on hand are dried herbs, go for it.

Buckwheat pancakes GF

Use all buttermilk and no other liquid, and all buckwheat flour. Their texture is a little thicker, and you will see tiny little holes forming all over the tops. You might want to make them tiny and use them for hors d'oeuvres, topped with caviar filling (below). In this case, fit 5 to 6 tiny pancakes at a time in the skillet.

Caviar filling GF, P

Fold the finished crêpe and top with a little plain yogurt and a good-quality caviar or smoked salmon.

Jam filling GF, P

Spread some good-brand all-fruit jam on a finished dessert crêpe. All-fruit jams and preserves are fantastic: half the calories, double the taste, and all natural.

Nut butter filling GF, P

Spread your favorite nut butter or peanut butter chocolate spread on a finished dessert crêpe.

Apple filling GF, P

Use with dessert crêpes.
3 tablespoons vegetable oil
4 Granny Smith (green) apples, peeled and cut in thin wedges
1 tablespoon grated lemon zest
3 tablespoons Sucanat
1 tablespoon rum or brandy

Heat the oil in a skillet. Add the apples and sauté at high temperature until golden. Add remaining ingredients and cook one more minute.

OMELETS

If you are making more than one omelet, use a larger skillet, and double, even triple, the recipe. You can use all the same sweet and savory fillings and toppings used in crêpes (which will come in handy on Passover: no crepes, but plenty of omelets with exciting filling). Here the secret is to never let the custard overcook, or it will toughen.

2 eggs, or 4 egg whites (No question of flax egg replacement here, sorry: an omelet is an omelet!)
¼ cup milk or dairy-free milk, low-fat OK, or water (Don't skip it. It makes the eggs much lighter and fluffier.)
Salt and pepper to taste

Dessert omelets: no ground pepper, 1 teaspoon sugar, dash vanilla extract

Omelet fillings

Same as the crepe fillings.

Whisk all ingredients together. Spray a 10-inch nonstick skillet with vegetable spray; heat until very hot. Pour the mixture in the skillet, swirling it evenly. Lift the edges with a knife to shift the mixture from the top to the bottom; repeat in several spots. As soon as the mixture looks barely firm, turn off the flame.

Use your favorite fillings before folding. If scrambled eggs is what you prefer, put in your filling and egg mixture, and scramble the mixture only until the mixture is barely set.

GRILLED CHEESE SANDWICHES AND PANINIS GFA

To toast the bread and melt the cheese just right, use a panini machine or a grilled sand-wich machine. Let me say this straight: I would never grill any meat or fish items with these machines. First of all, we all have a broiler in our oven that was made for grilling, but too many of us seem to have forgotten that fact, I wonder why. Second, I hate the way the machines close on the fish or meat like a ton of bricks, draining off all the good moisture and flavor that makes fish or meat so succulent. However, they're perfect for grilled sandwiches.

No Panini machine? No time to grill? No problem: make plain sandwiches!

8 slices good whole-grain bread, gluten-free OK
2 cans good tuna in oil, undrained
2 tomatoes, very thinly sliced
4 ounces good cheese, freshly slivered or grated
Ground pepper to taste

Place 4 slices of bread on the bottom side of the machine.

Drizzle the tuna oil on top of the bread. Top with the tuna. Top with the tomatoes, then cheese, then ground pepper, and finally the remaining slices of bread. Close the top part of the machine on the sandwiches. Let the sandwiches grill 2 to 3 minutes. For easier—and neater—eating, cut the sandwich in half or in four with a sharp knife. Eat hot.

Variations

- Use any fillings you like: leftover grilled vegetables, leftover cooked fish or chicken, sardines, roasted peppers, salad greens, olives, basil, etc.
- Use your favorite bread: whole-grain baguette, ciabatta, focaccia, seven grain, etc.
- Spread the bread with any interesting condiment you might have on hand: pesto, olive spread, even harissa (page 34), if you want the extra kick.

SMOOTHIES GF, P

Smoothies are a wonderful way to sneak in all the nutrient-rich foods your family and friends would ordinarily eat only sparingly, if at all, and you can make endless variations. My trick is to use frozen fruit instead of ice. In one fell swoop, you get the fruit and the ice and so much more flavor. Plus, frozen fruit often tastes even better than fresh because it is picked at its ripest and sweetest, and it requires no cleaning or rinsing. Bananas got too ripe? Just stick them in the freezer—the riper the better—and when you are ready to use them, run them under warm water. The peels will come right off (I absolutely love them smeared with peanut butter and drizzled with honey: Try it!). Make a large smoothie batch and refrigerate the rest right in the blender for later. If the mixture separates, give the blender a few turns again.

Can I interest you in bottled unsweetened fruit concentrates? The whole gamut: cranberry, blueberry, grape, pomegranate, mango, etc. They are heavenly, packed with good nutrition, and easy to find in your health food stores. They will at first seem pricey to you, but you will quickly change your mind when you realize a little goes a really long way.

If you are thinking of offering grown-up brunch drinks, don't even look for other recipes: Simply add half a cup of vodka or rum (a chocolate liqueur for the chocolate smoothie) to the mix!

BERRY SMOOTHIES GF, P

1 cup cranberry or pomegranate juice

1 cup plain yogurt, dairy-free yogurt, silken tofu, milk or dairy-free milk, low-fat OK

2 cups frozen berries (strawberries, blueberries, raspberries, blackberries, alone or in any combination)

2 tablespoons honey, maple syrup, or natural 100 percent pure fruit concentrate (health food stores), only if you like it sweeter

Mix all ingredients in the blender a full minute at high speed until smooth and frothy. Makes 5 cups.

Smoothies

GREEN SMOOTHIES GF, P

Try your best to stick some of the fruit in the freezer before blending, even for an hour or so. No need to have all of these fruit on hand; even a combination of two in larger amounts will be delicious. By the way, these fruit and the mint will make you a wonderful "green" fruit salad, all diced, minus the grape juice, plus a little maple syrup to taste.

1 cup green grapes
1 large pear or green apple, unpeeled, cut in chunks
3 ripe kiwis, peeled
1 cup chunks honeydew melon
1 cup white grape juice, lychee juice, or natural apple cider

A few leaves fresh mint, if you have them on hand
Mix all ingredients in the blender a full minute at high speed until smooth and frothy. Makes 5 cups.

CHOCOLATE ALMOND DATE SMOOTHIE GF, P

Consider this a whole meal. Nutritious and fabulous! This is the only smoothie I use ice with, to chill the heated mixture.

½ cup whole almonds
1 cup pitted dates, packed
⅓ cup cocoa powder
1 cup boiling water
1 cup plain yogurt, dairy-free yogurt, silken tofu, milk or dairy-free milk, low-fat OK
A dozen ice cubes

Place the almonds, dates, cocoa, and boiling water in the blender. Cover and let the mixture rest, unblended, 5 to 10 minutes. Add the yogurt, tofu or milk, and ice and blend a full minute at high speed until thick and frothy. Makes 5 cups.

TROPICAL SMOOTHIES GF, P

Canned pineapple does the job here. Only make sure it's minimally processed and unsweetened.

2 cups canned unsweetened pineapple chunks, juice and all
1 cup coconut milk, low-fat OK
3 cups cubed mango, papaya, or peaches (frozen is best)
1 banana (frozen is best)

Mix all ingredients in the blender a full minute at high speed until smooth and frothy. Makes about 6 cups.

BEET SMOOTHIES GF, P

LISA'S TIP

Beets contain healthy doses of iron, the B vitamin folate, and fiber. Red beets offer betacyanin, a plant pigment, which may protect against colon cancer.

Here is your chance to eat your beets! Who knew they were so delicious? I did—we grew up eating them every day. Here in America, they are virtually the stepchild of the vegetable family, and I wish them to be totally and wholeheartedly adopted.

They are so delicious, and so good for you!

I don't expect you to cook beets for a smoothie. I don't know anyone so devoted. Canned beets with nothing added are perfectly acceptable.

1 small can beets, juice and all
1 cup plain yogurt, silken tofu or unflavored soy, or coconut yogurt, low-fat OK

Mix all ingredients in the blender a full minute at high speed until smooth and frothy. Makes 1 serving.

HOT WHOLE-GRAIN CEREAL GF

This is the food of my lean student years, wearing a dozen hats. Not only did I never get sick of it, but I remember it fondly and with no grudge whatsoever; in fact, I still enjoy it regularly.

Forget about rolled oats, quick oats, instant oats, just-add-water oats (shudder, unless you are in the mddle of nowhere!). Steel-cut oats are cut in such a way (like tiny round pebbles) that they are soft and chewy without ever getting mushy. And they are so delicious and nutritious. As you will see throughout the book, you can make a soup, even a dessert, using steel-cut oats. Ignore the expensive drum box somewhat mysteriously marked "Irish" (what do you need Irish oats for?) and buy it loose in your health food store.

Basic preparation (serves 4 for breakfast)

1 cup steel-cut oats
4 cups water
Salt to taste

Place all ingredients in saucepan, bring to a boil, reduce to low, and let the mixture cook covered for 10 minutes. Serve it plain, or choose one of the following variations for a richer meal:

- For a richer breakfast, substitute 2 cups of milk or dairy-free milk (low-fat OK) for some of the water (2 cups milk, 2 cups water).
- Add a little sugar, honey, agave, or maple syrup in each serving.
- Stir in some low-fat vanilla yogurt, finely diced apple or fruit, grated coconut, raisins, or other dry fruit. Delicious cold too as a dessert!

- Spice it up with some ground cinnamon, ginger, or cardamom.
- Sprinkle each serving with toasted nuts.
- Do what my friend Kayla does (she turned me on to it as well: fabulous). Soak the oats in natural apple cider overnight in the pot you will be using to cook them, and add your favorite seasoning and toppings: raisins, cinnamon, etc. In the morning, all you need to do is bring the pot to a boil, and it's ready!
- Use other grains than steel-cut oats: thick corn grits, buckwheat, millet, amaranth, teff, etc. (Did you ever wonder why all running champions are Ethiopian? I heard it is because teff is their staple grain: the tiniest and most nutritionally concentrated grain of all!) Proceed just as above.

GRANOLA GF

Nothing like a good granola stirred into plain yogurt, or on your favorite frozen dessert, mixed with milk and eaten as cold cereal, or even eaten out of hand. Many of the commercial granolas are loaded with too much sugar and fat. Making granola is a snap and could be a real showcase for you: Put in exactly the sweetener you want, the nuts you want, the grain you want, and so on.

Here is a basic recipe that you will enjoy taking places.

I much prefer the slow-baking method in a low-temperature oven: This is the best way to ensure your dry fruit won't harden.

4 cups old-fashioned rolled (*not quick or instant*) oats
1 cup rice flour, or other gluten-free flour
1 cup chopped nuts: walnuts, pecans, cashews, almonds, etc.
1 cup unsweetened grated coconut, optional
Optional: 1 cup dry fruit, chopped if larger: raisins, cranberries, apricots, apples, blueberries, prunes, figs, dates, etc.
1 cup seeds: flax, sesame, pumpkin, sunflower, chia, hemp, poppy, etc.
¼ cup vegetable, flax or coconut oil
¾ cup honey, or maple syrup, or agave (less if you are restricted)
½ cup natural fruit juice of your choice
1 teaspoon salt

Spices of your choice: vanilla extract, cinnamon, ginger, cardamom, nutmeg, etc.
Preheat the oven to 275°F. Place the first set of ingredients in a mixing bowl. Whisk the second set of ingredients thoroughly in another bowl, and pour over the grain-seed mixture, mixing thoroughly until the mixture is evenly coated. Arrange the mixture on a large cookie sheet in one layer (if you need 2 sheets, use one extra), and bake a total of 1 hour, stirring once during the baking to ensure even baking. If it is not crunchy enough after it cools, return to the oven to crisp, just a few more minutes. Let the granola cool completely before storing in glass jars at room temperature. Makes about 9 cups.

DRINKS

I never drink soda, and I never serve soda, and nobody ever complains. Au contraire! They all clamor for one of my drinks, in pitchers, which I fill and refill in the wink of an eye. For large parties, I serve my drinks in a fun diner-style three-gallon cold drink dispenser. So move over soda and other store-bought un-goodies!

LEMONADE GF, P

Each variation is a snap to make, and fabulous. With each mixture, adjust the water and the lemonade mixture to your own personal taste. Please don't be shocked at my suggesting you settle for bottled lemon or lime juice in a pinch: Like me, you will notice at your health food store some very decent unprocessed or minimally processed brands that will do the trick when fresh lemons get too expensive to use in large amounts.

Basic:

> 4 cups fresh lemon or lime juice (settle for a good-brand bottled)
> 2 cups sugar

Bring the juice and sugar to just below a boil and turn off the heat. Cool and transfer to a glass jar. In a 2½-quart pitcher, put one cup lemonade mixture and 3 cups water and complete with ice all the way up. Mix thoroughly from the bottom up.

Note: If you get your hands on superfine sugar, use it instead of the regular sugar, and no heating: It dissolves instantly.

Maple lemonade: GF, P No boiling. In a glass jar, mix 4 cups lemon juice with 2 cups maple syrup. Use exactly as the basic mixture, but stir the mixture thoroughly before using (maple syrup tends to settle in the bottom).

Ginger lemonade: GF, P Same as for the basic mixture, but add ¼ cup grated fresh ginger to the sauce pan and strain.

Pineapple ginger lemonade: GF, P In the pitcher, 1 cup ginger lemonade mixture, 3 cups pineapple juice, complete with ice.

Green tea lemonade: GF, P Steep 6 bags green tea in 6 cups boiling water for about 15 minutes, then discard the tea bags. In a pitcher, 1 cup basic lemonade, 3 cups tea, and ice.

Raspberry lemonade: GF, P Steep 12 bags raspberry (or other herbal tea of your choice: passion fruit, apple cinnamon, etc.) in 6 cups boiling water for about 15 minutes, then discard the tea bags. In a pitcher, 1 cup basic lemonade, 3 cups raspberry tea, and ice.

ICED COFFEE GF, P

While I wouldn't dream of serving instant coffee (call me a snob, but really, why should I, with all the great real-coffee selection?), I have no problem using it in baking or in making iced coffee.

Put in a pitcher: 1 quart milk or dairy-free milk (low-fat OK), ⅓ cup instant coffee powder mixed with a few drops hot water, and complete with ice. Mix thoroughly. Let every guest sweeten his/her drink to taste.

ICED MOCHA GF, P

Just ask any of my guests: I make semi-industrial amounts of this drink at home! Same as in iced coffee above, using natural chocolate-flavored milk or dairy-free milk, low-fat OK.

ICED TEA GF, P

I find that intensifying herbal tea with real tea (decaf if you are looking to reduce your caffeine) results in a much more interesting drink, with a much deeper flavor. You have a nice variety to choose from: black, green, white, rooibos, kukicha, bancha, to name just a few.

> **LISA'S TIP**
>
> **Rooibos tea** is becoming popular among health-conscious consumers, due to its high level of antioxidants, flavonoids, its lack of caffeine, and its low tannin levels compared to fully oxidized black tea. It is purported to assist with nervous tension and digestion.

Steep 6 regular or decaf tea bags (black, green, white, rooibos) and 10 bags of your favorite herbal tea in 6 cups boiling water for about 30 minutes (of course, longer is OK too).

Whenever possible, use loose tea. About ¼ cup total. Strain the loose tea mixture and pour into a 3-quart pitcher. Complete with ice and sweeten if desired with sugar, maple syrup (my favorite), or agave syrup.

SANGRIA GF, P

A great party attraction. The classic favorite with a super-healthy twist. I find that using firm fruit (citrus, green apples) makes the sangria easier to keep up to 4 days than if you use berries, mango, or pineapple.

2 cups very strong hot tea (green, black, red, white), decaf OK
A dozen cloves
5–6 cinnamon sticks
A few pieces fresh ginger
1 dozen peppercorns
2 bottles dry red wine, chilled
1 12-ounce can pineapple juice concentrate with no sugar added (or any other juice concentrate)
1 each: orange, green apple, and lemon or lime, cut into medium-thin half slices

Mix the first set of ingredients in a teapot, and let it steep and cool completely. Strain the mixture into a large pitcher. Add the wine and fruit. Keep chilled. No ice. Serve with some of the sliced fruit in each glass.

Variation: White sangria GF, P

Green tea, dry white wine, light-colored juice concentrate (no cranberry, red grape, or pomegranate). Proceed just as above.

SAKE PUNCH GF

Fabulous! I get endless requests to share this recipe, so here comes!

4 cups very hot strong green tea, decaf OK
2 large pieces ginger, peeled and chopped
1 bunch lemongrass, roughly chopped (or 3 tablespoons powder)
3 cups vodka (inexpensive brand OK)
6 cups dry sake (inexpensive brand OK)
8 cups unsweetened lychee juice (health food stores)
1 cup maple syrup
½ cup lemon or lime juice

Steep the first set of ingredients in a tight-lid teapot until it cools. Strain the mixture into a large pitcher or punch bowl and stir in the second of ingredients. Chill. No ice.

COFFEE AND TEA GF

I make myself the best cup of coffee in the mocha machine, a stove-top mechanical marvel equipped with the most rudimentary yet foolproof percolating system.

Place water in the bottom, coffee in the middle filter insert, lock the top and bottom parts, and put on the fire. The water will percolate through the filter insert upward, and the finished coffee will be in the top part, ready to be poured into cups.

I also love the French press: Put in your coffee and boiling water, let it steep 2 to 3 minutes, then bring the filter down to separate the coffee from the grounds. Same goes for loose tea.

In the absence of a coffee- or tea-making device, the simplest way of all is to mix tea leaves (black, red, white, or green) or ground coffee with boiling water. Let the mixture sit 2 to 3 minutes or so and strain with a little fine-mesh strainer. Only make it good and strong. Anytime my mother tastes a bad cup of coffee or tea, she says scornfully, "Too much water!"

VEGETABLE JUICES GF, P

Wondering how to use all those leftover fruit and vegetables? Just juice 'em! Delicious and powerful, and much leaner than fruit juice. A juicer will be infinitely easier to use if you get one equipped with a large opening, which will allow for whole carrots, whole cucumbers, large beet chunks, reducing the cutting considerably, often eliminating it altogether. Almost anything is suitable, so play with what you find, and mix and match until you find your favorites: Leaves (all leaves), ginger, beets, carrots, celery, tomatoes, etc. Apples, pears, grapes, kiwis, papaya, etc. To mitigate the intensity of juice made from very intensely flavored leaves, add a green apple if you like.

INFUSED WATER GF, P

How about this: A pitcher cold water with some added (one at a time please!) sliced lemon, lime, mint, basil, sliced cucumber, sliced apples, ginger, lemongrass, rosemary, and nothing more but some ice if desired (I don't use any)? So pretty, simple, refreshing, and delicious: yum!

Infused Water

BREADS AND FLAT BREADS

I t is easy enough—but it often turns out totally futile—to promise ourselves to stay away from bread: As soon as we catch some of the intoxicating aromas wafting out of a bakery, all bets are off. Let's admit it: We all love a delicious slice of bread—as part of a sandwich, to mop up some sauce, or to eat with a good dip. However, many of us can't tolerate so much gluten, and then some can't have any gluten at all. Plus, many store-bought breads come with unwelcome additives. As my—and, it turns out, countless others'—love for all white starches grew increasingly unrequited, I came to see this "rejection" as an exciting challenge to come up with dishes that were both easily digested, and of course delicious: Good flavor is *not* negotiable!

In this chapter, I am including all low-gluten choices and gluten-free adaptations wherever applicable.

LISA'S TIP

HEALTHY GRAINS

Including whole grains in your diet is a great way to boost your nutrient intake. They are loaded with vitamins and minerals, including B vitamins, vitamin E, magnesium, selenium, and protective phytonutrients. A good source of fiber and complex carbohydrates, they are relatively low in calories and fat. It is no surprise that diets rich in whole grains may offer protection against heart disease, stroke, type 2 diabetes, hypertension, and certain cancers.

Whole grains are healthier than processed grains because they provide many more nutrients. They also offer a greater sense of fullness in people who eat them. Whole grains are made from the whole kernels of grain, including both the inside part of the grain and the outer covering. Processed grains remove the outer covering along with a lot of the nutrition and fiber. Fiber helps prevent constipation, and may cut the risk of heart disease, diverticulosis, and certain cancers.

Most Americans do not consume enough whole grains. For many of us, eating more whole grains requires learning about foods rarely seen in the traditional American diet. As you will see below, many delicious and nutritious grains exist. And, if you are gluten free, no need to worry, as many terrific and versatile grains are now readily available on the market.

Skip the white pasta and white rice and include healthy grains instead: brown rice, kasha, quinoa, spelt, and whole wheat pasta, to name a few. Here are some nutritional benefits of some healthy, tasty, and versatile grains:

Amaranth is a great grain for those with gluten intolerances and wheat allergies. It also has a terrific nutritional profile. One cup of cooked amaranth delivers lots of fiber, protein, and is rich in minerals, including iron, magnesium, manganese, and phosphorus. It also contains betalains, a class of antioxidants that may help reduce inflammation.

Barley is a good source of soluble fiber that may reduce cholesterol and stabilize blood sugar levels. Barley contains B vitamins, and the minerals selenium and copper. While pearled barley is not technically a whole grain, as it is polished, and some nutrients are lost, hulled barley is healthier, and contains more fiber, vitamins, and minerals. However, even pearled barley is a healthier alternative to refined grains such as white rice, couscous, or pastas made from white flours.

Brown rice is a much better choice than white rice. It contains fiber, B vitamins, and a variety of minerals. It contains nearly three times the fiber as white rice. A mere ½ cup serving of cooked brown rice contains nearly a half day's worth of the mineral manganese that works with various enzymes facilitating body processes.

Buckwheat, brought to America by Russian and Polish immigrants who called it "kasha," is a good source of the minerals manganese, magnesium, and zinc, as well as flavonoids like quercetin and rutin, which contain antioxidant and anti-inflammatory properties. A great choice for those following a gluten free diet. One cup cooked kasha contains 5 grams of fiber.

Bulgur wheat is higher in fiber than most grains. One cup cooked bulgur contains 8 grams of fiber. The insoluble fiber it contains is helpful in preventing constipation and diverticular disease. It also contains iron, magnesium, manganese, and B vitamins. Because bulgur is made from precooked wheat berries, it can be reconstituted by soaking or by simmering. Its wonderful nutty flavor and light texture makes it a great choice for salads and side dishes.

Farro is chock-full of minerals, antioxidants, lignans, phytonutrients, and fiber.

Millet contains manganese and phosphorus, which may contribute to bone health. It is also rich in B vitamins, especially niacin, B6, and folate. Added bonus: it is gluten-free.

Oats are a good source of soluble fiber and contain beta-glucans, which helps lower cholesterol and stabilize blood sugar levels. They also contain insoluble fiber that prevents constipation and promotes regular bowel movements. Moderate amounts of *pure, uncontaminated oats* are tolerated by most people with celiac disease, but it is important to be aware that many commercial oat products on the market have been cross-contaminated with wheat, barley, and/or rye.

Quinoa is a nutrition treasure and has a protein content that is superior to that of most grains, because it contains all the essential amino acids. It is high in the amino acid, lysine, which is important for tissue growth and repair. It is also rich in the minerals iron, magnesium, manganese, phosphorus, and copper, and is a great choice for the gluten free.

Spelt has gained popularity as a healthy and delicious grain due to its nutty flavor, high protein, and nutrition content. It is low in fat, high in fiber, and contains B vitamins and minerals, including potassium, magnesium, manganese and copper. And it has gained a following for those intolerant to wheat. Many people with wheat allergies can tolerate spelt well.

Teff is a champion grain. It is chock-full of minerals including calcium, iron, magnesium, manganese, and phosphorus.

Whole wheat products are not stripped of nutrients and fiber like refined products. Whole wheat foods such as whole wheat pastas, breads, and couscous contain insoluble fiber, which prevents constipation and may be protective against certain cancers. They also contain an array of vitamins and minerals.

Aim for *100% whole wheat products* such as whole wheat pasta and couscous.

Wild rice is high in protein and fiber and low in fat. It also contains the minerals potassium and phosphorus and B vitamins.

Savvy shopping tip: Choose grains that are 100% whole grain. When reading food labels, look out for words such as "multigrain" or "stoneground" that do not necessarily mean whole grain. And the phrase "made from whole grain" is generally used on products that aren't 100% whole grain.

BLUEBERRY SCONES GFA

3 cups flour: all-purpose, whole wheat pastry, or spelt (gluten-free: GF flour plus 1 teaspoon xanthan gum)

¼ cup sugar

⅓ cup margarine spread, or butter if you are making them dairy

4 teaspoons baking powder

1 teaspoon baking soda

½ teaspoon salt

1 tablespoon grated orange zest

1 cup plain yogurt or dairy-free yogurt, low-fat OK

1 egg, lightly beaten

2 cups fresh blueberries, or frozen and unthawed

Preheat oven to 400°F. Mix the flour, sugar, and margarine spread with a pastry cutter or two knives until mixture resembles coarse meal. Add baking powder, baking soda, salt, and orange zest and mix. Add the yogurt and egg and mix until just combined. Fold in the blueberries very gently, so as not to extract their moisture.

Roll out the dough on a very lightly floured board to ½-inch thickness. Cut out with a 2-inch cookie cutter or a glass (or quite simply, as I do, shape little balls and flatten them with your hands). Place the scones on a cookie sheet lined with foil or parchment. Bake about 15 minutes, or until lightly colored. Makes about 20 scones.

CORN BREAD GFA

Ready in a snap: So nice to know we have options that are dairy-free, low-gluten, and gluten-free. The secret of good corn bread is to stick your empty greased pan in the oven while you whip up the batter to get it really good and hot. This way the baking gets a huge head start as soon as the batter is poured, and the bread gets all those lovely trademark cracks all over.

2 cups plain yogurt or buttermilk, low-fat OK (dairy-free: soy or coconut plain yogurt, or 2 cups soy milk mixed with 2 tablespoons lemon juice or vinegar)

2 eggs

⅓ cup vegetable oil

2 cups medium cornmeal (fine cornmeal if you like a smoother texture)

1 cup all-purpose, whole wheat pastry, or spelt flour (gluten-free: brown rice flour or any other GF flour)

2 teaspoons baking powder

2 teaspoons baking soda

1 teaspoon salt

⅓ cup sugar

Preheat oven to 425°F. Grease a heavy 9- or 10-inch round (*real, not disposable*) pan and put it in the oven while you mix the bread. Mix the first set of ingredients in a bowl. In another bowl, mix the second set of ingredients thoroughly with a spoon. Pour the egg mixture into the flour mixture and mix until just combined. Immediately pour the mixture into the hot pan. Bake about 25 to 30 minutes, or until the top is cracked and golden. Serve warm or at room temperature.

Corn Bread

Variations

Corn muffins: GFA Grease a muffin pan and place in the oven while you prepare the batter. Proceed exactly as above. Bake 20 to 35 minutes.

Cheddar dill cheddar corn bread or muffins: GFA No sugar. Throw in ½ cup minced dill and 1 cup grated cheddar.

Smoked salmon corn bread or muffins: GFA No sugar and no salt. Throw in ½ cup shredded smoked salmon.

Tex-Mex corn bread or muffins: GFA No sugar and no salt. Throw in 1 cup frozen corn kernels and add 1 cup grated cheddar or kashkaval, minced onion, 3–4 tablespoons chopped cilantro, 1 tablespoon cumin, 1–2 tablespoons bottled hot sauce.

CHICKPEA LENTIL PARATHAS (FLAT BREADS) GFA

As if I needed more reasons to love Indian food, other than that it is sensible and delicious. I have generously shared throughout the book, but still, here are two more reasons right off the bat: There is no flour from any grain Indians don't cook with, so the selection is wonderfully exciting even for those of us who don't need to make gluten-free choices; the flat breads are whipped up in no time and need very little oil.

1½ cups each: chickpea flour and lentil flour (or choose from any whole grain flour you like), 3 cups total
¾ teaspoon salt
1 cup warm water

Optional (only if you are eating them alone): 2 tablespoons zaatar
Vegetable oil or ghee (page 278) for brushing the skillet

Mix all the dough ingredients together and knead just a few minutes, adding a little flour if necessary to make it firmer. Brush the dough with oil and let it rest a few minutes. Divide in 8 balls.

Heat up a nonstick skillet until very hot and brush it with oil or ghee. Roll out each ball on a lightly floured board, about 5 inches in diameter, and add to the skillet. Fry a minute or two on each side, brushing the skillet each time as you go. Eat with curries and soups, or even alone.

IRISH SODA BREAD

Dairy please: No substitutions here; they won't be nearly as good. Irish soda bread has two trademarks you shouldn't try to forgo: caraway seeds and the cross marks on top.

¾ stick unsalted butter, divided in three
3 cups flour (all-purpose, whole wheat pastry, or spelt)
1 teaspoon salt
1 tablespoon baking powder
1 teaspoon baking soda
½ cup sugar
1¾ cups buttermilk or plain yogurt, low-fat OK
2 eggs, beaten
2 tablespoons caraway seeds
1 cup currants or raisins

Preheat oven to 350°F. Grease a 10 inch skillet with a third of the butter.

Using two knives or a pastry cutter, work ⅓ of the butter, the flour, salt, baking powder, baking soda, and sugar, until the mixture resembles coarse meal. Mix the buttermilk and eggs well in a bowl. Add the caraway seeds and raisins and combine again. Add the egg mixture to the flour mixture, mixing only until combined. Pour the batter into the skillet. Cut the remaining butter into tiny pieces and drop evenly over the bread. With a sharp knife, make 2 perpendicular gashes over the bread, like a cross. Bake for about 1 hour, until the top looks golden and firm. Eat preferably warm.

MUSTARD CARAWAY BREAD GFA

You will love the funky caraway-mustard seed combination. This bread comes out firm enough for slicing and toasting and is a good match for both sweet and savory toppings.

3 cups flour: all-purpose, whole wheat pastry, or spelt (gluten-free: GF flour plus 1 teaspoon xanthan gum)
⅓ cup sugar
1 tablespoon baking powder
1½ tablespoons caraway seeds
2 tablespoons mustard seeds
1 teaspoon salt
3 eggs, beaten
1½ cups milk or dairy-free milk, low-fat OK
½ cup vegetable oil

Preheat the oven to 350°F. Mix the first set of ingredients in a bowl. In another bowl, mix the second set of ingredients thoroughly with a spoon. Pour the egg mixture into the flour mixture and mix until just combined. Pour the batter into a greased loaf pan. (If you have used GF flour, don't make the loaf, make only muffins.) Bake for 1 hour or until a knife inserted in center of loaf comes out clean.

Mustard caraway muffins: Pour the batter into about 18 muffin molds and bake 20 to 35 minutes, or a little longer, until the tops are firm.

VEGETABLE PANCAKES GFA

These are lots of fun, and quite adaptable. They are substantial enough to be a significant part of a main course. The kinds and amounts of spices and vegetables suggested are totally flexible. No problem making them in advance (even freezing them) and reheating them.

Pancake mixture:

1½ cups flour, any flour
1 cup milk or dairy-free milk, low-fat OK
1 egg, or ¼ cup flax mixture (page 224)
2 tablespoons vegetable oil
Salt and paper to taste
1 teaspoon baking powder
1 tablespoon curry
1 teaspoon cumin

4 scallions, sliced very thin
1 medium carrot, grated fine
¼ cup frozen corn kernels
¼ cup frozen peas

Olive oil, or ghee (page 278)

Mix all pancake ingredients in a blender or food processor. Fold in the vegetables by hand.

In a large nonstick skillet, heat just a few drops of olive oil or ghee. When the skillet is really hot, add the batter in small mounds, trying to fit 2 to 3 pancakes in the skillet. Cook about 1 minute on each side. Serve hot. To reheat, warm covered in one layer in a 300°F oven for about 10 minutes (a little longer if they were frozen).

BASIC BREAD

Consider this the mother recipe. You will be amazed at how many variations on this recipe you can make. Multiply the dough and play with it! My son Yakov can't live without this bread: Growing up at home, a loaf a day was the very least he was satisfied with. "This bread rules, this bread rocks," he would always say with delight. He used to tell me, "If everyone would have as much of your bread as I did, and you would market it, you would be a millionaire." Still, I wouldn't charge him!

Some very useful tips for successful bread baking:

- *Hot and cold temperatures and drafts kill the action of yeast and inhibit the rising of the dough, so make sure the water you mix with the yeast is warm and that you let the dough rise covered in a draft-free area.*
- *Not too much salt, please! Remember you are going to eat this bread with other foods, which are often salty, such as cheese, lox, and various spreads.*
- *When making bread, do not be tempted to add more flour as you go: that's what makes bread heavy. The gluten in the flour expands during both the kneading and the rising process and absorbs the liquids in the recipe, eliminating stickiness and yielding a light dough.*
- *Check for doneness. A well-baked bread will sound hollow when tapped on its bottom.*
- *As soon as you take the loaves out of the oven, turn them upside down to cool to avoid having moisture condense on the bottom crust, making it soggy.*
- *Wrap the cooled loaves tightly in plastic wrap. If you are not serving the bread on the day you are making it, freeze the wrapped loaves.*
- *Rather than get those pesky, hard-to-open individual yeast envelopes, get a jar at health food stores.*

1½ tablespoons active dry yeast
½ cup warm water
1 tablespoon sugar
4 cups flour: all-purpose, whole wheat pastry, or spelt
1¼ teaspoons salt
1 cup warm water
2 tablespoons olive oil

Mix the yeast, ½ cup water, and the sugar in a big bowl. Let the mixture sit for about 5 minutes: It will bubble. Add the flour, salt, 1 cup of warm water, and the oil. Mix by hand until just combined. Turn the mixture onto a lightly floured flat working surface and knead for 10 minutes, turning the dough a quarter of a turn every 2 to 3 minutes and punching it down often to eliminate any air pocket (or transfer the mixture to the bowl of an electric dough maker and set for 5 minutes of kneading). Transfer the kneaded dough into a big mixing bowl (remember, the dough will expand). Let the dough rise in a warm, draft-free area for 2 hours. It will have about doubled in size. Shape the bread into 3 to 4 long skinny loaves.

If you like your bread to have less crust and more crumb, shape the dough into 2 medium loaves. If you want a loaf with no crust and all crumb (like a Pullman loaf), place the dough in 2 lightly greased loaf pans. Place the loaves on a foil-covered cookie sheet, about 2 inches apart. Slash each loaf on the diagonal in several places with a very sharp knife. Bake in a preheated 400°F oven for about 40 minutes, a little longer for larger loaves.

Variations

Oat bread: Substitute ¾ cup rolled oats for ¾ cup flour in every four cups of flour (in other words: 3¼ cups flour plus ¾ cup oats instead of 4 cups flour).

You can also substitute semolina, fine cornmeal, or buckwheat flour in the same proportions as the oats. Bake as for basic bread.

Herb-and-cheese bread: Add to the dough 1 cup plain yogurt, ½ cup chopped dill, and 1 cup grated cheddar. Knead all additions into the dough before letting it rise. Proceed as for basic bread. Makes 2 round loaves.

Caraway or poppy seed bread: Knead ¼ cup caraway or poppy seeds thoroughly into the dough before you let it rise. Bake as for basic white bread.

Walnut raisin bread: Add to the dough ¾ cup dark raisins, ½ cup chopped walnuts, and 2 tablespoons dark molasses. Knead all three additions into the dough before letting it rise. Shape into 2 loaves. Bake as for basic white bread.

Zaatar bread: Roll the risen dough about ½ inch thin into a rectangle or round, brush lightly with olive oil, and sprinkle generously with zaatar (a delicious Israeli mixture of sesame seeds, oregano, and sumac). Bake only for 15 to 20 minutes. Do not let the dough get crisp, or it will harden.

Focaccia: Roll the risen dough about 1 inch thick, oblong or round. Poke it all over with a finger. Brush with olive oil, and if desired choose one or two of the following toppings, just a light smear: crushed tomatoes, oregano, ground pepper, finely chopped onion, grated cheese, and chopped fresh herbs (thyme, rosemary, sage, etc.). Bake in a preheated 350°F oven for about 40 minutes.

Water challah: If eggless challah is what you prefer, as I do, make the basic bread dough and shape and bake as in the challah recipe (page 247).

MOROCCAN BREAD (KHOBZ)

In Morocco, bread is not just the outside of a sandwich; it is sustenance itself. Every single morning, Moroccans make bread. They mix the dough, shape the loaves, let them rise, and wait for the young boy who will take them to the municipal oven, then back to the house just in time for lunch. No wonder the city streets are so fragrant and the local children so well coordinated: They're always racing around barefoot with huge trays balanced on their heads! You will not even find instructions for baking bread in most Moroccan bread recipes. They simply end with, "Let the loaves rise and send them to the oven." Here, then, a recipe for my native bread, baked right at home.

When I was growing up, we had a rich cousin who had a masseuse come to her house twice a week to help reduce her unsightly bulges. Once her maid, intrigued, asked her, "What is it that this lady does to you each time she comes?" To which my cousin answered self-consciously, "You know, if you massage a fat area often enough, you end up reducing it." The maid looked horrified and replied vehemently, "Oh, no, madame! When you knead the dough, it grows, and grows, and grows!"

In Morocco, no one bothers to wrap the bread. What for? There won't be a crumb left, and anyway, a fresh batch will be made the next day. Bread is stored for the day in flat wicker platters topped with dome covers called tbikas *to protect them from dust and humidity. But I am not about to bake bread every day, so I make a big recipe and freeze.*

Makes 2 loaves, enough for 8 ample servings.

1¼ tablespoons active dry yeast
½ cup warm water
1½ teaspoon sugar
4½ cups flour: all-purpose, whole wheat pastry, or spelt
1 cup warm water
1 teaspoon salt
1 tablespoon fennel or anise seeds
3 tablespoons sesame seeds

Dissolve the yeast in ½ cup water. Add the sugar and let the mixture "proof" for a few minutes; the yeast mixture will bubble, "proof" that it is active. Put the flour in a mixing bowl and add the yeast mixture, 1 cup warm water, salt, fennel, and sesame seeds. Turn the mixture onto a worktable or board and knead it for about 15 minutes, making sure you work on every corner, punching it down regularly to expel any air bubbles, until you have a firm but pliable dough (or place in the bowl of a dough maker and process for about 5 minutes). Divide the dough in half. Shape each half into a flat circular loaf, about 9 inches in diameter. Arrange the loaves far enough apart on a cookie sheet to give them room to rise. Let rise, covered with a clean cloth, in a warm, draft-free place, about 2 hours. Prick the tops of the loaves all over with a fork. Bake in a preheated 375°F oven for about 35 minutes.

Variation: For a coarser texture, you can substitute 1 cup semolina flour for an equal amount of flour.

CHALLAH

This is the traditional Jewish bread served on Shabbos and holiday celebrations. Person-
ally, I don't like bread that tastes like cake, so my recipe contains just enough oil and eggs to
enrich it and make it festive yet let it retain a bread texture. Here's a large recipe: It freezes very
well; just be sure to wrap the loaves very tightly. As always, my flour of choice is spelt.

4 tablespoons active dry yeast
4 cups warm water
½ cup honey or sugar
4 eggs
½ cup vegetable oil
1 tablespoon salt
12 cups flour: all-purpose, whole wheat pastry, or spelt
Topping:
1 egg, beaten with ¼ cup water
sesame or poppy seeds (optional)

Mix the yeast, water, and honey or sugar in a big bowl and let the mixture bubble for
about 5 minutes. Add the eggs, oil, and salt and beat. Add the flour and mix thoroughly.
Transfer the mixture to a lightly floured flat working surface and knead for about 20
minutes, turning the dough a quarter of a turn every 2 to 3 minutes and punching it down
often to eliminate any air pockets (or transfer the mixture to the bowl of a dough maker
and set for 10 minutes of kneading). Transfer the kneaded dough into a large mixing bowl
(remember, it will expand). Let rise, covered with a cloth, in a warm, draft-free area for 2
hours.

Preheat the oven to 350°F. Shape the challah: Divide the dough into 5 equal pieces.
Divide each piece into thirds and roll each third into a long thin rope. Pinch the 3 ropes
together at one end to hold them in place. Braid and place the braid on a foil-covered
cookie sheet. Repeat with the rest of the dough. Place the loaves well apart in the pans (you
might need 2 in all). Brush each loaf with the egg-and-water mixture and top with seeds if
desired. Bake 45 minutes to 1 hour.

Variation: Raisin challah

Served on Rosh Hashanah. Add two cups of raisins to the dough and shape it into 5
round loaves (make a long thin rope with each of the 5 equal pieces of dough and roll it
into a coil).

PIZZA AND ASSORTED TOPPINGS

I used to have qualms about making nondairy pizza at my demos, fearing my students might find my suggestion slightly disingenuous, until one of them recently exclaimed vehemently, "Why can't we find cheese-less pizza in the States just as we do in Europe? Where is it written that pizza must always have cheese?"

That just did it. That's right: Traditionally, only a few pizza varieties are topped with cheese, or even tomatoes, and there are quite a few wonderful toppings you can choose from: olives, anchovies, onions, artichoke hearts, eggs, roasted peppers, mushrooms, tiny meatballs, you just name it.

Dough:

> 2 tablespoons dry yeast
> 2 cups warm water
> 1 tablespoon sugar
> 5 cups flour: all-purpose, whole wheat pastry, or spelt
> 1 teaspoon salt
> ¼ cup olive oil

Mix the yeast, water, and sugar in a bowl. Let the mixture "proof" about 5 minutes; it will start bubbling. Add the remaining ingredients. Turn out onto a lightly floured board and knead by hand or in a dough maker about 10 minutes. Cover the dough and let it rise about 1 hour in a draft-free place. On a very lightly floured board, roll out the dough very thin onto 2 greased 16-inch round pans, leaving a slightly thicker rim all around.

Preheat the oven to 475°F. Brush the tops very lightly with olive oil. Spread the toppings (suggestions below) on the dough, leaving the rim blank. Bake about 15 minutes. Cut in wedges and serve hot.

Toppings: Short and sweet selection

- Tomato sauce, with added oregano, basil, or other favorite seasonings
- Very thinly sliced vegetables: tomatoes, zucchini, red onion, mushrooms, eggplant, etc.
- Roasted red peppers (bottled OK), sliced thin
- Capers (watch the salt)
- Pitted oil-cured olives (watch the salt)
- Anchovies (watch the salt)
- Flaked mock crab
- Artichoke hearts
- Diced natural (no nitrites) smoked turkey
- Dairy: 1 to 2 cups freshly grated strong cheese—Parmesan, kashkaval, etc. (you will need less with a milder cheese such as mozarella)—or soft cheese such as feta (watch the salt)
- Sliced spinach or arugala leaves

GLUTEN-FREE BREAD GF

This might well be the solution to your gluten-free bread cravings. Here's all I ask if you want to pull this off perfectly: Don't shape the dough into loaves. Rather, shape into rolls. There will be much less room to end up with a dried-out bread.

1½ cups warm water
1 tablespoon dry yeast
1 tablespoon sugar or honey
3 cups gluten-free flour (teff, rice, millet, buckwheat, etc.)
1 cup tapioca flour
¼ cup flax meal (health food stores)
½ cup soy or rice milk powder
3 tablespoons olive oil
2 teaspoons xanthan gum
1 tablespoon salt

Preheat the oven to 425°F. Mix the water, yeast, and sugar in a bowl and let the mixture foam. Add all remaining ingredients and knead 1 to 2 minutes. Let the mixture rest about 30 minutes.

Preheat the oven to 350°F. Shape small rolls and placc on a cookie sheet lined with foil or parchment (you will get about 2 dozen). Bake about 30 minutes until golden.

Variations: All variations of basic bread are applicable.

GLUTEN-FREE PIZZA GF

Use the gluten-free bread dough, roll it about ⅓ inch thick (remember, it won't rise!). Proceed exactly as for the pizza recipe and toppings.

DESSERTS

When my daughter was about ten years old, she told me once: "Mommy, you are the fattest skinny person I know. Make sure you don't gain any weight now, or you will become the skinniest fat person I know." You have guessed it: a slender and fit young mom, she is a tough act to follow, as is everyone else in my house. Still, I am happy to report that after all these years of cooking and baking up a storm, I have never stepped out of the dread borderline my daughter has set up for me. Thank you, Bella poupée, for keeping me on my toes! What do you know, my kids are watching *my* weight!

I devote much time to developing recipes for baked goods that would be interesting, natural, and delicious without being prohibitively rich. At the risk of sounding immodest, I might add I am told I always reach my goal, and then some. For years, I have experimented and played with ingredients that many cooks have ignored until they (the ingredients, not the cooks) recently became hip, such as dairy-free milks, nut butters, flours, and alternative sweeteners. Every ingredient I use stands on its own merits as a delicious, natural, wholesome addition to a recipe that a reader may not have thought possible.

My dessert repertoire is simple yet politically correct through and through, from a nutritional as well as a kosher standpoint.

One of my friends calls my baking "La cuisine sans beurre." Well, almost. In our early bakery days, most of our customers avoided dairy products for a wide variety of reasons and could never find dairy-free desserts worth eating or serving, and were delighted with our baked goods: just what they wanted to make themselves at home but couldn't find the time. We sold our carrot cake, chocolate cake, honey cake, chocolate chip cookies, oatmeal cookies, and many other desserts to numerous restaurants and specialty food stores.

In fact, who won Best Carrot Cake in the City in *New York Magazine* thirty-odd years ago? Levana's Bakery. Back in those days, as start-up bakers, our main goal was to construe simple, delicious, natural dairy-free desserts that could be served at the end of a meat meal for kosher kitchens and to lactose-intolerant diners. We were amazed by our success. The kosher public represented even then only a small part of our clientele. Only very few recipes, about half a dozen in all, didn't yield good results with oil and therefore contain the butter, which I use very sparingly. Margarine, one of my culinary nemeses, has been replaced in the last few years by several good brands of natural non-hydrogenated spreads that are much healthier and much superior in flavor. They are widely available in health food stores, and they are what I use in every recipe that lists margarine.

The desserts I am sharing with you in this chapter are the culmination of many years of mad-scientist experimenting. I even remember fondly my first concoctions, which brought quizzical looks and then the indulgent smiles that, instead of telling me to give up, spurred me on; and before long, they brought delighted grins to everyone's face. The success we have had with our line of homemade desserts, both when the former Levana Restaurant was just a bakery and in all the years I have had my catering business and cooking classes, are ample proof that I didn't work hard for nothing. Check out the line of all-natural spelt desserts I have just launched, called, what else, Levana!

Spelt

The flour of choice I use in all my baked goods is spelt: While I see no reason to put the whole nation on a gluten-free diet (you will see throughout my book that I make ample prevision for our gluten-free friends and offer gluten-free adaptations of countless dishes), I find that the idea of lowering gluten in our diet makes us not only explore the whole gamut of good grains but optimizes our nutrition: My tagline is "Enjoy spelt —less gluten, more protein, more fiber, delicious flavor."

My daughter-in-law Ruthie recently quoted a cute line her babysitter told her after sampling some institutional commercial desserts she had bought for the sake of comparing them with mine: "Ruth, your mother-in-law is going to be one rich lady if this is all the competition she has!" Amen: maybe one day, G-d willing!

Sugar

The sugar I use is always evaporated cane juice for white, and Sucanat for brown— both totally unrefined and minimally processed. Please note that all my dessert recipes contain on average a third less sugar than the traditional American cookbook recipes we are used to: These reduced amounts, by the way, are closer to the time-honored European tradition. You will see for yourself that good desserts made with real flavorings and extracts can easily do away with a good portion of that sugar.

You will be pleased to note I have made ample previsions for people with egg allergies and gluten allergies. No, I am not including vegan-gluten-free-sugar-free-fat-free-nut-free desserts. I just want to share a cute cartoon I recently saw in the *New Yorker* magazine. It was titled "Land of milk and honey. Day 1." One angel is holding a glass of milk and tells the other, "I can't drink this! I am lactose-intolerant!" To which the other replies, "What about me? I am lactose-intolerant *and* diabetic!" You get the point: One problem at a time, please! Those of us with multiple diet restrictions and extra-special needs warrant extra-special attention and serious and personalized experimenting. This is no joke! I cook and bake quite often for just such people, so I know!

Servings

You will notice all my dessert recipes serve a dozen or more. All of them keep at room temperature (cookies) or in the refrigerator (cakes, pies, puddings) and freeze perfectly, so why divide them since you got everything going? I am nothing if not utilitarian, so here are all the options:

1. Do as I instruct you in each dessert recipe and refrigerate (if using within a few days) or freeze (if using later: up to 3 months) the unused portion of pie, cake, cookies, bars: You will be delighted to find them on a day you are too harried or just too lazy to bake!

2. Serve one, freeze one: Make the pies in two 9-inch pans instead of in one 12-inch pie pan. Likewise, make the cakes in two loaf pans instead of in a larger round pan.

3. Divide the recipe in half (I pray you don't!).

Sugar

Americans have a sweet tooth. As a nation, we consume too much sugar and our intake has skyrocketed in recent years. On average, we guzzle down more than 20 teaspoons per person—over 350 calories worth—of added sugar per day! Much of that sugar comes from sugar-sweetened beverages such as soda. Excessive consumption of added sugar has been associated with an increased incidence of obesity. But small amounts of sugar will do no harm. It is OK to indulge in an occasional modest portion of your favorite dessert. And use the real thing instead of banning sugar altogether.

When selecting a sugar, it is best to choose unrefined sugars like honey, maple syrup, and molasses. They contain some antioxidants and minerals, and also have a richer flavor, so you will probably use less. But they still do provide calories so do not consume them—or any other sugar—in excess.

Here is the scoop on some sugars:

Fructose is found naturally in fruits along with fiber, vitamins and minerals. Unfortunately, however, we get most of our fructose from **high-fructose corn syrup (HFCS)**, which is basically corn syrup with some of its glucose converted to fructose. The biggest problem with HFCS is that it is cheap and ubiquitous, is often found in foods with little nutritional value such as soft drinks and processed foods, and we guzzle down way too much! It contains the same amount of calories and carbohydrates as table sugar.

Honey is made by honeybees from plant nectar and contains the same sweeteners—glucose and fructose—as table sugar. It is slightly sweeter than table sugar so you will probably use less.

Maple syrup is the boiled-down tree sap that comes from the sugar maple tree. The darker grade B maple syrup has a strong maple taste as well as hints of caramel and is often used for baking.

Molasses is a brown syrup produced during the sugar-making process. **Blackstrap molasses** is the darkest, thickest, and most nutritious. It contains several minerals such as iron and calcium.

Sucanat is an abbreviated term for "Sugar Cane Natural." It is pure, unrefined, dried sugarcane juice that, unlike white sugar, has not had the molasses removed. Sucanat's sweetness level allows it to be substituted at a one for one ratio in place of sugar and yields a slight molasses flavor.

White table sugar also known as **sucrose** is refined from sugarcane or beets and breaks down into half glucose and half fructose. It is the most popular form of sugar. **Brown sugar** is white sugar with the addition of molasses. It comes in both light and dark versions. The dark brown sugar contains more molasses, has a stronger flavor, and is moister.

CONSUMER CORNER

- Choose **naturally occurring sugars** coming from whole foods such as fruits, 100% fruit juice, and low-fat dairy.
- When shopping, choose **unsweetened foods** such as breakfast cereals and yogurts. It is better to add a small amount of sugar yourself if you must. You will use a lot less than the manufacturers use.
- When selecting a sugar, it is best to choose **unrefined sugars** instead of refined sugars. Unerefined sugars include honey, maple syrup, molasses, sucanat, date sugar, and maple sugar. A small amount goes a long way.
- **Limit artificial and non-nutritive sweeteners** such as saccharin, aspartame, stevia, and sucralose. While they do not promote tooth decay and are not a significant source of calories, they tend to taste funny and, on the whole, have done little to help us slim down. Further, the long-term health effects are unknown. Stick with **moderate portions** of the real thing. (One teaspoon of sugar contains 16 calories.)
- **Limit sugar-sweetened beverages.** They contain empty calories. A 12 oz can of soda, for example, contains nearly 10 teaspoons of sugar!
- **Limit sugar alcohols** such as xylitol, maltitol, sorbitol. Sugar alcohols are not well absorbed by the body and contain fewer calories than table sugar. They also do not promote tooth decay. But they still do contain calories and large amounts may have a laxative effect and cause abdominal discomfort.

MUFFINS, QUICK BREADS, AND HAND-MIXED CAKES GFA

This is my master muffin recipe, complete with all its variations. Mix and match, and get different results each time. You will never ever eat a store-bought muffin again, let alone use a muffin mix: I am not even going there! This recipe makes a dozen and a half medium muffins, in ten to fifteen minutes' preparation time.

All these muffin batters are mixed by hand, no need for a mixer. They can all be made with flax mixture (page 224) instead of eggs, and they are all gluten-free friendly. Just one useful piece of advice: When adapting these recipes to egg-free or gluten-free, always make muffins out of them, not larger cakes: The smaller the eggless or gluten-free item, the more manageable and the less room for flopping and crumbling.

You say cupcakes, I say muffins! My granddaughter Musia recently described to me a birthday party she went to and said to me, "The only thing I didn't like is I had to wipe off all those blue and green and red creams off the tops. Bubbie, why do they need it?" Yes, why indeed? I make muffins—yes, muffins—and make them festive in ways that are not expressed in extra sugar or fat, or added colorings, to name just a few examples: I make mini muffins; I use multicolored muffin liners; I sprinkle the muffins with miniature chocolate chips, grated coconut, grated apple, blueberries, or chopped peanuts; I stick cute flags and candles into them at display time.

This said, if you absolutely must, top the muffins (excuse me, the cupcakes) with icing or frosting or whatever. I trust you will find recipes for that everywhere. I hope you don't . . .

Vegetable spray

⅔ cup milk or dairy-free milk, low-fat OK

2 large eggs

⅔ cup vegetable oil

1 cup sugar

3 Granny Smith (green) apples, unpeeled, cored, and grated coarse in a food processor

1 cup old-fashioned oats

3 cups all-purpose, whole wheat pastry, or spelt flour

1½ teaspoons baking powder

1 teaspoon baking soda

½ teaspoon salt

½ cup raisins

½ cup chopped walnuts or pecans

1 tablespoon cinnamon

My granddaughter Sarah enjoying her muffin

You say cupcakes, I say muffins!

Preheat the oven to 375°F. Spray about 18 muffin molds with vegetable spray.

Combine the milk, eggs, oil, Sucanat, and apples and mix thoroughly but gently in a bowl, making sure not to extract more moisture from the apples. In another bowl, combine the oats, flour, baking powder, baking soda, salt, raisins, and nuts. Add the dry mixture to the milk mixture, combining gently but thoroughly with a spoon, taking care not to overmix, which toughens the batter. Pour the batter into the prepared muffin pans. Bake for about 30 minutes, or until a toothpick inserted in the center comes out clean. Makes about 18 muffins.

All substitutions in equal amounts:

- For the all-purpose flour, substitute whole wheat pastry or spelt flour.
- For gluten-free, **GF** substitute any GF flour plus 1 teaspoon xanthan gum. Make sure the mix includes a third of tapioca flour.
- For the oil, substitute coconut or flax oil, or olive oil marked "light."
- Use 4 egg whites instead of the 2 eggs, if you are watching your cholesterol.
- For raisins, substitute dried cranberries or other chopped dried fruit (prunes, apricots, dates, figs, etc.).

- For grated apple, substitute 2 cups packed grated carrots or zucchini, or 2 cups unflavored plain canned pumpkin, or 3 ripe bananas diced small, or 2 cups fresh or frozen blueberries marked IQF or IFF (see box on frozen blueberries, page 293).
- For walnuts, substitute almonds or pumpkin, flax, sesame, chia, hemp, poppy, or sunflower seeds.
- For the sugar, substitute Sucanat, rapadura, date sugar, maple sugar, or malt sugar (health food stores). Just be advised that some of these sugars are expensive!
- Throw in 1 cup semisweet chocolate chips.
- For cinnamon, substitute ground ginger, cardamom, or allspice, lemon zest, or orange zest.
- For rolled oats, **GF** substitute barley, quinoa, spelt, soy or other flakes.
- If you are egg restricted, use ½ cup flax mixture (page 224).
- Throw in a cup of unsweetened grated coconut.
- **To make a quick bread loaf or a round cake:** Only if using eggs and regular flour (all-purpose, whole pastry, or spelt), in other words not for egg-free and/or gluten-free batters. Pour the batter into a greased round pan or tube pan, or into a greased 11-by-14-inch baking pan, and bake in a preheated 350°F oven, about 1 hour, or a little longer until a knife inserted in the center of the loaf comes out clean.

COOKIES AND BARS

All cookies freeze perfectly, so be sure not to divide any of the recipes: Wait till they cool completely, store them in zipper bags, freeze them, and take them out as you go. Their thawing time is very brief.

Mixing cookie or cake dough in a food processor

The food processor will be your best friend when mixing a cake or cookie batter, if you keep this crucial rule in mind: When you mix in the dough, make absolutely certain you pulse it in, as opposed to using the mix button. Pulsing allows you to mix the flour in short and sweet spurts, only until the flour is combined, never allowing overmixing, as the flour would lose all its grit, and your batter would be ruined.

Assorted Cookies

CHOCOLATE CHIP COOKIES GFA

This recipe is in all my cookbooks, but how can I not include it here? I can never make enough of these; and apparently, neither can thousands and thousands of people. A few years ago, I was involved with a few friends in a massive fund-raising project and made a million cookies (yes, a million, and then some!). You would think I would get tired of them. Absolutely not! The egg-free version is almost as good—I make them for my egg-allergic granddaughter all the time. Besides, high-quality ingredients, the secret of a good chocolate chip cookie, is a soft and chewy texture, achieved by baking them only until they are just cooked, not a second longer. Remember, they continue to cook for a minute or two even as they cool. No problem mixing this dough by hand, and no mixer or food processor. A good cookie sheet makes a difference too: The heavier the better, as a heavy sheet will distribute the heat evenly and gradually.

This cookie has recently won Best Recipe award in a health and nutrition site called Health Castle. Upon reading this, my friend Eve wrote me: "May your delicious cookies—we can attest to how delicious they are—melt in the mouths of millions with nary a hint on the hips!"

2 eggs (only if you are restricted: use ½ cup flax mixture page 224)
½ cup sugar
1 cup packed brown sugar or Sucanat
¾ cup plus 2 tablespoons vegetable oil
1 tablespoon vanilla extract
2½ cups flour: all-purpose, whole wheat pastry, spelt (gluten-free—any GF flour)
¾ teaspoon baking powder
¾ teaspoon baking soda
½ teaspoon salt
1½ cups semisweet chocolate chips, best quality
½ chopped nuts, optional

Preheat the oven to 375°F. Cream the eggs and sugars in a food processor or with an electric mixer until light and fluffy. Add the oil and vanilla and mix in thoroughly. Add the flour, baking powder, baking soda, and salt and pulse (or mix at low speed) until just combined. Fold in the chips and nuts (if using) by hand. Drop the cookies in heaping teaspoonfuls onto a cookie sheet lined with parchment paper, 1 inch apart.

Bake 10 minutes. The cookies will firm up as they cool, so do not be tempted to bake them longer, or they will harden. Bake only one tray at a time. Store at room temperature in tin boxes. Separate each layer of cookies with foil or wax paper so they don't stick together. Makes about 4 dozen.

OATMEAL COOKIES GFA

This gem of a recipe does all my bidding: added nuts and seeds, gluten-free, different kinds of oil, you name it! I use the recipe in a dozen permutations and get a different cookie each time, all fun and exciting. They are so crunchy you can crumble them and use them as granola over yogurt. Couldn't live without them! Don't even bother with a mixer: All ingredients aboard, mix, that's the whole story! Occasionally I have an urge to eat more of them than is good for me, and I forgo a whole meal so I can splurge and have four or five of them instead, with a cup of tea. In this case, I call them lunch: They are real food!

2 eggs (only if you are restricted: use ½ cup flax mixture page 224)

¾ cup vegetable oil

½ cup sugar

¾ cup packed brown sugar or Sucanat

½ teaspoon salt

3 cups old-fashioned oats (gluten-free: make sure it is clearly stated on the container)

1 cup flour: all-purpose, whole wheat pastry, spelt, or gluten-free

1 teaspoon baking soda

1 teaspoon baking powder

1½ teaspoons cinnamon

1½ teaspoons allspice

¼ teaspoon nutmeg

Preheat the oven to 375°F. Place all ingredients in a mixing bowl and combine thoroughly by hand.

Drop by heaping teaspoons on a cookie sheet lined with parchment paper, 1 inch apart. Bake one sheet at a time. Bake 18 minutes. The texture will be crisp. Leave one baked cookie out a few minutes: If it is not perfectly crisp, return the cookies in the oven to crisp 1 to 2 more minutes. Store at room temperature in a cookie tin.

Variations: Short and sweet selection please!

- Use flax oil or coconut oil or other nut oil instead of vegetable oil.
- Use all Sucanat and no white sugar: total 1¼ cups. You can substitute maple sugar or date sugar: It will be delicious but more expensive.
- Throw in 1 cup of unsweetened grated coconut.
- Throw in ½ cup nuts (pecans, walnuts, hazelnuts, peanuts, etc.) or seeds (sunflower, pumpkin, flax, poppy, chia, hemp, etc.).
- Throw in ½ cup raisins, cranberries, or other dry fruit, larger ones chopped.
- Throw in 2 cups best-quality chocolate chip cookies. In this case, lower the sugar in the basic recipe to 1 cup total.

SUGAR COOKIES GFA

Children never seem to tire of this treat. Tapioca flour gives the cookies their ethereally light texture. They are bland and lend themselves to lots of playing and decorating: This diehard baker hates all frills, so I will just suggest brushing the tops with egg wash (egg mixed with a little water) and topping with sprinkles, coarse sugar, and tiny chocolate chips just before baking, or flavoring the dough with cinnamon, ginger, cardamom, lemon zest, etc. (1 to 2 tablespoons, 1 flavor at a time).

2 eggs (only if you are restricted: use ½ cup flax mixture, page 224)
¾ cup sugar
½ cup oil
¼ cup orange juice or water
2 teaspoons vanilla extract
2 teaspoons baking powder
½ teaspoon salt
2 cups flour: all-purpose, whole wheat pastry flour, spelt flour, or gluten-free flour
1 cup tapioca flour

Preheat the oven to 375°F. With an electric mixer at high speed, or in a food processor, mix the eggs, sugar, oil, juice or water, and vanilla until light and fluffy. Reduce the mixer speed to low; add the baking powder, salt, and flour; and mix one more minute until well blended (or add to the food processor, making sure you use the pulse button and pulse only until combined).

Divide the dough into 4 pieces. Roll out each piece on a very lightly floured surface about ⅛ inch thick, making sure the thickness is even so they bake evenly. Using assorted cookie cutters, cut in different shapes. Place the cookies on a parchment-lined cookie sheet. Bake 8 to 10 minutes until crisp and golden. Makes about 4 dozen. Store in an airtight cookie tin.

Ice cream sandwiches: Spread your favorite ice cream or sorbet on one sugar cookie, and top with another cookie. Repeat with as many cookies and ice cream as you like. Freeze until serving time.

BISCOTTI GFA

If there was only one cookie recipe left for me to make, biscotti would be it, hands down, and not only because it is so simple and delicious but because it is so versatile. From the basic dough, you could go into so many exciting directions. You might even consider multiplying the basic dough then dividing it again and add different flavors to each portion.

I have provided here my great favorites, but if you come up with exciting flavors of your own, go ahead and add them where you think they will fit best—just go with your personal preference, one flavor at a time please: cinnamon, ginger, cloves, natural extracts such as caramel, maple, lavender, geranium, jasmine, juniper, etc. (getting racy!), all available at health food stores or online. Just a few drops of these extracts are ample enough for a whole batch as they are very potent and impossibly delicious!

Basic dough:

3 eggs (only if you are restricted: use ¾ cup flax mixture, page 224)
1 cup sugar
1 cup vegetable oil
2 tablespoons juice or water
3 cups flour: all-purpose, whole wheat pastry, or spelt (gluten-free: skip the juice or water, and raise the flour to 3⅓ cups)
1 tablespoon baking powder
¼ teaspoon salt

Additions

Choose from the following.

Hazelnut cranberry: Add to the basic dough: ¾ cup dried cranberries, 1½ cups chopped hazelnuts, 1 tablespoon cardamom, 2 tablespoons orange zest.

Anise sesame: Add to the basic dough: 3 tablespoons anise seeds, 1 cup sesame seeds.

Almond: Add to the basic dough: 1 tablespoon vanilla extract, 1½ cups whole almonds, ¾ cup golden raisins (optional), 1 teaspoon almond extract.

Mocha: Add to the basic dough: 2 tablespoons instant coffee powder (decaf OK) mixed with a few drops warm water, 3 tablespoons cocoa powder, ¼ cup sugar.

Lemon coconut: Add to the basic dough: 2 cups unsweetened grated coconut, ¼ cup sugar, 2 tablespoons lemon zest.

Chocolate chips: Add to the basic dough 1½ cups semisweet chocolate chips.

Ginger: Add to the basic dough: ½ cup preserved ginger, packed, finely chopped; 1 tablespoon grated fresh ginger; and 1 tablespoon ginger powder.

Make the basic dough: Mix the eggs, sugar, and oil by hand or with a mixer, until well combined. Add all remaining dough ingredients and mix to make a smooth dough. Fold in the ingredients of your selected flavor by hand and mix again until well combined. The dough can be made up to 2 days in advance and refrigerated.

Preheat the oven to 375°F. Divide the dough into 4 pieces. On a very lightly floured board, roll each piece into a 12-inch cylinder. Transfer each cylinder onto a cookie sheet lined with parchment paper and flatten into a log about 2½ inches wide and ½ inch thick. Make sure the shaped logs are at least 1 inch apart, as they will expand. Bake for 20 minutes. Reduce the oven temperature to 325°F. When the logs are cool enough to handle, carefully move them onto a cutting board. Cut ½-inch slices with a very sharp serrated knife; put the slices back on the cookie sheet, cut side down, and bake again for 20 more minutes or until golden brown and very crisp. (Take one out and let it cool and then taste it. If it's not very crisp, return the biscotti to the oven for 2 to 3 more minutes.) Store at room temperature in an airtight cookie tin. Makes about 4 dozen.

BROWNIES GFA, P

Here comes the timeless classic, the little black dress of your dessert repertoire. I whip them up at the drop of a hat: I am often asked to do just that, so I double the recipe and pour the batter into a (real, not disposable) large cookie sheet with sides, and show up at the party with my goodies. You won't feel any difference whatsoever in the flavor or texture if you make them gluten-free or with potato starch on Passover.

I have included all the fixings: Play with a different one each time and get different results, and look like a real pro! My all-time favorite is caramel sea salt. Two simple secrets for the success of this dessert: very good chocolate for this and absolutely every chocolate dessert, and not a second more baking time. Even if they look barely set to you, the residual heat will do the rest.

I love to make them in a round tart pan and cut them into wedges; but of course, any baking pan will do.

8 ounces best-quality dark chocolate, chopped, or 2 cups best-quality semisweet chocolate chips
1 cup margarine spread
4 eggs
1 cup sugar
1 tablespoon vanilla extract
½ cup flour, any flour (Passover: potato starch)

Preheat oven to 375°F. Melt the chocolate and margarine spreadin a small saucepan over very low heat or in a microwave for 1 to 2 minutes. In a food processor or with an electric mixer, beat the eggs and sugar until light and fluffy. Add the chocolate mixture and mix. Add the flour and vanilla and mix, pulsing until just combined. Pour the batter into a greased 12-inch round spring form tart pan or a 12-inch square pan, and bake for 35 minutes until the top is barely firm. It will set completely with the residual heat sticking to the pan. Chill before cutting, so you can cut them neatly. Store refrigerated in a sealed container. Makes about 3 dozen.

Variations

Sea salt and caramel: Bring the salt to 1 tablespoon and add 1 tablespoon caramel extract (available in health food stores or online).

Espresso and brandy: Include 1 tablespoon instant espresso or coffee powder (decaf OK) and 3 tablespoons rum, brandy, or bourbon.

Peppermint: Add a few drops peppermint extract (health food stores).

Peanut butter: Instead of 1 cup margarine, use ½ cup margarine spread plus ½ cup peanut butter.

Pecan brownies: Add ¾ cup chopped pecans (or any nut you prefer), toasted 12–15 minutes in a 325°F oven.

Dark chocolate

Dark chocolate not only tastes delicious but also imparts many health benefits. They are rich in antioxidants and polyphenols that may contribute to heart health, reduce blood pressure, and lower cholesterol. Look for products with at least 60% cocoa. But stick a small flavorful portion! And be sure to balance the extra calories by eating less of other treats.

CHOCOLATE PEANUT BUTTER COOKIES GFA

Chocolate and peanut butter: A marriage made in cookie heaven! These are so much fun, cracked all over and forming dark ridges on the white-dusted tops.

1 cup crunchy peanut butter, try your best for unsalted (smooth is OK too, but you won't get the crunch)
1 tablespoon instant coffee powder, decaf OK
1 cup best-quality semisweet chocolate chips
1 cup sugar
¼ cup cocoa powder
2 eggs
½ teaspoon salt (skip if you used salted peanut butter)
1 teaspoon baking soda
1 teaspoon vanilla extract
2½ cups flour: all-purpose, whole wheat pastry, or spelt (gluten-free: use any GF flour)
Powdered sugar, sifted

Preheat oven to 375°F. Melt the peanut butter, coffee powder, and the chocolate chips on a very low flame in a saucepan. It will only take a minute or two, so please watch it carefully. Turn off the flame and add all remaining ingredients. Mix thoroughly by hand. Form little balls and roll them in the powdered sugar. Place on a foil-lined cookie sheet and flatten slightly. Bake 8 to 10 minutes until they look cracked all over. Makes 4 dozen. Store in an airtight cookie tin.

COCONUT COOKIES GFA

I am a total nut for coconut. Another terrific refrigerated cookie dough. Make the dough and refrigerate or freeze and take out the logs as you need them.

2 eggs
1¼ cups sugar
1 cup vegetable oil
2½ cups flour: all-purpose, whole wheat pastry, or spelt (gluten-free: use any GF flour)
¾ teaspoon baking powder
¾ teaspoon baking soda
½ teaspoon salt
1 tablespoon lemon zest
2 cups unsweetened grated coconut, packed
½ cup chopped pecans, optional

In a food processor, cream the sugar, margarine, baking soda, and flavorings until fluffy and lemon-colored. Add the eggs and cream again until fluffy. Add the flour gradually and pulse each time only until just combined. Transfer to a bowl and add all remaining ingredients, combining thoroughly. Shape the dough into 4 to 5 logs about 2 inches in diameter, wrap them in plastic, and tie both ends with twisters. The dough will look very loose: that's OK, it will firm up as it chills. Refrigerate 2 hours or longer, until you are ready to use them, up to 3 days (or freeze up to 4 weeks).

Preheat the oven to 325°F. Unwrap the rolls and slice ¼ inch thick using a sharp serrated knife, making sure they are all the same thickness so they bake evenly. Place the slices 1 inch apart on a cookie sheet lined with parchment paper. Bake 20 minutes. If they haven't crisped once they cooled, return them to the oven for just 2 to 3 minutes longer. Store at room temperature in an airtight cookie tin. Makes 3 dozen.

CHINESE COOKIES GFA

Who knew they could be made right at home? And who knows why they are called Chinese cookies for that matter? I don't think the Chinese have ever even heard of them. It's a little like French kiss or French laundry or French goodness knows what else, which always leaves the French scratching their heads as to what that could possibly mean. Anyway, who cares what their name is, all they need to be is fabulous! Fabulous and streamlined, as here. The almond extract is their trademark, so don't skip it.

I am giving you a large recipe, because the rolls you might want to leave unbaked will keep in the freezer a few weeks, and you will be happy to find them when you need them.

1½ cups sugar
2 cups margarine spread
1¼ teaspoons baking soda
1 teaspoon salt
1 teaspoon vanilla extract
1 teaspoon almond extract
2 eggs (only if you are restricted: use ½ cup flax mixture, page 224)
4 cups flour: all-purpose, whole wheat pastry, or spelt (gluten-free: use any GF flour)
1 cup tapioca flour
⅔ cup semisweet chocolate chips, melted (very low temperature in a small saucepan or 1 minute in a microwave)

In a food processor, cream the sugar, baking soda, salt, and extracts until fluffy and lemon-colored. Add the eggs and cream again until fluffy. Add the flour gradually and pulse each time only until just combined. Put the dough on a sheet of plastic wrap and flatten it out with your hands. Drizzle with the chocolate and fold the dough over twice to get a marbled effect. Shape rolls about 10 inches long and 2½ inches in diameter, wrap them in plastic, and tie both ends with twisters. You will get about 6 rolls total. Refrigerate 2 hours or longer, until you are ready to use them, up to 3 days (freeze the rolls you intend to use later up to 4 weeks).

Preheat the oven to 350°F. Unwrap the rolls and slice ¼ inch thick with a sharp serrated knife, making sure they are all the same thickness so they bake evenly. Place the slices 1 inch apart on a cookie sheet lined with parchment paper. Bake 25 minutes. They will crisp while they cool; if they didn't get crisp enough return them to the oven 2 to 3 more minutes. Makes about 6 dozen total. Store at room temperature in an airtight cookie tin.

HAMMANTASCHEN GFA

The signature triangle-shaped fun Purim cookie, with three points pinched around a jam filling. It matters not at all if you don't celebrate Purim—you will love 'em!

Dough:

4 cups flour: all-purpose, whole wheat pastry, or spelt (gluten-free: any GF flour)
1 tablespoon baking powder
½ salt
4 eggs
¾ cup sugar
1 cup vegetable oil
1 tablespoon vanilla extract
¼ cup orange juice
Grated rind of 1 orange

Fillings:

Choice of

- Prune butter (lekvar), poppy seed (mohn) filling, apricot, or strawberry preserves (try your best for all-fruit, available at health foods stores)
- ½ cup brown sugar or Sucanat, 1 cup raisins, ½ cup walnuts, 1 tablespoon cinnamon (pulse in a food processor just long enough to get a fine but not mushy grind)

Make the dough: Combine the flour, baking powder, and salt in a bowl and set aside. Beat the eggs, sugar, and oil in a food processor or with an electric mixer (or even by hand) until light and fluffy. Add the vanilla, juice and rind, and the flour mixture, mixing at low speed (in a food processor, use the pulse button and pulse only until combined) or by hand until well combined. Let the dough rest in the refrigerator for 1 hour or up to one day.

Preheat the oven to 350°F. Cut out a portion of dough and roll out evenly on a very lightly floured board, ⅛ inch thin. Cut out 3-inch circles with a scalloped cookie cutter. Place a heaping teaspoon filling in the center of each circle. Bring up the sides at 3 equidistant points, pinching firmly and leaving the centers exposed. Repeat with the rest of the dough and filling, using the scraps of the previous portion of cut-out dough with the next piece of dough you cut out, taking care to flour the board very lightly so the dough will not get too heavy.

Place the cookies on a cookie sheet lined with parchment paper, 1 inch apart. Bake about 20 minutes, or until lightly golden. Store in tins, do not refrigerate. Makes 3 dozen.

ALMOND SHORTBREAD CRESCENTS GFA

A great Sephardi favorite, called ghriba. *Traditionally we make them round and top them with a little cinnamon, but I find that no matter how carefully I store them, the tops always start crumbling and looking ragged, so I shape them in crescents, and they behave themselves and keep their shape very neatly. These melt-in-your-mouth gems are totally suitable for gluten-free and have no eggs whatsoever.*

1 cup margarine spread
¾ cup powdered sugar
2 cups flour: all-purpose, whole wheat pastry, or spelt (gluten-free: use any GF flour—I make them with chickpea flour)
¼ teaspoon salt
¼ to ½ teaspoon almond extract
1 cup sliced unpeeled almonds
Powdered sugar for dusting the cookies, optional

Preheat oven to 325°F. In a food processor, cream the margarine spreadand sugar until very light and fluffy. Add the sugar, flour, salt, and almond extract and pulse just 2 to 3 times. Transfer the mixture to a bowl. Add the almonds and mix by hand only until the dough comes together in a ball. Form small crescents. Place on a cookie sheet lined with parchment paper. Bake about 20 minutes, until just golden. Do not allow the cookies to get dark, or they will toughen. If desired, sift some powdered sugar, using a small strainer, over the cookies while still warm.

Store at room temperature in an airtight cookie tin. Makes about 3 dozen.

Orange flower water, rose water

Orange flower water, also called orange blossom water, is a clear, perfumed distillation of fresh bitter-orange blossoms.

Delightful in many Mediterranean and French dessert preparations, it is inexpensive and easy to find at specialty food stores, ethnic grocery stores, or online. You won't be at a loss about what to do with it: Include it in all the desserts I have suggested—add a few drops to mint tea and fruit salads or use it to rinse your face! Use rose water in the same way—the ancient beauty secret.

FRENCH ALMOND MACARONS GF, P

You will never think of macaroons as institutional fare after you taste these elegant and easy treats, close cousins of the amaretto cookies. Gluten-free without even trying! If you get lazy and would rather use store-bought ground almonds, also called almond flour (warning: you will pay dearly for the extra "convenience"), use 3½ cups ground and mix everything by hand.

If you are fond of hazelnuts, or pecans or cashews, simply substitute them for the almonds.

The trademark of macarons is their sandwiched presentation, with very simple fillings just to make them stick together: Jam, or melted chocolate.

3 cups unblanched almonds
1 cup powdered sugar
1 tablespoon lemon zest, or other flavoring of your choice, such as orange flower water, vanilla extract, coffee
3 egg whites
Good pinch salt
⅓ cup sugar

Preheat the oven to 325°F.

In a food processor, grind the almonds, powdered sugar, and flavoring to a fine powder, making sure you do not over mix. Beat the egg whites and salt in a bowl with an electric mixer, then add the sugar and beat again until the mixture is firm. Fold in the almond mixture until thoroughly combined.

Line 2 cookie sheets with parchment paper. Drop the cookies through a pastry bag fitted with a plain round tip, the size of walnuts. Bake 20 minutes, until golden. Do not allow the cookies to darken. Let the cookies cool. Spread half the cookies with jam or melted chocolate and top them with another cookie. Store at room temperature in an airtight cookie tin. Makes 18 macarons.

Variation: amaretto cookies GF, P

No sandwiching. Skip the flavorings, and use 2 to 3 tablespoons amaretto liqueur. Makes 3 dozen amaretto cookies.

SPICY NUT TRUFFLES GF, P

For nut lovers only: the famous Pfeffernusse, Sephardi style. My daughter-in-law Ruthie's favorite cookie in the whole world. Perfect for Passover too, and gluten-free. Don't try to bake them in a disposable cookie sheet, or the bottoms will burn.

1⅔ cups unblanched almonds
1⅔ cups walnuts
¾ cup sugar
2 teaspoons ground cloves
1 teaspoon baking powder
Good pinch salt
1 egg, or a little more
Powdered sugar, sifted (do not skip the sifting)

Preheat the oven to 400°F. In a food processor, place all ingredients, except the egg, and grind until you obtain a finely ground but still textured mixture. Do not grinder finer or you will get a greasy mixture. Transfer to a mixing bowl.

Add the egg and mix by hand until the mixture is smooth and malleable, adding just a little more egg if necessary. Shape the mixture into little balls. Pour powdered sugar over the balls (as opposed to rolling them into the sugar, which might make them look greasy), shaking off the excess sugar. Place the balls on a *real* cookie sheet lined with parchment paper. Bake 15 minutes, not a second longer. Let the truffles cool completely before storing in an airtight tin.

Spicy Nut Truffles

APRICOT OAT BARS GFA

Incredibly easy and wonderful! There is nothing I don't do with oats, even mudpacks and hair rinses (which of course I don't eat—relax!).

Fine grating and zesting

Use a long narrow zester: It is the best. No more bloody knuckles. It is so narrow it allows room only for the item you are grating, and it is razor-sharp. It will also grate cheese and citrus zest in a flash.

¾ cup margarine spread
¾ cup brown sugar or Sucanat
1½ cups old-fashioned oats
1½ cups flour: all-purpose, whole wheat pastry, or spelt (gluten-free: use any GF flour)
1 teaspoon baking powder
½ teaspoon salt
2 tablespoons orange zest
1½ cups apricot jam (try your best for all-fruit)

Preheat the oven to 350°F. Put all but last ingredient in a mixing bowl and work the mixture by hand briefly, only until it comes together into a smooth dough. Spread two-thirds of the mixture onto a greased cookie sheet, pressing hard to compact it. You will get a layer about ½ inch thick. Don't worry if it doesn't cover the whole surface of the sheet, just ignore the empty space. Spread the jam evenly over the dough. Crumble the remaining dough, adding a little flour if necessary, to resemble coarse meal and sprinkle it over the jam. Bake about 40 minutes. Cool slightly before cutting into bars or squares. Store at room temperature in an airtight cookie tin. Makes about 3 dozen.

DATE POWER BARS GFA

Have you ever taken the time to read the ingredient list in some commercial brands of granola bars? I am sorry to say they are not the healthy snacks they are cracked up to be. By contrast, just look at this lineup of flavors: Why even bother shopping for snacks if ten minutes of work will get you dozens of these scrumptious bars? Each one is like having a meal. You just can't miss! When I am on the road, they are my best friends. They keep very well in a tin or in the freezer—no need to wipe them all out, so behave please!

4 cups soft and plump pitted dates, packed (about 1½ pounds)
½ cup agave
1 cup tahini (sesame paste)
1 cup flax meal
3–4 cups *crunchy* granola (page 231, or settle for a good store-bought crunchy brand), finely crumbled

In a food processor, process the dates and agave until a perfectly smooth paste forms. Transfer to a bowl and add all but last ingredient. Combine thoroughly (it will be sticky, be patient). Press the mixture firmly into a greased cookie sheet, about ½ inch high. Refrigerate until firm. Cut into 1-inch x 3-inch bars. Store refrigerated in airtight tins. Makes about 5 dozen.

Variations:

- Substitute other dry fruit for the dates
- Substitute chopped toasted nuts for the granola, in equal amounts
- Throw in 2 cups unsweetened grated coconut
- Substitute other ground seed or nut flour for the flax meal
- Substitute any nut butter for the tahini

CHOCOLATE SALAMI GFA

These delightful confections have a funny name, because each slice is specked with the nuts and graham crackers and looks as funky as salami. No problem making them gluten-free! No need to slice all of them, leave the unused logs in the freezer or refrigerator until ready to use: They keep very well.

¾ cup sugar

1 cup margarine spread

3 tablespoons rum, bourbon, or unflavored brandy

2 cups best-quality semisweet chocolate chips or grated chocolate

¼ cup cocoa powder

2 tablespoons instant coffee powder, decaf OK

1 egg (or 2 egg whites; if you must, settle for ¼ cup flax mixture, page 224)

1 cup toasted pecans or hazelnuts, coarsely chopped

½ box (7½ ounces) unflavored graham crackers, gluten-free OK, broken by hand into small pieces

Melt the first set of ingredients on a very low flame, stirring. Turn off the flame and quickly whisk in the egg until incorporated. Add the nuts and graham crackers and combine thoroughly. Refrigerate briefly to let the mixture firm up so it's easier to handle. Shape into logs about 2 inches in diameter and wrap tightly in plastic, securing the ends with twisters. You will get 5 to 6 logs total. Refrigerate the logs 2 to 3 hours, until firm (or freeze the logs you will use later). Unwrap and slice ½ inch thick with a sharp serrated knife. Makes about 6 dozen slices (each log makes about a dozen slices). Keep the slices refrigerated until serving time.

Chocolate Salami

QUICK HALVAH BARS GFA

We all love the wonderful taste of halvah but hardly ever get near it because of the prohibitive amount of sugar it contains. I tinkered with the flavors until I obtained this delicious approximation. It takes no time and doesn't even cook or bake, and keeps refrigerated for weeks. Attack of the munchies? A little chunk will hit the spot! If you are making this treat on short notice and don't have time to let the mixture firm up, don't worry about a thing and serve it with a spoon.

1½ cups tahini (sesame paste)

1½ cups *"toasted wheat germ and honey"* (that's the exact name of the product) in the cereal section of the supermarket (gluten-free: use crunchy granola—page 231, or good-quality store-bought, ground medium-fine in a food processor, using the pulse button)

1½ cups unsweetened grated coconut, packed

1 cup toasted sesame seeds or chopped almonds or pistachios (10–12 minutes in a preheated 325°F oven)

1 cup agave syrup (try not to substitute honey or maple syrup unless that's all you can find, as they will add a delicious but unnecessary layer of flavor)

½ teaspoon salt

1 tablespoon vanilla extract

Mix all ingredients by hand. Press firmly and uniformly into a 10-inch square baking pan. Refrigerate until firm. Cut into squares or bars.

Variation: Chocolate-covered halvah GF

Reduce the agave to ⅔ cup. After the mixture firms up, melt 1 cup semisweet chocolate chips with 1 tablespoon oil and spread over the top of the mixture. Let the chocolate layer firm up before cutting into squares or bars.

DESSERTS AND PIES

HONEY-ROASTED BANANAS WITH COCONUT SORBET GF, P

Fun and delightful treat, best served warm. A sort of tropical "a la mode" dessert.

6 medium-ripe bananas, or ripe plantains, split lengthwise

⅓ cup maple or agave syrup, or honey

2 tablespoons vegetable oil

2 tablespoons grated fresh ginger

2 tablespoons rum

Juice and zest of 1 lemon

½ cup unsweetened grated coconut, packed

Coconut sorbet, for garnish

Chopped toasted nuts, or granola, for sprinkling (optional)

Preheat the oven to 400°F. Place the banana halves tightly side by side in a baking pan just large enough to fit them all in one layer. Mix all remaining ingredients thoroughly in a bowl and pour the mixture evenly over the bananas. Roast 15 minutes. Serve warm with a scoop of coconut sorbet. Sprinkle with the nuts or granola if desired.

CHESTNUT CHOCOLATE MOLDS GF

I fervently hope this cookbook gives any of my recalcitrant American readers a real taste, maybe even a yen, for chestnuts—and not only from a street cart but right at home, in desserts and in savory dishes. We ate them so often growing up. I never bother with boiling whole chestnuts, as I am afraid you will find the peeling a real imposition—vacuum-packed roasted and peeled work perfectly (I get them online).

Kosher gelatin

I have always used unflavored kosher gelatin in many exciting desserts but had never offered any of them in my cookbooks and my demos, as it was available only in bulk for food service.

Recently food service has finally made kosher gelatin available for retail to the public. You will find this really exciting news as it is absolutely dairy- and meat-free (although it is derived from cow's bones, bones are considered thoroughly pareve, or meat-free), and perfectly reliable in your preparations.

---

1 envelope unflavored gelatin
½ cup cold water
1 cups dairy-free milk, low-fat OK, heated to just below boiling
4 cups vacuum-packed roasted peeled chestnuts
1 cup dairy-free cream cheese
1 cup sugar
¼ cup brandy or rum
Good pinch salt
Good pinch nutmeg

Sprinkle the gelatin over the cold water and let it rest a few minutes. Transfer the gelatin mixture to a food processor and add the hot milk and chestnuts. Process a full minute until perfectly smooth. Add all remaining ingredients and process again until smooth. Spray 8 to 10 small ramekins with vegetable spray, or use small glasses and pour the mixture into them. Chill. Serve alone or with chocolate sauce (page 48) or caramel sauce (page 49). Makes 8 to 10 servings.

MIXED BERRY KANTEN GF

Consider kanten the Jell-O of champions: kuzu is the starch of the kuzu plant, is a wonderful thickener, and is easy to get in health food stores. Kanten, the dessert made with kuzu, is quick and delicious, and does wonders for upset stomachs. You can eat it warm too. If you wanted a real quick kanten, make this dessert without berries using just the kuzu and the juice of your choice.

⅔ cup kuzu
4 cups unfiltered apple cider, pomegranate or cranberry juice
6 cups mixed frozen berries
⅔ cup maple syrup

In a medium saucepan, mix the kuzu and cider until dissolved. Turn on the flame and cook on medium-high flame until thickened, just a few minutes. Add the berries and maple syrup and cook a few more minutes until the mixture is heated through and loses its cloudy shade. Transfer to a mold or individual cups and chill. Makes 8 to 10 servings.

LYCHEE KANTEN GF

This is a white version of the berry kanten above. Sometimes we get lucky and find fresh lychee, that wonderfully intriguing Chinese fruit with the fuzzy skin and incredibly fragrant meat.

4 cups unsweetened lychee juice (health food stores)
⅔ cup kuzu
3 cups lychee nuts, peeled and coarsely chopped (settle for 1 large can lychees—try your best for unsweetened—juice and all, fruit chopped)
2 tablespoons grated fresh ginger
2 bags green tea, decaf OK
Maple syrup to taste (wait until you taste the finished dessert: you might find it sweet enough as is)

In a medium saucepan, whisk the juice and kuzu until dissolved. Turn on the flame, add the remaining ingredients, and bring to a boil. Lower the flame and cook, whisking, 4 to 5 more minutes, until thickened. Discard the tea bags. Add a little maple syrup if it needs it. Transfer the mixture to a mold or individual cups and chill. Makes 8 to 10 servings.

Green tea

Green tea contains heart-healthy flavonoids known as catechins and other antioxidants that may offer protection against certain cancers and Alzheimer's, and improve cardiovascular and bone health.

SPICY TAPIOCA ALMOND PUDDING GF

Overlaid with my favorite Indian flavors. Another perfect example of great results with plebeian ingredients. Gluten-free without even trying.

3 cups dairy-free milk, low-fat OK, plus a little more to thin the pudding if necessary (wait till it's done before adding)

½ cup tapioca flour

½ cup brown rice flour

1 15-ounce can coconut milk

1½ cups finely ground (whole, not blanched) almonds

1 cup sugar

1 tablespoon ground cardamom

1 tablespoon ground ginger

Good pinch ground cloves

Good pinch saffron threads

½ teaspoon salt

1 cup golden raisins

Whisk half the milk with the tapioca and brown rice flour in a saucepan until smooth. Turn on the flame, add all but the last ingredient, and bring to a boil. As soon as it comes to a boil, turn the flame to very low and cook covered for 10 minutes. Stir in the raisins and cook 5 more minutes. Thin the mixture if necessary. Transfer the mixture to a bowl or individual cups. Chill before serving. Makes 8–10 servings.

Ghee (clarified butter)

Clarified butter is known as ghee, an essential ingredient in many Indian dishes and desserts. It tastes wonderful, good and strong and nutty, so a little goes a long way and needs no refrigeration. Buy it in a health food store, or just make your own: Cook it in a skillet just a few minutes and strain it into a jar, leaving the brown sediment behind. If you use it on toast or tossed into pasta, you will be pleased to find that you only need about half of the plain butter you normally use.

INDIAN SWEET POTATO PUDDING GF

A nice way to get you to eat your vegetables! Everyone in my family is a sweet potato nut: We love them in every way, shape, or form. The molasses are a nice counterpoint to the mildness of the sweet potatoes.

4 medium sweet potatoes, grated (about 6 cups packed)
⅓ cup vegetable oil or ghee (page 278, or store-bought)
1 cup coconut milk
1 cup dairy-free milk, low-fat OK
Good pinch saffron
2 tablespoons orange flower water or rose water
¾ cup dark molasses
1 tablespoon cardamom
2 tablespoons ground ginger
3 tablespoons rum
Good pinch salt

Preheat the oven to 350°F. Combine all ingredients well in a mixing bowl. Pour the mixture into a greased 9-by-13-inch baking dish. Bake 1 hour or a little longer until the top looks set. Let the pudding cool. Serve warm or at room temperature. Makes 8–10 servings

Variation: Corn amaranth pudding GF

Omit the sweet potatoes, use 1 cup each amaranth and coarse cornmeal, and bring the milk to 3 cups. Proceed just as above.

CHOCOLATE ESPRESSO MOUSSE GF

Ridiculously simple and incredibly delicious: I whip it up in minutes. Who would believe it has no eggs and no cream and tastes so rich? No trace of the tofu's controversial heritage, it's all eclipsed by the other wonderful flavors! Tofu contributes only its bulk and great texture.

1 cup semisweet real chocolate chips, only the best
2 tablespoons instant coffee powder, decaf OK
¼ cup hot water
⅔ cup pure cocoa powder
⅔ cup sugar
¼ cup vegetable oil
2 tablespoons brandy or rum
1 pound silken tofu, drained

In a small saucepan, over a very low flame, heat all but last ingredient until the chocolate is melted and the mixture looks smooth (or microwave 2 minutes). Transfer the mixture to a food processor, add the tofu, and process a full minute until perfectly smooth. Transfer to a bowl or to small individual cups. Chill until firm. Makes 8–10 servings.

HAZELNUT MOUSSE GF

Hazelnut butter

Hazelnut butter is heavenly but can be hard to find (although I always find it online). In this case, just use 3 cups toasted hazelnuts and grind them to a paste, then use 1 cup of that mixture as the hazelnut butter listed in the recipe, storing the rest in a glass jar for future use.

This is even simpler than the chocolate mousse above. Please do look for superfine sugar in your supermarket, at its very fine texture will blend with the other ingredients without any gritty texture.

1 cup hazelnut butter
1 cup superfine sugar
1 pound extra-firm tofu, drained and blotted dry with paper towels

Place all the ingredients in a food processor and process a full minute until perfectly smooth. Transfer to a bowl or to small individual cups. Chill until firm. Makes 8–10 servings.

Chocolate hazelnut mousse parfaits: layer small amounts of chocolate mousse and hazelnut mousse in small clear glasses, and chill. At serving time, sprinkle with granola or chopped nuts.

CHOCOLATE OATS POTS DE CRÈME GF

Long before the whole-grain fashion began (I am not telling you how long, I heard ladies don't do that, but I will give you a hint: circa my ultra-lean student years, the very years that inadvertently turned me into a cook, as I was constantly bartering all kinds of favors for a good homemade dinner), I was exploring ways to eat nutritious food for pennies and in minutes, and subsist on a low-low budget. Oats and all their possibilities were, as they still are, at the top of my list. You would think I would at all costs stay away from the struggling-student association they inevitably conjure up in my mind. Exactly the opposite is the case, I assure you: Now I can jazz them up with some really fabulous and easy-to-find ingredients and end up with an elegant comfort food. The lean years were fun and creative and made me the nutritious-delicious-inexpensive cook that I am: Forgive me if I say it with great pride as I go down memory lane!

3 cups milk or dairy-free milk, low-fat OK
1 cup steel-cut oats
⅔ cup cocoa powder
⅔ cup maple syrup or agave, or a little more to taste (wait till you taste the finished dessert before adding)
2 tablespoons instant coffee powder
3 tablespoons rum or brandy
1 cup coconut milk

Bring all ingredients to boil in a saucepan. Reduce the temperature to medium low and cook covered for about 20 minutes. Thin with a little more milk if you like it a little looser. Pour into a bowl, or a dozen individual bowls, and chill.

Chocolate Oats Pots De Crème

RICOTTA YOGURT BERRY PARFAITS GF

One of my rare dairy desserts. No one ever believes me when I say it took five minutes to make eight or more servings. This dessert never fails to make me look good! You will experience firsthand the magic of berries: Remember you will not *be settling if you use frozen berries, au contraire!*

4 cups fresh or frozen mixed berries, larger ones cut up
3 tablespoons crème de cassis
¼ cup maple syrup or honey
1 tablespoon balsamic vinegar
3 cups vanilla yogurt, low-fat OK
3 cups ricotta cheese, low-fat OK
1½ cups crunchy granola, large clumps broken up

Mix the berries, cassis, maple syrup, and vinegar in a bowl and set aside. Prepare 8 wine or martini glasses. Combine the ricotta and yogurt and divide the mixture among the glasses. Top with the berry mixture, juice and all. Just before serving, sprinkle the granola over all.

BREAD BERRY TRIFLE GFA

I think you will be berry-ed out after this recipe. Or will you? I only call it trifle because it is layered and is made in a trifle dish, not because it has custard, which it absolutely doesn't need to be fantastic. This stunning dish never fails to get raves at every demo I make it at. The trifle dish adds greatly to the drama, as the see-through glass allows you a real glimpse of the coming attractions! Gluten-free bread will work here just as well as the regular kind.

> 1 cup cranberry or pomegranate juice
> ¼ cup arrowroot or tapioca flour
> 8 cups frozen mixed berries
> ⅔ cup maple syrup, or a little more (don't add more until you taste the finished berry mixture)
> ¼ cup crème de cassis (liquor stores)
> Juice and grated zest of 1 lemon
> 1 loaf sliced bread, any kind, included sprouted or gluten-free

Whisk the juice and arrowroot in a saucepan until smooth. Turn on the flame. Whisk in the berries, maple syrup, crème de cassis, juice, and zest, and bring to a boil. Reduce to low and cook 5 more minutes.

Place one layer bread slices in a 9-by-13-inch pan or in a trifle mold, making sure you cover the bottom completely. Pour a third of the berry mixture evenly to get the bread thoroughly soaked. Repeat 2 times: one layer bread slices, berry mixture (total: 3 layers breads, 3 layers berry mixture). Cover and chill the mold. Makes a dozen ample servings.

CHOCOLATE TERRINE WITH CRANBERRY COULIS GF

Chocolate and cranberry: Just can't resist! This terrine has the seductive texture of chocolate truffles. Get ready for the treat!

> ½ margarine spread
> 2 cups best quality semisweet chocolate chips
> ¼ cup cocoa powder
> ½ cup powdered sugar
> ½ cup soy or rice milk powder
> ¼ cup crème de cassis (liqueur stores)
> ½ cup red currant jelly, or natural jellied cranberry sauce (health food stores)
> 1 egg yolk

Melt the margarine spread, chocolate chips, cocoa powder, sugar, and milk powder on a very low flame until just melted (or microwave 2 minutes). Add the liqueur, jelly, and egg yolk and whisk until just heated through. Transfer the mixture to a food processor, and process a full minute, until perfectly smooth. Pour the mixture into a small greased loaf pan or small greased ramekins. Refrigerate until firm. Unmold, slice (if you used a loaf pan), and serve with cranberry coulis (page 50). Makes 8 or more servings.

LEMON COCONUT MOUSSE GF

Another treat born of good flavor matchmaking!

1½ envelopes unflavored gelatin
¼ cup cold water
1 15-ounce can coconut milk
½ cup fresh lemon juice
3 tablespoons lemon rind
¼ cup rum
1 cup light agave syrup
1 pound silken tofu
1 8-ounce container dairy-free cream cheese
1 cup toasted coconut for topping (about 15 minutes in a 325°F oven), optional

Dissolve the gelatin in the water. Bring the coconut milk and the lemon juice to just below boiling. Transfer to a food processor with the gelatin mixture and process about 30 seconds. Add all remaining ingredients and process until perfectly smooth. Pour into a bowl or small individual cups and chill. Top with toasted coconut, if desired. Makes a dozen servings.

Variation: Lemon coconut pie GFA

This will make for a more dramatic presentation, with just a couple minutes more work, for the crust. Grind about 12 ounces graham crackers (gluten-free OK) with ⅓ cup oil in a food processor and press firmly into a 12-inch pie plate and then pour the mousse batter on top and chill. Cut into wedges. Makes a dozen servings.

Lemon Coconut Mousse

CRANBERRY PEACH CRUMB PIE GFA

No need to wait till summer for this wonderful treat. Frozen cranberries and peaches are wonderful year-round. This pie is best served warm, alone, or a la mode, with a scoop of sorbet or vanilla ice cream.

Fruit mixture:

2 cup dried cranberries, or 3 cups fresh or frozen (in this case, add more sugar to taste)
4 cups fresh or frozen peaches, cut in small chunks
¼ cup arrowroot or kuzu
½ cup brown sugar or Sucanat
2 tablespoons lemon juice
1 tablespoon lemon zest
2 tablespoons brandy or rum

Topping:

1 cup old-fashioned oats
½ cup flour, any kind
½ cup walnuts or pecans, chopped coarse
¼ cup margarine spread
¾ cup brown sugar or Sucanat

Preheat oven to 350°F. Mix the fruit mixture ingredients gently so as not to extract moisture and pour into a greased 12-inch pie pan. Mix the topping ingredients lightly with your fingers until you get a mealy texture. Sprinkle the crumb mixture evenly over the cranberry mixture, using it all up. Bake for about 45 minutes, or a little longer, until the top is bubbly and golden. Best served warm, alone or with vanilla ice cream or sorbet.

Variation: Apple crumb pie GFA

Substitute 6 Granny Smith (green) apples for the peaches and cranberries, peeled and diced medium small. Substitute lemon zest for the orange zest and add 1 tablespoon cinnamon. Proceed just as above.

Cranberry Peach Crumb Pie

CHOCOLATE COCONUT TART GFA

For this fabulous tart, celebrating another great love match—chocolate and coconut—you are under no pressure whatsoever. Make the crust a couple days before dessert time and make the filling even a few days before serving, then pour the filling over the crust the day you are serving the dessert. Of course there is no problem making both the crust and the filling on serving day, just as long as you allow the filling to set.

Crust:

½ cup margarine spread
¾ cup powdered sugar
2 egg yolks
¼ cup cocoa powder
2 cups flour, any flour, a little more if needed

Filling:

¾ cup coconut milk
⅓ cup tapioca flour
½ cup margarine spread
1½ cups semisweet chocolate chips, only the best
¼ cup cocoa powder
2 tablespoons rum
½ cup sugar
3 eggs
2 cups unsweetened grated coconut (health food stores)

Preheat the oven to 350°F. Make the crust: In a food processor, cream the margarine, sugar, and egg yolks until fluffy. Add the cocoa and flour and pulse just 3 to 4 seconds, adding a little flour if needed to make a smooth-firm dough. Working quickly, starting from the center toward the sides, spread the crust evenly in a 12-inch spring form pie pan, coming up the sides, patting firmly. Prick the crust with a fork all over. Bake about 30 minutes. Store covered at room temperature up to 2 days before filling and serving.

Make the filling: In a saucepan, whisk the coconut milk and tapioca flour until smooth. Turn the flame on low and add the margarine, chocolate chips, cocoa, rum, and sugar. Whisk only until the chocolate is melted and the mixture is smooth. Quickly whisk in the eggs one at a time and whisk 2 to 3 minutes, until the mixture is smooth and thick. Turn off the flame and fold in the coconut. Refrigerate the filling until firm and pour over the baked crust. Serve at room temperature, alone or with coconut sorbet.

PLUM CUSTARD TART GFA

Easy and wonderful, and a really nice way to use plums in the spring. The granola crust makes it extra special.

Granola crust:

1½ cups granola
1½ cups flour, any flour
½ cup oil
½ cup almonds
¼ cup agave, honey or maple syrup
2–3 tablespoons fine cornmeal
10–12 dark plums, sliced thick

Custard:

1½ cups milk or dairy-free milk, low-fat OK
½ cup soy milk or rice milk powder
3 eggs
¾ cup sugar or Sucanat, plus a little more for sprinkling
¼ cup crème de cassis (liquor stores)

Preheat the oven to 375°F. Make the crust. Grind all the crust ingredients in a food processor, using the pulse button, making sure not to over mix. Spread thin onto the bottom of a 12-inch spring form pie plate, patting firmly.

Sprinkle the bottom of the crust with the cornmeal. Spread the plums evenly in the bottom.

Make the custard: Process or whisk all custard ingredients until smooth and pour gently and evenly over the plums. Sprinkle lightly with additional sugar. Bake 40 minutes, or just a little longer, until the custard is barely set. Makes a dozen ample servings.

LEMON BLUEBERRY TART GFA

Another wonderful and low-maintenance dessert. Bake the crust all by itself up to a couple days ahead, cover tightly, and store it at room temperature. A few minutes before serving, pour the lemon curd into it, and top with fresh blueberries. Yum!

Crust:

½ cup margarine spread
½ cup sugar
¼ teaspoon salt
2 eggs
2 teaspoons vanilla extract
1 tablespoon grated lemon zest
2½ cups flour, any flour

1 recipe lemon curd (page 46)
2 cups blueberries

Preheat the oven to 350°F. Make the crust: In a food processor, cream the margarine, sugar, and salt. Add the eggs one at a time and mix each time until just incorporated. Add vanilla, zest, and flour and mix just a few more seconds using the pulse button. Working quickly, starting from the center toward the sides, spread the crust evenly in a 12-inch spring form pie pan, coming up the sides, patting firmly. Prick the crust all over with a fork. Bake for 30 minutes or until golden brown—don't allow it to darken. Let the crust cool completely. At serving time, fill the crust with the lemon curd and top with the berries. Makes a dozen ample servings.

Variation: Lemon bars

This is how my daughter-in-law Ruthie served them at a party, and we watched them disappear. Same pie crust, but bake it flat (no sides) in an 11-by-14-inch baking pan. Same baking time. At serving time, spread with the curd, top with the berries, and cut in squares. Another option: No berries, just the curd, and sift powdered sugar lightly over the top.

RICOTTA ALMOND PIE GFA

Anyone looking for a nice departure from the traditional all-American cheesecake? This is for you! Light and ethereal, with a wonderful almond crust and scented with lemon peel.

Almond crust ingredients

½ cup almonds
¼ cup brown sugar or Sucanat
Good pinch salt
2 cups flour, any flour
1 tablespoon vanilla extract
⅓ cup cold unsalted butter, cut in pieces
1–2 tablespoons cold water, only if you need it to make a smooth dough

Filling ingredients:

3 cups ricotta, low-fat OK
4 eggs
1 cup sugar
2 tablespoons brandy or rum
2 tablespoons lemon zest

Preheat the oven to 350°F. Make the crust: Finely grind the almonds with the sugar. Add the salt, flour, vanilla, and butter and pulse just until the mixture resembles coarse meal. Add a little water only if you need it so the dough comes together. Working quickly from the center toward the sides, spread into a 12-inch spring form pie plate, coming up the sides.

Whisk all the filling ingredients together. Pour into the pie crust. Bake about 40 minutes, or until set. Let the pie cool and cut in wedges. Makes a dozen ample servings.

CHOCOLATE PEANUT BUTTER PIE GFA

This star was born just recently, on a crazy-hot day, where I was ready to go to all lengths to avoid using the oven. I just mixed everything, poured, and prayed. I fretted all day and sampled smidgens of the mixture a dozen times to see if it was setting. I needn't have worried! This dessert has all possible assets besides being heavenly and totally wholesome: No baking needed, dairy-free, no eggs, and easily adapted to gluten-free. Any leftovers will keep perfectly several days in the refrigerator, or up to a month in a freezer.

3 5-ounce packages graham crackers (gluten-free OK)
½ cup vegetable oil
3 cups best quality semisweet chocolate chips
½ cup pure cocoa powder
2 tablespoons instant coffee powder
¼ rum or brandy
½ cup sugar
1 8-ounce container dairy-free cream cheese
1 pound silken tofu, drained
¾ cup peanut butter

In a food processor, finely grind the crackers with the oil. Press the mixture very firmly onto the bottom of a 12-inch pie plate.

On a very low flame, melt the chips, cocoa, coffee, and rum in a saucepan (or microwave 2 minutes). Transfer to a food processor with all remaining ingredients and process until perfectly smooth, a full minute. Pour the mixture over the crust. Chill a few hours to let the mixture set. Cut the pie in wedges. Makes a dozen ample servings.

CRANBERRY APRICOT BREAD PUDDING GFA

I often whip up this treat after a party, when I look to recycle my leftover bread: gluten-free. This is for you too!

Any bread will do as long as it is not too crusty (in other words, don't use baguette or ciabatta!). You will love the kick and the bold ruby-colored specks the cranberries add. Nothing to it: All aboard—one step and you're done! Individual desserts: Pour into greased muffin molds and reduce the baking time to about 45 minutes.

1-pound loaf bread, gluten-free OK, cut up in large chunks
3 cups milk or dairy-free milk, low-fat OK
4 eggs
2 cups all-fruit apricot preserves
½ cup sugar
1 cup oil
2 tablespoons orange flower (settle for 2 tablespoons orange zest)
3 tablespoons apricot brandy or rum
3 cups fresh or frozen cranberries, coarsely chopped (food processor)

Preheat oven to 375°F. Mix all ingredients except cranberries by hand in a bowl, breaking up the bread and preserves as you go. Fold in the cranberries. Pour the batter into a greased 9-by-13-inch pan, or a greased 10-inch round pan. Bake for about 1 hour, or a little longer, until the pudding looks nice and puffy, and the center is firm. Serve warm or at room temperature, alone or with a scoop of sorbet or vanilla ice cream.

Variation: Apple bread pudding GFA

Skip the cranberries and the orange flower water and reduce the milk to 2 cups. Add 4 Granny Smith (green) apples, unpeeled and coarsely grated, and 2 tablespoons cinnamon. Proceed just as above.

Apple Bread Pudding with Caramel Sauce and Coconut Sorbet

BREAD AND CHOCOLATE PUDDING GFA

Another wonderful way to use leftover bread, perfectly adapted to gluten-free and a snap to prepare. The black-and-white alternating pattern is fun and takes only a few more minutes.

1-pound loaf bread, gluten-free OK, cut up in large chunks
4 eggs (only if you are restricted: use 1 cup flax mixture, page 224)
4 cups milk or dairy-free milk, low-fat OK
1½ cups sugar
1 cup vegetable oil
¼ cup rum or brandy
1 tablespoon vanilla extract
½ teaspoon nutmeg
½ cup pure cocoa powder
1 tablespoon orange zest
¾ cup golden raisins

Combine the first set of ingredients in a bowl, breaking up the bread as you go. Divide the mixture into two bowls. Add the cocoa in one bowl; add raisins and orange zest in the second bowl. Combine each mixture thoroughly in their respective bowls.

Preheat oven to 375°F. Grease a 9-by-13-inch baking pan. Layer half the black evenly in the pan, top with half the white mixture. Repeat with the remaining black mixture and the remaining white mixture, spreading gently and evenly so as not to disturb the bottom layers.

Bake for about 1 hour, or a little longer, until the pudding looks nice and puffy and the center is firm. Serve warm or at room temperature, alone or with caramel sauce (page 49).

CAKES
BLUEBERRY CAKE WITH ALMOND STREUSEL

Blueberries: You just say the word, and I wax lyrical. All of my friends who used to summer with us in the mountains think of me fondly each time they make this cake. I can't remember how many thousands I made; I still have pictures of all of us wearing huge hats and carrying huge pails, picking blueberries. What fun!

If you decide to forgo the streusel step, the cake will be slightly less dramatic but just as delicious.

¾ cup vegetable oil
1½ cups sugar
4 eggs
1 tablespoon baking powder
1 tablespoon grated orange zest
3 cups flour: all-purpose, whole wheat pastry, or spelt
2 tablespoons triple sec, kirsch or cassis (liquor stores)
3 cups blueberries, rinsed and dried thoroughly (place in a large cookie sheet lined with several layers of paper towels), or frozen marked IQF or IFF (see box on blueberries)

Blueberry Cake with Almond Streusel

Streusel:

½ cup ground almonds
¼ cup oil
½ cup flour, any flour, a little more if needed
¼ cup sugar or Sucanat
2 teaspoons cinnamon

Preheat the oven to 350ºF. Grease and flour a 10-inch round or tube pan, or an 11-by-14-inch baking pan.

Cream the oil, sugar, and eggs in a food processor until light and fluffy. Mixing the whole cake by hand is OK too. Add all but last ingredient and pulse 3–4 times, until just combined.

Transfer to a mixing bowl. Very gently stir in the blueberries with a spoon. If using frozen, take them out of the freezer at this point, but not before. Pour the batter into the prepared pan.

Mix the streusel ingredients lightly with your fingers until the mixture looks like coarse meal, adding a drop more flour if necessary. Sprinkle evenly over the cake, using it all up. Bake about 1 hour or until a knife inserted in the center of the cake comes out clean. Invert the cake and let the steam escape, then invert again streusel side up. Makes a dozen ample servings

IQF blueberries

If you happen, as I always do, to have an unseasonable yen for blueberry cake or muffins, simply use frozen blueberries (try your best for the ones marked Maine wild blueberries: delicious!) marked IQF (individually quick frozen) or IFF (individually flash frozen). This means that the berries (or any other fruit, whole small fruit or larger fruit cut in chunks) are first frozen very briefly in one layer, then conditioned into their final packaging. The step of freezing them individually before freezing them in a group affords you the possibility of taking out only the amount of berries you need (perfect for smoothies and fruit sauces), saving the rest for next time; it also means they won't make a mess and turn your whole batter purple. Simply leave them in the freezer until the minute you need to fold them into your batter; they have ample time to thaw during baking.

SEMOLINA ALMOND CAKE WITH LEMON SYRUP GFA

This improbable ingredient combination results in an incredibly moist and fragrant cake. It is important to use a shallow mold here, like a pie plate, no higher than 2 inches, so the syrup that is poured on the baked cake reaches all the way to the bottom.

4 eggs whites
¼ teaspoon salt
¾ cup sugar
4 egg yolks
¾ cup olive oil
1 tablespoon baking powder
Zest of 1 lemon
1½ cups finely ground almonds (use a food processor)
1 ½ cups fine semolina flour (gluten-free: use fine cornmeal)
1 cup flour, any flour

Preheat the oven to 325°F. With an electric mixer, whip the egg whites and salt at high speed until soft peaks form. Add the sugar gradually and whip until stiff. Switch to low speed, allowing only enough time to combine the ingredients, beating in one ingredient at a time, just a few seconds each time, the yolks, then the oil, etc., until all ingredients are incorporated.

Pour the batter into a greased 12-inch round pie pan. Bake 40 minutes or until a knife inserted in the center comes out clean. Immediately poke the cake all over with a toothpick or skewer, and pour the syrup (recipe follows) all over the cake, using it all up.

Syrup:

¾ cup light agave syrup
Juice and zest of 2 lemons
Heat the ingredients over a low flame until just warm (or microwave 30 seconds to 1 minute).

BOURBON APPLE PECAN CAKE

The combination of the apples, bourbon, and pecans is a classic. Mix by hand in minutes.

4 eggs
1 cup vegetable oil
2 cups packed brown sugar or Sucanat
¼ cup bourbon
½ teaspoon salt
1 teaspoon baking soda
3 cups flour: all-purpose, whole pastry, or spelt
1 tablespoon cinnamon
¼ teaspoon nutmeg
4 Granny Smith (green) apples, unpeeled, cored, and diced small
⅔ cup pecans, chopped coarse

Preheat oven to 350°F. Grease and flour a 10-inch round pan or tube pan, or 11-by-14-inch baking pan. Mix the first set of ingredients thoroughly in a bowl. Mix the second set of ingredients thoroughly in another bowl. Combine both mixtures thoroughly with a spoon, taking care not to extract moisture from the apples. Pour the batter into the pan and bake 1 hour, or a little longer, until a knife inserted in the center of the cake comes out clean. Invert the cake to cool on a rack. Makes 16 ample servings

BANANA CHOCOLATE CHIP CAKE

Children adore it, and of course so will you. Bananas got too ripe? Don't even think of chucking them as they make the greatest smoothies, muffins, and cakes, their flavor reaching their sweetest and most intense peak! The riper the better: Freeze them, and when ready to use, run them under warm water; the peel will come right off.

½ cup very strong Earl Grey tea, decaf OK (steep 2 tea bags in ½ cup hot water)
1½ cups sugar
4 eggs
1 cup oil
1 tablespoon vanilla extract
3 cups all-purpose, whole wheat pastry, or spelt flour
2 teaspoons baking soda
½ teaspoon salt
1 cup old-fashioned rolled oats
4 very ripe bananas, mashed or diced small
1 cup semisweet chocolate chips, best quality

Preheat oven to 350°F. Mix the tea, sugar, eggs, oil, and vanilla in a bowl. Mix the flour, baking soda, salt and oats in another bowl. Mix both mixtures only until combined. Fold in the bananas and the chips with a spoon, mixing gently but thoroughly. Pour the batter into a greased 10-inch round or tube pan, or in a greased 11-by-14-inch pan, and bake 1 hour, or until a knife inserted in the center comes out clean. Invert to cool on a rack. Makes 16 ample servings.

CHOCOLATE BEET COCONUT CAKE GFA, P

It is unfortunate that in America, beets invariably conjure up loaded remarks about, uhmmm, never mind . . . I am always looking for ways to sneak them in, as in this cake, where they do their magic even while they totally escape detection: The result is this dense, moist, and deliciously funky cake. This is one of those rare times I use cans, because beets' long cooking time could be a deterrent, and because they taste pretty decent, especially in this cake, where they will be combined with all the other goodies.

4 egg whites
Good pinch salt
1½ cups sugar
4 egg yolks
1 cup oil
3 cups good-quality natural canned beets, drained, juice reserved, mashed with a fork or potato masher
2 cups flour: all-purpose, whole wheat pastry, or spelt (gluten-free: any GF flour. Passover, 1½ cups potato starch)
1 tablespoon baking powder
1 cup juice from the canned beets (add a little water to complete 1 cup if necessary)
1 cup cocoa powder
1½ cups unsweetened grated coconut, packed

Preheat the oven to 350°F. With an electric mixer, whip the egg whites and salt at high speed until soft peaks form. Add the sugar gradually and whip until stiff. Switch to low speed and, allowing only enough time to combine the ingredients, beat in one ingredient at a time, just a few seconds each time—the yolks, then the oil, etc., until all ingredients are incorporated. Pour the batter into a greased tube pan or a 10-inch round pan or 11-by-14-inch pan, and bake for 1 hour or until the point of a knife inserted in the center comes out clean. Invert and cool on a rack. Makes 16 ample servings.

HONEY CAKE

Honey cake is the traditional cake of the Jewish New Year, but you will be making it year-round: It's that good! I actually succeed in turning quite a few people on to my honey cake. Mine is moist and spicy and easy to love; I trust it will make you forget all the indignities of past dried-out and brittle honey cakes. I make it several ways, all scrumptious, but this is one of my favorites. The secret ingredient, orange marmalade, was shared by my dear friend Leah.

1 cup oil
⅔ cup sugar
1 cup dark honey
1 cup orange marmalade, try your best for all-fruit (page 44, or store-bought)
4 eggs
¾ cup strong coffee at room temperature
3 tablespoons rum or brandy
3 cups flour: all-purpose, whole wheat pastry, or spelt
2 teaspoons baking powder
1 teaspoon baking soda
Good pinch salt
1 teaspoon each cinnamon, allspice and ginger
½ cup sliced almonds (optional)

Preheat the oven to 350°F. Mix the first set of ingredients in a food processor.

Mix the second set of ingredients in a bowl, and add in 3 additions to the egg mixture, using the pulse button, mixing each time only until combined. If you are adding the almonds, fold them in by hand with a spoon.

Pour the batter into a greased tube pan or 10-inch pan, or 11-by-14-inch pan, and bake 1 hour, or a little longer until a knife inserted in the center comes out clean. Invert on a rack to cool. Makes 16 ample servings.

ALMOND STREUSEL COFFEE CAKE

Yum! Lemon and almonds: Outrageous match! Wonderful brunch choice as it has the look and texture of a yeasted pastry. Don't hesitate to go dairy-free.

Filling and topping:

1 cup whole unblanched almonds (pecans or walnuts are great too)

½ cup sugar

⅓ cup flour: all-purpose, whole wheat pastry, or spelt

2 tablespoons cold unsalted butter, cut small (dairy-free: natural margarine, health food stores)

½ cup butter, at room temperature (dairy-free: natural margarine, health food stores)

1 cup sugar

3 eggs

2½ cups flour: all-purpose, whole wheat pastry, or spelt

2 tablespoons grated lemon zest

1 teaspoon baking soda

1 teaspoon baking powder

¼ teaspoon salt

1 cup plain yogurt (dairy-free: plain soy or coconut yogurt, or 1 cup soy milk mixed with a tablespoon lemon juice)

Preheat the oven to 350°F. Make the topping: In a food processor, coarsely grind the almonds. And the remaining topping ingredients and pulse briefly, until the mixture looks like coarse meal. Reserve.

Butter and flour a 10-inch spring form pan or a tube pan. Cream the butter and sugar until smooth. Beat in the eggs, one at a time, until light and fluffy. Combine the flour, lemon zest, baking soda, baking powder, and salt in a bowl and add alternately with the yogurt to the batter, pulsing each time 2 to 3 times, only until just combined.

Pour half the batter into the pan. Sprinkle evenly with half the filling. Pour the remaining batter gently and evenly, then sprinkle with the remaining topping, using it all up. Bake about 45 minutes, or until a knife inserted in the center comes out clean. Invert and cool on a rack. Makes a dozen ample servings.

CHOCOLATE JASMINE MARBLE CAKE

Submit to the seduction of jasmine in this gorgeous cake!

3 cups flour: all-purpose, whole pastry, or spelt
1 tablespoon baking powder
Good pinch salt
1½ cups sugar
1 cup oil
4 eggs
1 tablespoon vanilla extract
3/4 cup strong jasmine tea (2 jasmine tea bags or 2 teaspoons jasmine tea leaves steeped in boiling water and strained)
¼ rum or brandy
⅓ cocoa powder
⅓ cup sugar
1 tablespoon coffee powder
2 tablespoons oil

Preheat the oven to 350°F. Mix the flour, baking powder, and salt in a bowl and set aside.

In a food processor, cream the sugar and margarine spreaduntil light and fluffy. Add the eggs one at a time, pulsing each time only until incorporated. Add the vanilla. Add the flour mixture alternately with the tea, starting and ending with the flour mixture, pulsing only 2 to 3 times after each addition. Pour the batter into a greased and floured 10-inch spring form cake pan or tube pan, leaving about 1 cup batter in the processor. Add the cocoa, sugar, coffee, and oil to the food processor and pulse 2 to 3 times, until just combined. Pour the cocoa mixture gently and evenly on top of the batter, then swirl it with a knife to get a marbled effect. Bake 1 hour or until a knife inserted in the center comes out clean. Invert on a rack to cool. Makes 16 ample servings.

MOLTEN CHOCOLATE CAKES GFA, P

If there is anyone who doesn't go gaga over these little gems with the runny gooey centers, I have never met them! Alas, no baking in advance and no reheating, or they won't be, well, molten chocolate cake: runny and gooey!

The great news is, (a) they are nothing to prepare even though they look and taste as if they came out of the best restaurant, and (b) the batter can be made and poured in advance in individual ramekins or muffin molds and refrigerated until ready to use, and I mean it literally: You could stick them in the oven as you are resetting for dessert—they will be ready in minutes.

3 cups semisweet chocolate chips, best quality
½ cup margarine spread
1 tablespoon coffee powder, mixed with a few drops hot water
3 tablespoons cocoa powder
6 eggs
1 cup sugar
2 tablespoons flour (Passover: potato starch)
1 tablespoon vanilla extract

Preheat oven to 375°F. Melt the chocolate, margarine, coffee, and cocoa over very low heat, or microwave in a bowl for 1 to 2 minutes. In a food processor, beat the eggs and sugar until light and fluffy. Add the chocolate mixture and mix. Add the flour and vanilla and pulse until just combined. Pour the mixture into 8 to 10 greased ramekins or muffin molds and bake about 12 minutes, or until the top is barely set and the center is still slightly wet. Watch the baking closely after the first 12 minutes: Do not overbake, or the center will solidify. Err on the side of caution and bake rather less than more: Invert just one on a plate—if it's too runny, don't worry, just stuff it right back in its mold and return all the molds to the oven for another couple minutes. Invert the cakes onto dessert plates and serve *immediately* while hot, alone, or with vanilla or coffee ice cream or coconut sorbet. Makes 8 to 10 servings.

Variations:

In an adventurous mood? Take a look at all the exciting flavor variations in brownies (page 264) and use them in equal amounts. No added nuts please, just extracts and spices, so as not to change the runny texture.

TROPICAL FRUIT CAKE

Sometimes I take my playing with food a drop further than even I myself dare, tinkering endlessly, picking my family and friends as willing victims as I subject them to constantly evolving batches and asking them to please forget they ever tasted something if it was just way too wacky. This cake is a perfect example of getting a drop too adventurous. But here is the unanimous verdict on the last (this) try: It's fabulous, like having a cocktail in a plate instead of in a glass. This fruit cake will not be passed around like other fruit cakes: It's for keeps!

½ cup preserved ginger (health food stores), packed
1 large navel orange, skin and all, quartered and seeded
1 lemon, skin and all, quartered and seeded
1 cup oil
¼ cup dark rum
1½ cups sugar
4 eggs
3½ cups flour: all-purpose, whole wheat pastry, or spelt
2 teaspoons baking soda
¼ teaspoon salt
1 ripe banana, diced small
1 cup golden raisins

Preheat oven to 350°F. Finely grind the ginger in a food processor. Add the citrus and pulse until finely ground but not mushy. Set the mixture aside in a mixing bowl. In the same food processor bowl (no need to rinse), cream the oil, rum, sugar, and eggs. Mix the flour with the baking soda and salt in a bowl. Add the flour mixture in three additions, pulsing only until well combined. Pour the mixture over the citrus mixture. Add the banana and raisins and combine thoroughly. Pour the batter into a greased 10-inch tube pan (if you think you might have too much batter, pour the excess into a smaller mold or muffin molds). Bake 1 hour or until a knife inserted in the center comes out clean. Invert to cool on a rack. Makes 16 ample servings.

CHOCOLATE CAKE

This is the only chocolate cake you will ever need to make. The mixture of soy milk and lemon juice curdles and yield a cake as tender and moist as chocolate cakes made with yogurt or buttermilk, only this one has the advantage of being dairy-free. No problem replacing this mixture with 1 cup yogurt or dairy-free yogurt, and proceeding with the recipe as instructed. Do not be alarmed at the large amount of sugar used (this cakes yield about 20 servings!) and do not try to reduce it or the cake will be bitter.

1 cup soy milk
1 tablespoon lemon juice
4 eggs
2 ⅔ cups sugar
1 cup vegetable oil
2 ⅔ cups flour: all-purpose, whole-wheat pastry, or spelt
1½ teaspoons baking powder
1½ teaspoons baking soda
Good pinch salt
1 ¼ cups best quality cocoa powder
1 cup hot water
3 tablespoons instant coffee or espresso powder
3 tablespoons brandy, rum or bourbon

Preheat the oven to 325°F. Mix the soy milk and lemon juice, and set aside. Mix the flour, baking powder, baking soda, salt and cocoa in a bowl, and set aside. Mix the hot water with the coffee, brandy and vanilla in another bowl, and set aside. In a food processor, beat the eggs and sugar until light and fluffy. Add the oil and beat. Add the flour mixture to the egg mixture alternately with the coffee mixture, beginning and ending with the flour mixture, just incorporating the addition each time, 2–3 pulses. Add the reserved soy milk mixture, and mix again a few more seconds. The batter will be very runny: don't worry! Pour the batter into a greased and lightly floured 10-inch spring form pan or Bundt pan. Bake for 75 minutes or until a knife inserted in the center comes out clean. Unmold and invert onto a cooling rack. Serve alone or with a drizzle of caramel sauce (page 49) or a dollop of chocolate espresso mousse or hazelnut mousse (page 279).

Chocolate Cake with Caramel Sauce

PRALINE "CHEESECAKE" GF

Consider this a party cake. I have a dairy-free cheesecake in my previous cookbook, Levana Cooks Dairy-Free. This praline variation on the classic is practically the only recipe in this book (indeed in my repertoire) that is very rich and more labored. I am including it as an occasional party treat for two reasons: (1) it's out of this world (pretty good reason, no?), and (2) in the past couple years, several good brands of healthy dairy-free cream cheese, sour cream, and yogurt have been developed, just check your health food store.

Although you will never miss the dairy version, if you would rather make this dessert with dairy ingredients, go right ahead and use real cream cheese, sour cream, and yogurt.

Hazelnut butter

Hazelnut butter can be hard to find in health food stores but very easy to find online, or just grind toasted hazelnuts into a paste in a food processor; no other nut butter will be as delicious here.

---

2 packages graham crackers (10 ounces total), gluten-free OK
⅓ cup vegetable oil, a drop more if necessary

Batter:

3 8-ounce containers dairy-free cream cheese
1 12-ounce container dairy-free sour cream (reserve ¼ cup)
⅓ lemon juice
¼ cup tapioca or arrowroot
1¼ cups sugar
4 eggs
1 tablespoon vanilla extract
1 cup hazelnut butter

Topping:

Reserved sour cream
1 cup coconut or soy vanilla yogurt (or 1 cup silken tofu plus 1 tablespoon sugar)
2 tablespoons instant coffee powder dissolved in a few drops of warm water
2 tablespoons rum
Toasted chopped hazelnuts for sprinkling the finished cake, optional

Preheat oven to 375°F. Grind the crackers with the oil in a food processor until fine. Press firmly into the bottom of a 10-inch spring form pan. Bake for 10 minutes. Take out of the oven, and reduce the oven temperature to 325°F.

Cream all the batter ingredients until smooth and pour half over the crust. Add the hazelnut butter to the remaining batter and process just a few seconds until combined. Pour gently and evenly over the white layer, then swirl it with a knife to get a marbled effect. Bake for 1 hour and 10 minutes. Turn off the oven and leave the cake in 2 more hours without ever opening the oven. Take out and chill completely.

Process the topping ingredients and spread evenly over the cake. Just before serving, sprinkle the ground nuts, if using, over the cake. Makes 20 ample servings.

Variation: Original plain "cheesecake" GF

Same crust, same baking time. Process the batter ingredients (using up all of the sour cream) and pour into the pan. No hazelnut butter, no topping. Same temperatures, same baking time, same method.

FROZEN COCONUT CRUNCH CHOCOLATE CAKE

I developed this wonderful recipe to accommodate kosher diners after a meat meal as well as dairy-intolerant diners. Although it is delicious as is, feel free to substitute dairy ice cream for the sorbet, keeping the color scheme monochromatic: vanilla, coffee, chocolate. I tried with a red layer (berry) and found it disrupted the earthy color and flavor theme.

Crust:

4 cups crisp rice cereal
2 tablespoons instant coffee powder, diluted in a few drops water
1 cup unsweetened grated coconut
½ cup cocoa powder
½ cup agave or maple syrup
3 cups coconut sorbet (first sorbet layer)

Cake layer:

1 pound sponge cake, good quality store-bought OK, sliced ½ inch thick
½ agave or maple syrup
3 cups coconut sorbet (second sorbet layer)

Top layer:

2 cups semisweet chocolate chips
½ cup coconut milk
1 tablespoon agave or maple syrup
2 tablespoons oil
¼ cup white or dark rum (don't skimp: this is what will keep the top layer from freezing solid)

Mix the crust ingredients thoroughly in a bowl. Press the mixture firmly into a 10-inch spring form pan. Spread the sorbet (first layer) over the crust. Spread the cake slices over the sorbet, compacting it, making sure you cover the whole surface. Pour the syrup slowly and evenly over the cake. Spread the sorbet (2nd layer) evenly over the cake. Place the cake in the freezer 2 to 3 hours to firm up.

Make the top layer: Melt all top-layer ingredients over a very low flame (or microwave 1 to 2 minutes), let it cool a few minutes and pour evenly over the cake. Cover the cake tightly with plastic wrap and return to the freezer. Freeze the cake 8 hours or more. Take out the cake a few minutes before serving, then cut in wedges. Makes 20 ample servings.

SUGGESTED MENUS

Here are some menus for all occasions. These are only suggestions of course, but I composed these menus with the main guidelines in mind—budget, colors, textures, preparation times, and as importantly, dietary preferences and special needs. I hope they will be great help to you when you plan your own menu.

A Moroccan Feast
Fish Soup
Dried Fruit Couscous with Lamb
Chicken Pie
Swiss Chard Carrot Salad
Grated Carrot Salad
Fennel Salad
Moroccan-Style Ratatouille
Semolina Almond Cake
Date Power Bars

A Vegetarian dinner
Kabocha Sweet Potato Soup
Panzanella
Millet Fritters with Red Pepper coulis
Minted Zucchini and Pea purée
Ricotta Almond Pie

A French Dinner
Herb White Bean Soup
Tilapia Niçoise en Papillotte
White Vegetable Purée
Apple Waldorf Salad
Bread and Chocolate Pudding

A Vegan Dinner
Thai Sweet Potato Peanut Butter Soup
Artichoke and Lima Bean Tajine
Stir-Fried Tofu, Vegetables and Seaweed on
    Soba Noodles
Spicy Chick Pea Lettuce Salad
Chocolate Peanut Butter Pie

An Italian Dinner
Chestnut Mushroom soup
Arborio Risotto with Spinach and Asparagus
Balsamic-Roasted Chicken Breasts
Baby Arugala, Avocado and Tomato Salad
Lemon Blueberry Tart

A Shabbos Dinner
Roasted Tomato Soup
Roasted Salmon with Maple Glaze
Herb Roast Chicken
Kasha with Mushrooms and Onions
Kabocha, Kale and Seaweed Stew
Chocolate Coconut Tart
Almond Shortbread Crescents

A Salad Dinner
Baby Spinach with Golden Beets and Fresh
    Corn
Vegetable Tuna Salad
White Bean Salad with Artichoke and Swiss
    Chard
Cabbage Salad with Garlic and Lemon
Green Fruit Salad

A Chocolate Lovers' Dinner
Black Bean Chocolate Soup
Chicken Breasts with Mole Sauce
Wild Rice and Chestnuts
Spicy Roasted Butternut Squash
Chocolate Terrine with Cranberry Coulis

An Israeli Dinner
Chickpea Soup
Fish Chraimi
Israeli Salad
Tabouleh
Quick Halvah Bars
Hammentashen

A Cold Summer Dinner
Cold Avocado Cucumber Soup
Chicken in Walnut Sauce
Roasted Vegetables
Summer Rolls with Thai Dipping Sauce
Bread Berry Trifle

An Old-Classics Dinner
Quick Borscht
Yerushlami Kugel
Cabbage Cucumber Apple Slaw
Roast Turkey with Barbecue Sauce
Chocolate Jasmine Marble Cake

A Children's Favorite Dinner
Baked Fish Sticks
Pea Soup
Cold Sesame Noodles
Cucumber Salad
Banana Chocolate Chip Cake

Dinner for a Crowd on a Budget
Hot and Sweet Parsnips
Moroccan Lentil Soup
Vegetarian Chopped Liver
Tofu Egg Salad
Moroccan Potato Pie
Shakshuka
Hummus
Braised Red Cabbage and Apples
Mixed Greens Salad
Barley, Lentil and Kale Pilaf
Carrot Cake
Brownies

Brunch Party
Iced Coffee and Iced tea
Sake Punch
Asparagus with Mock Hollandaise sauce
Mushroom Cheese Frittata
Herb-Roasted Salmon
Caesar's Salad
Blueberry Scones
Corn Bread
Yogurt Granola Berry Parfaits
Crêpes with Apple Filling

An Asian Dinner Party
Miso Vegetable Soup
Pad Thai
Steamed Vegetable Dumplings
Soba Noodles with Roasted Roots
Steamed Chicken Breasts with Baby Bok Choy
    and Shitaki Mushrooms
Sashimi Salad
Kale, Beet and Seaweed Salad
Chinese Meatloaf
Mixed Berry Kanten

The Fun Foods Dinner
Quick Minestrone
Spaghetti and Meatballs
Un-stuffed Cabbage
Sweet Potato Latkas
Eggplant Roulades
Spicy Bean Corn Salad
Chocolate Salami
Chinese Cookies

A Latin Dinner
Seviche
Oat Quinoa Chili with Guacamole
Creole Chicken with Rice
Plantains, Squash and Apple Bake
Pineapple Mango Salsa
Tropical Fruit Cake
Sangria

An Indian Dinner
Indian Red Lentil Soup
Chicken Curry with Tomatoes and Plantains
Chickpea Paratha
Cucumber Raita
Chai
Spicy Tapioca Almond Pudding

A Dairy-Free All-Dessert Party
Chocolate Chip Cookies
Oatmeal Cookies
Spicy Nut truffles
Apricot Bars
Apple Muffins
Anise Sesame Biscotti
Lemon Coconut Mousse
Frozen Coconut Crunch Chocolate Cake
Dairy-Free Cheesecake
Cranberry Peach Crumb Pie
Chocolate Espresso Mousse
Blueberry Cake with Almond Streusel

A Thanksgiving Dinner
Chestnut Mushroom Soup
Roast Turkey with Juniper Wine Gravy
Roasted Raddichio, Endives and Fennel
Cranberry Relish
Wild Rice Pilaf
Haricot Verts, Asparagus and Artichoke Salad
Mixed Greens with Fruity Shallot Dressing
Molten Chocolate Cakes
Coconut Cookies

A Seder Feast
Tricolor Fish Terrine with Watercress
    Horseradish Sauce
Russian Salad
Moroccan Eggplant Salad
Roasted Garlic, Artichoke, and Celery Root
    Soup
Roast Beef with Wild Mushroom Sauce
Herb Roasted Baby Potatoes
Zucchini and Brussels Sprouts in Tomato Sauce
Mixed Greens with Raspberry Vinaigrette
Chocolate Beet Coconut cake
Spicy Nut Truffles

ABOUT THE CONTRIBUTORS

Lévana Kirschenbaum was co-owner of Levana Restaurant on Manhattan's Upper West Side (alas, recently closed after thirty-two years), and the pioneer in Kosher upscale dining. She is a cooking teacher and cookbook author, and gets countless devoted fans for her fearless, practical, and nutritious approach to cooking. She gives weekly cooking demos and gets cooking demo engagements around the country. She has published *Levana's Table: Kosher Cooking for Everyone*, *Levana Cooks Dairy-Free!*, and a book-dvd set based on her demo series called *In Short Order*. She is launching a line of all-natural spelt desserts, called, what else, Lévana. Go onto her website to find out more about her demos, cookbooks, desserts, and entertaining stories at www.levanacooks.com.

Lisa R. Young, PhD, RD, CDN is a nationally recognized nutritionist in private practice and an adjunct professor of nutrition at New York University. She is the author of *The Portion Teller Plan: the No-Diet Reality Guide to Eating, Cheating, and Losing Weight Permanently*. She was named a Woman of Action by the Israel Cancer Research Fund.

Meir Pliskin photographs out of his studio in New York City. His talents cover a wide range of genres: commercial, events, and portraits. Visit his website at www.meirpliskin.com.

GLUTEN-FREE INDEX

This index contains the titles of recipes and their variations that are coded GF (Gluten-Free) or GFA (Gluten-Free Adaptable).

PASSOVER INDEX

This index contains the titles of recipes and their variations that are coded P (Passover).

GENERAL INDEX

Index by Bella Hass Weinberg, D.L.S.

This index includes the codes GF (Gluten-Free), GFA (Gluten-Free Adaptable), and P (Passover) only next to the titles of recipes.